Once Upon a Yugoslavia

When the American Way
Met Tito's Third Way

A Personal Journey

Once Upon a Yugoslavia

When the American Way
Met Tito's Third Way

A Personal Journey

Surya Green

Foreword by Dr. Henry Breitrose
Professor Emeritus of Communication
Stanford University

New Europe Books

Williamstown, Massachusetts

Published by New Europe Books, 2015
Williamstown, Massachusetts
www.NewEuropeBooks.com

Copyright © Surya Green, 2015
Cover design by Hadley Kincade
Interior design by Knowledge Publishing Services, 2015

ISBN: 978-0-9900043-4-9

Cataloging-in-Publication data is available from the Library of Congress.

Printed in the USA
First edition
10 9 8 7 6 5 4 3 2 1

In memory of
my mother, Florence Silberberg Eisner (1914–2012),
and my father, Bernard Eisner (1912–1994),
and all my relatives whose lives were sacrificed
in the Holocaust during World War II

CONTENTS

ACKNOWLEDGMENTS

For their help of whatever type during this book's gestation,
I thank wholeheartedly:

Rajesh Barya, Julia Beach, Dr. Henry Breitrose, Prue Breitrose, Jeroen Brouwer, Andrea Carlos, Bernard Chanin, Florence Eisner, Justin Folkers, Bonnie Gurian, Jason Gurian, Jane Harvey, Richard Hollaman, Dr. Poonam Kohli, Herm van Leeuwen, Sylvia Luetjohann, Bertram Mourits, Dr. Charles Onwulata, Nada Osmanovíc, Vijay Vipasha Pal, Ellen Perchonock, Manu van Poppel, Giri Prins, Vesna Sacks, Robert Silberberg, Richard J. Smit, Sri Swami Sarvatmanandaji Maharaj, Sri Sunirmalanandaji Maharaj, Daryl Gurian Stern, Colin Thomson-Hohl, Ineke Nur Kristal van den Broek, Bart Visscher, Elisabeth Visscher-Endeveld, Kitty WaBwanda-de Boer, Alexandra Wenta, Budhy Chen Wetters, Bhaskara Bas Wiersma, Rascha Wiesse, and Eddie Woods; Marquis, Levon, Garri, Ry, and Henderson at Apple in Bryn Mawr, Pennsylvania; and Esmir Majdanac, James, Stephan, and Hanneke at Apple in Amsterdam.

I offer my sincere apology to anyone whose name has been inadvertently omitted.

And wholeheartedly I thank Paul Olchváry, publisher of New Europe Books, and his team.

FOREWORD

Surya Green's fascinating book narrates two journeys undertaken simultaneously. The first was the author's unsought sojourn from Stanford, California, to Yugoslavia in 1968. Yugoslavia was then a socialist country led by Josip Broz Tito (aka Marshal Tito), World War II hero and dictatorial head of state. The second journey was an inner one that obliged her to scrupulously reexamine her most basic beliefs as a person and a citizen.

These parallel journeys are the elements of an intensely personal and perceptive story. It is often said that travel broadens the mind. In Surya Green's case, immersion in Tito's Yugoslavia served to deepen as well as broaden her knowledge of herself, and the social orders of both Yugoslavia and her American homeland.

The Sixties was a decade of explosive exploration, and documentary film was a means for making sense of the chaos. Stanford's graduate program in documentary was in its infancy when we admitted Surya Green. She was a bright and energetic Barnard College graduate with an intense curiosity and independence, and a considerable amount of fearlessness at a time when the revolutionary feminist thoughts of Betty Friedan's *The Feminine Mystique* had yet to become part of the general culture.

One of our Stanford film friends was Leo Dratfield, a pioneer in nontheatrical film distribution with excellent connections in Eastern

Europe. He was friendly with animators and studio heads on the other side of what was then known as the "Iron Curtain." One of his favorite studios was Zagreb, which made splendid animated films. He mentioned to Surya's film mentor, the late Janet Voelker Alexander, that there might be an interesting educational opportunity at the studio in Yugoslavia for a recent graduate.

A summer job at Zagreb Film, Yugoslavia's award-winning animation and documentary studio, was too tempting an offer for a bright and inquisitive film graduate student to refuse. Besides, 1968 was a terrible year in America. The assassinations of Martin Luther King and Robert Kennedy, and the seventh year of a seemingly endless war in Vietnam, must have made a summer in another culture very attractive for an adventurous young woman.

But in Tito's Yugoslavia, even more than in America, the personal was indeed political. It didn't take long for Surya to become intensely aware that customs and language presented extraordinary challenges. Moreover, Yugoslavia was very much the opposite of American consumer culture.

Reflectively examining everyday experiences of two contrasting cultures enhanced Surya Green's original way of looking at the world. Surya's experiences in a society that ran on "Yugo-slave" time also made her reexamine the conflicting values of personal security, which was what Yugoslavia offered its people, and the lack of personal freedom, which was the price. In theory it's an interesting dialectic, but a punishing one in actual practice.

Confronted with the harsh objective reality on the ground, many Americans of Surya's age and background would have fled on the next train. But through a combination of bravery, self-discipline, and unrelenting inquisitiveness, Surya navigated her way from one surprise or disappointment—often it is hard to determine which was which—to another.

Her eye learned to see the rewards in all her experiences. Among them: A week's visit by John Grierson, the father of the documentary film, gave Surya the benefit of a lifetime's wisdom, and poked at her established beliefs. Grierson was a wise man, irrepressibly optimistic, and he had a unique ability to inspire others, as his conversations with Surya insightfully attest.

Surya reciprocated his friendship by sharing her thoughts about life in Yugoslavia. He wrote her later in a letter: "I think of your reaction to Zagreb as an important testament, for I have not before heard the Yugoslav general condition made so plain. I now seem to understand Djilas a little better." Milovan Djilas was the high-ranking communist official whose criticism of the Yugoslav system landed him in prison, with his books banned in Yugoslavia for decades.

In the end, Surya Green's Yugoslav experience was enlightening in the truest sense. Gaining profound knowledge about herself as she overcame the struggles of being a stranger in a strange land was heroic and, I believe, ennobling. In my view, the need to gather inner strength and self-knowledge in the alien Yugoslav society is an early key to Surya's evolution as a truly humane and centered person.

Learning not to judge others, to seek balance, and to accept the truth that love is based on giving and not taking are difficult life lessons. So are the lessons of patience, aloneness, self-reliance, and reduced consuming. Then there are the lessons connected with being an aware citizen. Surya mastered them all during her transformational stay in Zagreb.

The story of Surya Green's two parallel journeys, outer and inner, is inspiring and uplifting. It is always fascinating to learn how seemingly accidental events affect people's lives, but Surya Green's book is full of extraordinary personal adventures. Observing Surya's ability to understand how everyday experiences have influenced her is to gain a very special insight into the evolution of a subtle and complex consciousness. *Once Upon a Yugoslavia* is a compelling story indeed.

—*Henry Breitrose (1936–2014), founder of the graduate program in documentary filmmaking and professor emeritus of communication, Stanford University*

INTRODUCTION

Seeing the Overview

*O*nce Upon a Yugoslavia describes my process of rethinking my good American life. What really constitutes a "good life"? What is "quality of life," and what is a "better life"?

An overwhelming urge to uncover life's whys and wherefores has impassioned me since childhood, propelling me increasingly onward and inward. At first my quest for the aim of life was instinctual and but dimly felt. Eventually the vague spiritual pursuit became a conscious adventure of enlightening discovery.

My search for life's deepest answers has situated me, for longer or shorter stays, in diverse parts of my native America, in Europe, and in Asia. The many visas and stamps in my passports to the contrary, by and by I learned: the ultimate answers are secreted in only one place, and we need not leave home to reclaim them. Unless we are born into a family that kindles our spiritual spark from our earliest breaths, the journey leading us to know our true nature will span many a sunrise.

In my case, at a certain point I had to find a personal balance within the unbalanced value system defining success and happiness in my homeland. I am full of wonder, gratitude, and humility that my ever-continuing odyssey guided me to a pot of gold most priceless: inner experience of life's nonmaterial purpose.

Once Upon a Yugoslavia relates an initial, preparatory stage of my ripening process from I to We to Thee-awareness. In a nutshell, and narrated in the present tense reflecting the immediacy of my Yugoslav experience to this day:

Nearing the completion of my master's degree studies in communication at Stanford University in 1968, I accept a summer writing job at a renowned film studio in socialist Yugoslavia—Zagreb Film by name, commonly dubbed "the Studio."[1] I have no particular interest in alternatives to the capitalist system but I *am* interested in people, and how peoples of other societies and cultures live. Yugoslavia will let me observe a society based on aspirations quite different from my traditional American ideals and ambitions.

Working and residing in Zagreb, in Croatia, a republic of the Socialist Federal Republic of Yugoslavia, will serve as a living textbook for a uniquely tailored postgraduate summer course: "Daily Life in a Developing Second World Country: Tito's Yugoslavia."

Once in Zagreb, I am simultaneously thrown into a 24/7 seminar foreign to the curriculum of any school I attended: "Beyond Material Awareness: Living Our Life in Relation to Attaining True Success in this World."

Up until my stay in Zagreb, I am immersed in the individualistic American Way of life and lack genuine understanding of myself. My challenging engagement with Yugoslav society forces me to recognize the narrow confines of my thinking.

Once Upon a Yugoslavia conveys my thoughts, feelings, and experiences while I am undergoing, unbeknownst to me, a de-education and re-education that is opening my mind and heart for a deeper and wider perspective.

Yu-go-*slave*-ia, as I call the country following local usage, compels me to spot the lessons presented every day for my inner maturation. I unlearn, while relearning, some basic principles needed to live an aware,

---

[1] Certain terms in this book are capitalized even where the lower case might be grammatically sufficient—to acknowledge, for example, the prominent role of the Studio in Yugoslavia's film industry, the Godlike dominance of the Party over Yugoslavia and the rest of the Eastern Bloc, or the central role of Sun and Earth in all our lives.

content, and fulfilling existence. My I-centered self receives twentieth-century lessons in what I trust can finally become the twenty-first century's We-focused lifestyle.

The transformation described in these pages begins in the past. Yet the narration also applies to the present as well as the future. My individual journey reflects changes I consider inevitable on our collective path to a humane tomorrow. The future of our global community depends on sharing, and sharing motivates my pen. Perhaps my mind-and-heart awakening discoveries will give readers a sense of "Aha, yes, of course!"

Once Upon a Yugoslavia is part of my projected series of books on the stages of personal transformation linked to a larger transformation. It speaks to the call of our times—trying times calling us to help effect a new way of living together on this planet for the good of all. *Once Upon a Yugoslavia* is one action and offering for a better world.

Surya Green
Amsterdam, the Netherlands

1

Venturing Out of the Comfort Zone

Once upon a time, in the summer of 1968, I am seated in a European train taking me toward the unknown: the mysterious country of Tito's Yugoslavia. I have no idea that my foreign travels will ultimately transport me beyond national borders to the furthermost limits of my mind.

The train chugs into the Zagreb train station on a fiery July day. I did not expect a welcoming committee, but there is absolutely no one to receive me. Thinking the Studio's rep is late, I find my way to the waiting room. Poorly dressed and gray-toned people occupy every inch of the cramped space. Some people squat on the ground.

The women wear dark-colored nondescript skirts, mainly long and loose, topped by blouses of coarse plain cotton. Kerchiefs cover many heads. Three small children huddle around a woman who breastfeeds a baby. Never before have I seen breastfeeding in public.

The men are clad in open-collared shirts or pullovers and loose trousers. Many of them sport short-cropped, heavily oiled hair. Several men are stretched out asleep on the wooden benches. One man sits in a corner slicing and giving chunks of greasy roast bacon and bread to the people gathered around him. His family?

The odor of stale sweat permeates the room. These people conform to the stereotype of disadvantaged communist citizens. Have I stepped onto the set of a European art house movie?

As strange as the scene looks to me, many eyes stare in my direction. Not that I am remarkably beautiful or ugly. Perhaps my clothing, of the latest American fashion, attracts their gaze. My minidress contrasts sharply to the modest attire of the Yugoslav women. The dress raised no eyebrows in the States. Here it evokes reactions of dismay.

Clicking sounds similar to "tsk, tsk" sting my ears. I assume this means pretty much the same as at home: "Pity! Pity! Shame! Shame!" The disapproval of the travelers, the stifling heat, the stuffy air, and the stench of the waiting room convince me to leave the train station.

After two days in transit, I rally the strength to go on carrying my suitcase and my portable typewriter. Family and friends, doubting the existence of quality goods in a communist country, persuaded me to pack a hearty supply of skirts, blouses, and dresses to remain my stylish self even in Yugoslavia. My parents stuffed nuts, dried fruits, and cookies into my suitcase. In these free-flying days when airlines do not strictly apply overweight penalty fees, and luggage manufacturers have yet to discover the wheel, my baggage weighs me down. I drag myself to a huddle of taxi drivers who scrutinize me thoroughly.

"Zagreb Film," I announce. The men act baffled.

"The Studio is well known!" I exclaim. The drivers do not understand English and I have not one phrase of Serbo-Croatian at my disposal.

"Okay, okay," I say, more to myself than to them. They snigger as they watch me search in my large shoulder bag crammed with everything I thought I might possibly need during the two days' journey from New York to Zagreb. One driver motions me to his car.

I show the precious letter sent by Zagreb Film confirming the summer job. "This is the address. *Vlaška 70*." The man shrugs and throws up his hands.

Another driver rubs his fingers together in the international gesture for money. Nowhere on my route have I been able to buy the

Yugoslav currency, the dinar. After more rummaging in my purse, I produce the German coins left over from the passage through Germany and the meal in the train. The driver, glancing at them, shakes his head unfavorably.

All except two of the men wander back to their cars. One of them makes a hand signal I interpret to mean I should just stand there and wait, because help will be coming, and I need not fret. The other driver walks off. It is almost high noon, and the blazing rays of summer Sun burn into my naked arms. Leaning on his taxi, the driver leers at my legs, all the while picking at his teeth. His face bears a mischievous grin. I wish I had worn slacks.

Finally, at last, the first driver returns in the company of an elderly fellow who seems to be in his seventies. He is bald and needs a shave. Gray stubble pops out helter-skelter. His round-rimmed eyeglasses remind me of my grandfather's classic pair. The seasoned recruit points to my suitcase, then to himself, and lifts my baggage with youthful agility. Smiling a broad, toothless grin, he walks away at a rapid pace. Astonished, I follow. The dynamic porter marches past the fleet of parked taxis and crosses the street. Running to keep up, I flap the Studio's letterhead address at him.

Not missing a step, he says "*Da, da*"—apparently "Yes, yes." He strides briskly toward a crowd of people pushing their way into a tram. A veritable battle tank, the old man rolls in among them and squeezes through the carriage. People struggling onto the tram shove me aside. Before I can board, the tram begins moving. I panic and shout in English, "Wait a minute! Wait for me!"

The tram continues. Reenergized by the need of the moment, I run in pursuit, waving frantically for the tram to halt. Passengers hanging out the windows wave gaily back. They seem to enjoy my inconvenience!

Huffing, puffing, and overheated, I catch the tram at its next stop. Adapting the local push-and-squeeze tactic, I burrow into the packed hotbox. The perspiring bodies melt us into a human soup. My nose does not have to be overly sensitive to note again that underarm deodorant may not be available to Yugoslavs.

I hold my breath and resort to the elbowing maneuver. Colliding into the old man, my baggage firmly in his grip, I sigh in relief. He breaks into his huge, toothless grin. Two slightly ripped tram tickets dangle from his shirt pocket. After long steamy minutes as one of the smelly horde, I am unsteadied when the tram jerks to a standstill. The old man gasps and joins the thrust to the nearest exit. I cling to his jacket, my determination to breathe fresh air growing stronger by the moment. Push changes to shove the instant the tram door opens. We land on the pavement as if by a cannon's discharge. I would relish a pause, but the energetic old man resumes his rapid gait.

He leads me to large wooden doors opening into a courtyard. Once inside, he places the suitcase and the typewriter on the ground quite gently. Then he collapses like a ragdoll.

"Are you okay, are you okay?" I cry, tapping his arm. He groans excessively, much more than my light touch deserves.

"Are you okay?" I ask again, forgetting he does not comprehend a single word I utter. His condition alarms me until he sticks his palm straight out.

"Oh, yes, yes, here," I pronounce, emptying my purse into his hand. I have no idea what price the old man sets for his labor, or what the tram tickets cost, but the German marks catapult him to his feet. He brushes himself off, flashes his infectious smile, bows slightly to me, and departs.

I see two buildings, one yellow and one gray. Perhaps the color attracts me; also, the yellow building is closer. A plaque displays the name "Zagreb Film" and the Studio's symbol, a fully maned prancing horse.

Entering, I spot a tiny cubicle. A small desk contains two old-fashioned black phones, an opened newspaper, and a copper pot of strong-smelling coffee atop an electric heater. Behind the desk sits a blonde-haired woman. Her chubby face, unaltered by cosmetics, is broad and plain. She is dressed in a dark blue smock that may be a uniform. Eyeing my baggage curiously, she says something in Serbo-Croatian.

"I am here to work at Zagreb Film," I respond in English.

Her expression is blank. I exercise my rusty French to no avail.

A man comes into the building and stops to watch the tiny drama in progress. His appearance distinguishes him from the Yugoslavs at the train station and in the tram. His slightly long hair, light gray-tinted sunglasses, deep blue tee shirt, and flowing cotton trousers create an artistic look I find appealing.

"Želimir Matko?" I ask.

"English?" he counters.

"American."

"Oh, *Američanka*. I not speak American, only English," he tells in all seriousness. "Matko meeting, many business."

"Will he be long?" I inquire.

"Oh, maybe two meters," he answers, raising his hand inches above his head. He entrusts my baggage to the receptionist and signals me to follow him. We walk along a gray hallway lined by offices on both sides. The hallway, its paint faded and peeling in spots, sorely needs a renovation. Possibly the corridor lighting is dim for good reason.

We enter a small, cramped room. "Matko office. Not like Amerika," says the man apologetically.

My rescuer is correct: This office "not like Amerika." Stacks of books carrying titles in various languages, correspondence, and reports crowd the room. Raggedy brown-edged papers, crumpled and worn, cover the window ledge. The window needs neither curtains nor shades since the papers block the sunlight. Matko's desk is another mountainous landscape of papers and books. Deftly maneuvering around the papers and books on the floor, I manage to reach the visitor's chair.

After months of corresponding with Želimir Matko, Director of Distribution for Zagreb Films, responsible for sales and marketing, here I am in the capital of Croatia. Matko's letters, typed on thin, onionskin paper, featured the logo of the prancing horse. In the upper left corner was a reproduction of the Hollywood Oscar and the caption "Academy Award 1961, Best Cartoon, *Surogat*, 'Ersatz,' by Dušan Vukotić." At first it puzzled me that an organization in a communist country placed a symbol of capitalism on its letterhead.

Pretrip research informed me that the Socialist Federal Republic of Yugoslavia (SFRY) is a communist state based on collective ownership and one-party rule. The Federation consists of six Balkan republics: Bosnia and Herzegovina, Croatia, Macedonia, Montenegro, Serbia, and Slovenia. Each republic contains much ethnic diversity, and each has the same degree of autonomy under the federal constitution.

Yugoslavia's leader since 1945, Josip Broz Tito, rejected the domination of his country by the Union of Soviet Socialist Republics (USSR). Differing with the methods of the USSR and its leader Joseph Stalin for attaining communism, Tito set Yugoslavia on a middle path balanced between Soviet-style communism and Western capitalism. He forged a "Third Way" between the Eastern and Western Blocs.

The Zagreb Film letterhead conveys that the Studio wants to present itself as an earnest competitor in the business of international film, able to meet the requirements of foreign markets and hard currency transactions. Nonetheless, in one of his letters Matko wrote: "I suppose that the main purpose of your coming to Yugoslavia is not to make money. In any case, Yugoslavia is wrong country for anyone to become rich!!!" His emphatic declaration made me wonder if even people in a communist country equate being rich with having money. He asked how long I could stay. "We have a considerable number of films for which we would like to have a commentary in English," he wrote. "We are only afraid to exhaust you while in Zagreb."

Now I sit alone in this communist country. On the wall behind Matko's desk hangs a photo of President Tito. His expression is serious, resolute. He is a man of peasant stock who became a national leader and international statesman.

Atop Matko's desk a round metal clock stands on thin, spindly legs. It ticks steadily as five minutes become ten, twenty. . . . I begin to fidget. Time is slipping away. Perhaps time may signify something different to Yugoslavs than to me. Despite having to dash behind the elderly porter, I sense that life here generally moves in the slow lane.

This thought actually came as my Zagreb-bound train left the Free West, *sooo verrrry slooooowly.*

After racing steadily through the cities and countryside of Germany and Austria, the train noticeably decelerated once it crossed into Yugoslavia. Languidly it rolled through the countryside, as if reluctant to reach the Croatian capital. The train's reduced speed let me observe the green and lush Yugoslav countryside in detail.

We passed through living Balkan picture books reflecting a traditional peasant society. Horse-drawn carts ambled alongside the train. In the fields, humans and horses were the sole workers, no tractors to be seen. As in an America gone by, the farms grew varied crops. I saw no monocultures. The farmers toiled the land using simple hand tools.

Eventually the snail's pace of the train turned my good humor to irritation.

Now, sitting and waiting in Matko's office, I am annoyed. I am accustomed to the dynamic go-go-go pulse of my hometown. If my life were a film, and the filmmaker used the slow motion technique to slow certain periods of time, that approach could achieve interesting cinematic effects. Doing things in slow motion might even, if my life were a film, make my existence in time appear to last longer.

But my life is not a film. My life is not a stream of light images flickering on a movie screen, giving the illusion of constant movement. I am alive in a flesh and blood body, living here and now in physical reality. Being stilled to slow motion in Matko's workroom is a huge waste of my time. How can life in slow mo, and now even no-mo, be anything except irksome to a born and bred New Yorker? My patience reaches an exasperation point. Just then a smiling man saunters into the room.

Indeed, he towers over me by at least nine inches. If his height intimidates me, his warm approach does not. He greets me with a friendly handshake and keeps pumping my hand, all the while continuing to smile. I estimate he is in his early fifties. His straight chestnut brown hair, combed back on the sides, frames the balding top of his head.

Broadly built, he wears gray cotton baggy pants, a long-sleeve brown-checkered sports shirt, sandals, and thin brown socks. I catch a whiff of aftershave.

"Miss Green? I am Matko," he states in a booming voice. He strikes me as someone rich with the confidence of being an expert at his job. "Welcome to Yu-go-*slave*-ia!"

2

Entering a Gray Existence

Matko speaks English with a thick accent and, curiously, he hammers the third syllable of his country's name. He pronounces it not as "slav," but definitely as the English word "slave." He laughs, greatly amused. Full and deep, his laugh charms me.

"I am not joking," he says as he maneuvers himself into his chair, a simple wooden chair quite unlike the posture-perfect desk chairs preferred in American offices. Settling into the seat, just wide enough for his ample body, Matko gives a mini history lesson.

"The English word 'slave' refers to the Slavic peoples, the Slavs of Eastern and Central Europe. Slavs were often enslaved during the early Middle Ages. The Romans used Slavs as slaves."

Matko explains that the Byzantine Empire, or the Eastern Roman Empire, trying to stabilize its German-Slav frontier in the early ninth century, captured Slavs and placed them in forced servitude. "As well, the Germans took Slavs as slaves," he continues. "And some Slavs themselves participated in the slave trade. The word 'slave' comes from 'Slav.' Well, actually, the word comes from a Latin term, *sclavus*, referring to those Slavs of Eastern and Central Europe who were forced into servitude by foreign invasion."

Matko's knowledge on the subject impresses me. "The words 'Slavs' and 'slaves' are certainly similar," I remark.

Do all Yugoslavs pronounce "Slav" as "slave," or is Matko transmitting a cryptic message of political critique? In the strictest meaning of the word, a "slave" is a dehumanized human being. A slave, bought and sold as property, is the possession of others and lacks the most basic human rights. Aside from sufficient food, water, clothing, and shelter needed to stay alive in order to carry out the required tasks of one's slavery, a slave does not even receive "slave wages." I want to ask Matko if he, as a Slav, really sees himself as a slave today. Does he truly consider himself to be a Yu-go-*slave*-ian?

Tito's photo watches us sternly. My questions may be too politically delicate to pose as a foreigner Matko does not know. Besides, his mini lecture is over. There is neither question-answer nor discussion in his history class.

"Now to business," Matko declares. "Please, I must apologize for my long meeting, but that's the influence of your capitalism, isn't it?"

Before I can respond, a woman enters the office. She wears the dark blue smock; the outfit does seem to be a uniform. "*Druže*! ('Comrade!') *Telefon*! *Beograd*!" she reports urgently. "*Beograd*!"

Beograd, Belgrade, is Yugoslavia's largest city and the federal capital. Located in the republic of Serbia, *Beograd* houses the national government and Tito's headquarters in the National Palace.

Matko shuffles through papers on his desk. "Back in a minute," he announces, papers stacked under his arm. His tone is cheerful despite the gravity the woman's voice conveyed.

Matko's "minute" ticks on. The Slav-slave issue absorbs me. Does Matko's reference to Yugoslavs being Yugo-*slaves* have solid historical reference, or is it simply a semantic correspondence? Are the Slavic peoples called this because they were slaves, or did the word "slave" evolve from Slavic people getting enslaved?

Even while caught up in the Slav-slave word play, I closely examine the plain and simple room in which I find myself. There is no decoration per se. The image of Tito and framed certificates fill the walls. The office boasts an imposing collection of Zagreb Film's awards, won at prestigious international film festivals. On Matko's desk, framed photographs depict him with men whose clothing suggests they are Westerners. Film people, I assume. Matko appears to have an extensive professional circle.

I look intently at the photos until my eyes flutter to a close. After the challenging arrival in Zagreb, and the precarious tram ride, tiredness sends me into a doze.

My eyes open sleepily on Matko's return, about fifteen minutes later. He apologizes for the inconvenience. "Well, Miss Green," he begins, "during the next few months we'll know exactly where you are, won't we?"

His statement, sounding suspiciously Big Brotherish, bolts me awake. I fake a smile and counter, "Well, Mr. Matko, it depends how you mean that."

My thoughts go quickly to my mother. When I informed my parents about my summer job, my mother commented: "I am scared of communism, but I feel safe in America."

My mother passed her fear of communism to me at a very young age. I grew up in the America of the conservative 1950s, the time of the anticommunist crusade and Republican Senator Joseph McCarthy.

The McCarthy anticommunism investigations have been likened to the witch trials held in colonial America. In Salem, Massachusetts, in 1692, an atmosphere of hysteria brought death by hanging to many innocent people found guilty of witchcraft. The mid-twentieth-century witch-hunts destroyed the lives of many Americans suspected of communist affiliations, based on flimsy evidence. Communist suspects had to contend with government investigation, especially during televised public hearings. Whether or not they actually had communist loyalties, sympathies, or membership in the Communist Party of America, they faced job dismissal, blacklisting, and social ostracism.

During the anticommunist hysteria, my parents regularly listened to the radio program "I Was a Communist for the FBI." The popular series dramatized the adventures of Matt Cvetic, a real FBI agent of Slovenian background. Cvetic infiltrates local cells of the Communist

Party of America to spy from inside and gather information on communist plots to destroy America. My father, I later found out, wanted to join the FBI. But an agent would have to know how to use handguns. My mother said no. Perhaps as recompense, every week we listened religiously to "I Was a Communist for the FBI." The ultrapatriotic radio program reinforced the message that Soviet communism was dangerously anti-American.

I learned to associate the word "communist" with "Big Brother" and an all-powerful Soviet state sharply monitoring its citizens while presenting a major peril to the American way of life and national security. Those were the Cold War days of political and military tension between the USA-led capitalistic Western powers and the USSR-led communist countries of Central and Eastern Europe. The threat of nuclear war hung in the air.

In my elementary school we practiced "taking cover" under our desks as a means of protecting ourselves in the event of a Soviet nuclear attack. We never thought to inquire: "Why? What good would it do to duck under our desks?" No one told us that Russian schoolchildren, taught to be frightened by America's nuclear capability, were possibly involved in a comparable exercise.

Now it is 1968 and we Americans still fear the "Red Menace." My mother unwittingly sums up mainstream opinion when she observes, in regard to my upcoming job in Zagreb: "I don't know anything about Yugoslavia. I suppose it is like Russia and the other communist countries." Her parents had emigrated from Eastern Europe in the early part of the century. "If you want to take the chance to go there, what can I say?"

Incredibly, my inherited fear of communism did not prevent my spontaneous "Yes!" to the Yugoslav job offer. Since my childhood, my parents encouraged me to make my own decisions. Those decisions, emanating from our American culture, motivated me to succeed in whatever I attempted. Like most Americans, I grew up a true believer that, as an American, I had the freedom to attain the success that is the hallmark of, well, "Success."

Fortunately for me, my white skin color does not call forth the racial prejudice obstructing black people in my country. I was raised, however, in the Judaic faith. Our family is not religious, attending synagogue mainly on the holidays, but culturally we are Jewish Americans. Besides having to endure occasional if camouflaged anti-Semitism, from a young age I have experienced the slings and arrows of bias against females. Despite the handicaps inherent to my religion and genitalia, I cherish the American ideal that any goal or dream can be realized through one's abilities, effort, and perseverance. This ideal, shining behind the charisma of my beloved country, gives the "American Way" a special importance in the world. Growing up, I had no doubts I would reach the heights of success in America.

Indeed, my high school graduating class voted me the female graduate "Most Likely to Succeed." The student voters and I myself thought of success as an achievement, as an attainment of the American Dream linked with material prosperity and position and fame in society. To justify the confidence of my schoolmates, I had to run the American race. No problem. Focused on material achievement as I was, I lived and labored triumphantly in the American system of persistent competition, rush, and stress. Because of my birth in Manhattan, the nation's economic heart, I benefited from my hometown's dominant thinking: "If you can make it in New York, you can make it anywhere."

My parents' open-minded reaction to the unusual venue of my summer employment both surprised and relieved me. Enthusiastically I dispersed my job news among my family, friends, and acquaintances. Only then did I learn that most of them faithfully considered the American Way to be "the only way." The "c" word unleashed fears of an evil enemy committed to destroying America. After I tired of defending my choice to work in a communist country, if only for a summer, I found myself practicing self-censorship.

Now I am sitting in Matko's office at Zagreb Film in communist Yu-go-*slave*-ia, and there is no escaping.

"Well, Miss Green," Matko continues, "knowing where you are while in Zagreb should be no problem, should it?"

Once more I hear the Big Brotherish implication of his previous statement. Again I force myself to smile. "What exactly do you mean?"

"Ah, you Americans have a curious way of speaking," comments Matko. "But that's why you're here, isn't it? We need good English—rather, American—versions of our films. Only an American can do that for us."

"I'll try my best, of course."

"As you know, we can't pay much. We're a poor country, Miss Green. Let me also point out that we're stuck in a lack of space and equipment. Your office will not be spacious and luxurious. I hope you don't mind. The job you're supposed to do is not typical office work, so you'll be able to work here at the Studio or at home."

"About a place to live, Mr. Matko, your letter said you would arrange accommodations for me in a private home or in a modest hotel. The journey has been very tiring. May I go to my room now?"

"Ah, Miss Green," begins Matko in a sugary intonation. "Well, you see, we've been so busy we weren't even able to come for you this morning. We received your cable with arrival time but we thought, since you are American, you'd be able to manage."

"Yes, but about a room . . ." Matko's indifference perturbs me. Furthermore, after my arduous trip he has not offered any refreshment, not even a glass of water on this sweltering day.

"Well, let's see. . . . A hotel would cost roughly two-thirds of your salary, so you should stay in a private home. I hope you don't expect luxury."

"I'm prepared to live the way you do. I'm willing to accept your lifestyle."

"That's interesting," remarks Matko, a wry smile slanting his lips. "Not all our own people are."

I find it necessary to remind Matko: "You wrote there should be no difficulty to arrange accommodations in the vicinity of your Studio."

"Ah, yes," sighs Matko. "Sorry to say no one has made any provisions for your stay. I will investigate." He leaves the room, promising, "Back in a minute."

Matko's "minute" ticks slowly and steadily into a next minute, on and on. Is the clock on Matko's desk only for show? As a native New Yorker, I am habituated to perpetual activity and movement at a galloping Manhattan tempo. Sitting still and waiting while "doing nothing" idles away my time. We Americans equate time with money. "Losing" or "wasting" time is tantamount to a sin. I cannot imagine I will ever say here, "Time flies."

Again I scan Matko's office. I check my wristwatch, repeatedly. I take deep breaths. I entertain myself by finger tapping a few of my favorite American songs on the arm of the chair. My self-styled music recital pulls me homeward, delivering some comfort. When my fingers ask for rest, I wonder: *What next?* Tired and thirsty, I puzzle over the Studio's neglect of my housing needs. A rush of impatience to get showered and settled follows a burst of annoyance. My hot Hungarian blood is nearing the boiling point. In this advancing state of upset, strangely, I get the unfamiliar thought: *Slow down.* Humph! Do I have a choice?

Eventually Matko returns and exclaims jovially, "You are very lucky! Come on, I will take you to your living quarters."

Matko drives a small gray automobile of an East European brand unknown to me. Compared to my "battle tank," the super-size powder blue Buick I sold before leaving the States, Matko's car is a mini model. Tiny though it is, the car roars to a start. Riding toward the outskirts of Zagreb, we pass an occasional horse-drawn cart similar to those I watched from the train window, and we drive by rows, endless rows, of gray, multistory apartment blocks. The bland vista is relieved here and there by young, fragile trees. They seem so weak, so vulnerable, exactly as I feel at this moment.

"Such gray buildings," I comment.

"Built in a period of rapid planning after the war," says Matko. "We are a developing economy, Miss Green. Urbanizing an old peasant economy is no easy task. Villagers flood into the cities to earn more money. We struggle with problems of an acute housing shortage, overcrowding, social adjustment, traffic—you name it. We lack cash. We can't do everything at once."

Block after block of the repetitive drab architecture bores my eyes. Matko explains that the buildings had to be built on the smallest budget.

Still, I think, were there no low-cost imaginative possibilities for enlivening the lackluster gray slabs? Is the resultant plainness due to a lack of construction materials or of creative design innovation?

The dismally uniform buildings and the look-alike people on the streets create a dull sameness. These people mirror the gray-shaded travelers I observed at the train station. A number of the older women dress entirely in black, from their headscarves to their laced walking shoes resembling men's oxfords. Some women balance food baskets on their heads.

"My Hungarian grandmother sometimes wore a *babushka*," I say, referring to the kerchiefs tied below the chin of many of the women in black.

"We call it a *marama*," Matko responds.

Even the dazzling afternoon sunlight cannot brighten the darkness of these surroundings. I get a premonition of doom.

We arrive at our destination, another identical block of the soulless gray apartment buildings. Matko parks the car on the sidewalk. My surprise at the unconventional parking spot amuses him. "Don't worry," he intones in his merry way, "it's our custom."

Matko and I walk to the courtyard of a large building. I am sweltering in the July heat. In the open area, a beefy man, perspiring heavily in a sleeveless undershirt, slops water over a car similar to Matko's. Like the Yugoslavs I have seen so far, he appears well fed.

At the courtyard's left side, Matko knocks at a door that needs sprucing up. A middle-aged woman wearing a *marama* opens the door while wiping her other hand across the apron around her waist. She is chewing on a piece of bread. Matko introduces himself. The woman ushers us into her apartment through a narrow, feebly lit entrance hall. We follow her to a door leading into a small, dark room. The room smells musty, as if long unoccupied. The furnishings could have been salvaged from the stage set of a film documenting the 1930s worldwide economic depression.

Against the left wall is a sofa bed covered by a threadbare fabric of dark maroon. Nearby stands a wooden chest of drawers topped by shelves displaying glasses and dishes behind glass doors. In one corner looms a tall, black metal heating stove fueled by wood or coal. Dominating the rest of the room, two straight-backed wooden chairs face each other around a heavy wooden table. An outdated landscape calendar nailed to the wall provides the sole decoration.

There is one window, and it is closed. As in Matko's office, it admits only half the daylight. No papers and books obstruct the bottom part of the window. Instead, a dark shade covers half the window's length. I could never sleep in this room.

The woman guides us down the hall. We enter a small space containing a sink with one faucet, a two-burner hot plate, and jars of homemade pickled cucumbers and peppers lined up on shelves. Matko translates the woman's comment: "You can use the kitchen."

The likelihood is inconceivable to me.

We follow the landlady further. She opens the door to a lavatory. There is a toilet bowl lacking a seat, and a small sink possessing only one faucet. A second faucet, on the wall, has a hose attached. I point to it: "Is that the hot water?"

After a small exchange with the woman, Matko discloses: "There is no hot water."

How can I live here?

We return to "my room." Matko and the woman engage in animated conversation. Discussing terms of the rental, are they? Nostalgia seizes me as I think of my sweet little walkup in Manhattan, sublet to a cousin for the summer.

The woman slides the cupboard's glass doors and removes a cut glass bottle and three matching small glasses. Pouring a colorless liquid from the bottle, she presents a glass to Matko and one to me. Matko raises his drink in a toast and clicks our glasses.

"*Živeli!*" he exclaims, as if announcing a victory. "*Živeli* means 'Cheers!' You always learn the most important words first," he declares, grinning. "*Živeli* comes from the verb *živeti*, 'to live.'"

The Yugoslav toast reminds me of the Hebrew toasting expression *l'chaim*, "to life!" I bring the glass to my nose. The scent is fruity, sweet, not unpleasant, but I do not rush the liquid to my lips.

"Some things take getting used to, Miss Green. This is *šljivovica*, our famous plum brandy." He pauses before saying, with a resolute finality, "Well, all you have to do is settle in."

Contesting Matko's housing solution will surely break up the *šljivovica* party. How to proceed and not insult Matko or the landlady? I begin hesitantly. "Mr. Matko, you know, well, I'm not certain this room is really good for me."

"I told you not to expect luxury," he responds in a slightly irritated tone.

"It's not that," I tell him. "The woman and I can't communicate, she has no phone, and the room is far out of town. Driving here, you said that the trams stop running in the evening. Wouldn't I be a little bit isolated?"

I do not mention the absence of hot water or shower or refrigerator or proper cooking stove. It had never occurred to me that the ordinary conveniences I automatically count on at home would be missing here.

"Miss Green, housing conditions are very difficult in this town," states Matko in a somber, admonishing tone. "People come from the countryside much faster than we can build houses to accommodate them."

"It's not that I am ungrateful, Mr. Matko. I will be cut off here."

The nonexistence of what I consider essential bathing and cooking facilities is secondary to the mood of isolation gripping me. At the Zagreb train station, where no Studio rep awaited me, I tasted the heart pain of being a stranger in a strange land. Now an intense sadness accompanies the lonely sensation.

"Isn't there any alternative to this place?"

"It won't be easy," replies Matko, "but you cannot be forced to stay where you do not want, can you? You are not a Yu-go-*slave*!"

During our exchange, the landlady has watched us, her lips puckered into a serious grimace and her broad arms akimbo. She has understood the gist of the conversation. Matko turns to her and speaks in a low and grave voice totally unlike the sparkling tone induced by the *šljivovica*. I hear the words "*Američanka*" and "*Amerika.*" The woman's disappointed look embarrasses me.

Back at the Studio, Matko escorts me to his office and asks me to wait. Before exiting, he promises: "I will inquire further." As in the rejected room, I feel isolated and lonely in the half-shade of Matko's workspace. Light has disappeared from the world. Sun presides over the July Yugoslav sky, yet a shadowy energy darkens the atmosphere. A gray cloud hangs over this society. Or has the long journey and the afternoon heat tumble-tossed me into over-tiredness and low spirits? Misgivings arise: "Have I made the right decision to come here?"

3

Remembering the Backstory

Actually, I never made a decision to work in Yugoslavia. I had not used my mind to weigh rationally the pros and cons of accepting the summer job. A spontaneous answer had simply emerged. Now I find my instant positive response inexplicable.

Surely my heart, feeling no connection to Yugoslavia, had not influenced the decision. Did my spontaneous "Yes!" spring merely from my attraction to adventure, from my curiosity to explore the unfamiliar? Or is there a deeper reason why I uprooted myself to come here? Why do I get the thought that some "decisive force" temporarily eradicated my negative preconceptions of communism? I recollect the California spring day that ostensibly launched my Yugoslavian odyssey.

I am walking across the Stanford University campus. Situated in a beautiful valley framed by rolling hills, the university nestles under the habitually clear blue California sky. The sheer physical splendor of the location never fails to impress me. When Stanford awarded me a fellowship for my master's degree, immediately I agreed. Around that particular snap decision hovers no mystery. Who would not want to attend the prestigious "Harvard of the West" offering top-notch education? Stanford's official motto, "The wind of freedom blows," also resonates with me. As a freedom-loving American, I take pride in my country's reputation as the "Land of the Free."

Additionally, Stanford's motto evokes the birth city of my maternal grandfather, in Latvia in northeast Europe. Liepāja, its location on the Baltic Sea affording a constant sea breeze, is known as "the city where the wind is born."

I stroll past Stanford's eye-pleasing buildings of sandstone masonry topped by red-tile roofs in Spanish-colonial style. Sun shines brilliantly, but I see this sunny California day through eyes clouded by a gloomy mental state. Apparently I inhale, riding on my breath, the disturbed energy pervading my homeland.

Turmoil engulfs America. The US government is militarily engaged in Vietnam to prevent a communist takeover of Southeast Asia. At home, the antiwar movement is growing. College protests against the Vietnam War have become commonplace. Every month, dozens more American schools erupt. Students and peace activists march against American troops fighting and dying for a questionable cause. I myself do not demonstrate for US departure from Vietnam even though I vehemently agree with "Stop All Wars!" Young men flee to Canada to escape the draft.

As well, the racial struggle between the people of color and the whites is continuing. Blacks strongly protest discriminatory practices based on race. Every summer since 1964, underprivileged inner-city black people have taken to the streets shouting out their general dissatisfactions. This energy of discontent sometimes explodes in wild, chaotic, and bloody rioting and looting. Especially the 1965 riots in the Watts neighborhood of Los Angeles highlighted the issues of racial discrimination and the huge disparity of wealth and opportunity between black and white Americans.

In 1966, the consummate American civil rights leader, Dr. Martin Luther King, Jr., complained of living in a sick and violent nation. "I'm sick and tired of violence," he declared. "I'm tired of the war in Vietnam.

I'm tired of war and conflict in the world. I'm tired of shooting. I'm tired of hatred. I'm tired of selfishness. I'm tired of evil."[2]

Not all of America's discontented citizens follow Dr. King's path of peace. The year 1967 witnessed a record number of destructive riots in inner cities.

Americans of African heritage, formerly called "Negroes" and now terming themselves "blacks," are asserting their distinctive identity as black Americans. The militant Black Panthers, formed in California in 1966 to combat white superiority and submission to the white man's system and to rally black people, coined such slogans as "Black Pride!" and "Black Power!" Enhanced racial pride and self-esteem empower black people to demand improved social conditions. All around us calls such as "Free the Blacks!" and "End Racial Discrimination!" ring in our ears.

In February 1968, the National Advisory Commission on Civil Disorders, also known as the Kerner Commission, appointed by President Lyndon B. Johnson to explain the riots plaguing American cities, releases the Report of the National Advisory Commission on Civil Disorders, aka the Kerner Report. The report indicts white society for isolating and neglecting African Americans, warning: "Our nation is moving toward two societies, one black, one white—separate and unequal."[3]

Martin Luther King is involved in his latest social reform campaign. His mission has become more inclusive than solely the integration and equal rights of black people. He is criticizing and challenging American war policies and the poverty at home. He seeks social justice for the most vulnerable in American society.

Making connections between Vietnam, racism, classism, and poverty in America, Dr. King aims to transform the economic situation of poor Americans. He strives for a broad national coalition of the working class and the poor of all races and backgrounds to join in a

---

[2] *At Canaan's Edge: America in the King Years, 1965–68,* by Taylor Branch, Simon & Schuster, New York, 2006.

[3] Kerner Commission, Report of the National Advisory Commission on Civil Disorders, Washington: US Government Printing Office, 1968.

Poor People's March to Washington, D.C. Preparing for the multiethnic march to America's capital city, Dr. King holds a summit meeting of Chicano farm laborers, Native Americans from the Plains (still called Indians), and white coal miners from Appalachia. The representatives sit together to explore the then-revolutionary idea that their peoples might have mutual grievances and causes.[4]

Before the mass demonstration takes place, and while he is readying a church sermon entitled "America May Go to Hell," Martin Luther King is killed in Memphis by a white assassin. It is the fourth of April in explosive 1968. Besides the general violence and unrest troubling the national scene, enraged black people riot and loot in over one hundred American cities.[5]

The assassination of Dr. King and the subsequent events temporarily pull my attention away from my Stanford classes in journalism, broadcast news, and film. Like most people I react with shock, rage, and sorrow, as I did five years earlier to the assassination of John F. Kennedy. Both JFK and MLK symbolized positive social change for America. Their assassinations signified the opposite. The media reminds us that in 1948 an assassin killed Mahatma Gandhi, India's great apostle of peace. Mahatma Gandhi led effective nonviolent resistance to racially discriminatory laws in South Africa and went on to guide India's struggle for freedom from British colonial domination. Mahatma Gandhi's example of nonviolent civil disobedience, peace marches, and hunger strikes inspired Dr. King. As at JFK's assassination, I mourn the passing of Dr. King as if he had been a family member or a personal friend.

Most of all, I mourn my country. I lament the steady downturning of the American nation that Dr. King's assassination represents to me. This current America differs markedly from the America I learned to love as a child. I grew up believing in the schoolbook truth of my country as the world's exemplary leader of freedom, justice, and liberty for all.

---

[4] "Dr. King's Complex Journey," by Leonard Pitts Jr., columnist for the *Miami Herald*, reprinted in the *Philadelphia Inquirer*, Philadelphia, January 16, 2006.

[5] www.historymatters, gmu.edu/d/6553

Now I am disheartened at my country's increasing violence, racism, divisions, imbalances, and war policies. As well, I feel uncomfortable with America's excessively consumerist orientation and emphasis on material wealth.

In these days of the late 1960s, while some Americans protest their abhorrence of reigning political and social conditions by demonstrating on the nation's campuses and streets, another stream of Americans is disillusioned that social change will or can be activated by the governing authorities. Young people, especially those from white, educated, and middle and upper class families, challenge the emphasis on materialism. Searching for deeper values, they are discovering yoga and meditation, holistic natural medicine, soft drugs for mind expansion, and mystical and spiritual practices outside the Judaic-Christian tradition. Pioneering alternatives to the secular, materialistic good life root into the California soil.

During San Francisco's 1967 "Summer of Love," up to one hundred thousand young people had gathered in the San Francisco Bay area. Together they had celebrated the new "hippie" counterculture focused on the ideals of harmony, love, and sharing.

Shortly afterward, I arrived at Stanford.

Visionary young people, concentrated in San Francisco in the Haight-Ashbury hippie district, about a half-hour drive from Stanford, dream of an altruistic humanity creating a humane society on a peaceful Mother Earth. They release their ideas and ideals into the California atmosphere, where some open minds are receptive to these seed-thoughts, even if unconsciously. I am on the scene as California sees the beginnings of the "alternative natural lifestyle" and the environmental movement. But the "counterculture" cannot grab my interest. I am happily immersed in my graduate studies.

Every day I stroll to Redwood Hall for classes in the Department of Communication. Today I decide to visit first at the office of Janet Voelker, my film mentor.

"Hi Jan," I say, greeting her in the informal California style whereby professors are addressed by their first names.

"Remember Leo Dratfield?" she asks. Sure, he is the respected distributor of East European nontheatrical films who guest-lectured to our film class. Introducing him, Dr. Henry Breitrose, head of the film department, declared Dratfield "a pioneer in nontheatrical film distribution." His firm, Contemporary Films, started distributing short films, animations, documentaries, and foreign films at a time when one could see such works only at film societies. Dratfield established a San Francisco branch of Contemporary Films in the early 1960s. Visiting Stanford, he met Jan and other faculty. During his postlecture Q and A, Leo and I enjoyed a short exchange.

"Leo wants to know, want a summer writing job in Yugoslavia?"

"Yes!" I exclaim.

My "Yes!" emerges spontaneously. "Who, what, where, when, why, how?" I pose the six basic journalistic questions in joking fashion.

Jan laughs and fires back: "Interesting educational opportunity. Two months at the renowned Zagreb Film in Croatia, Yugoslavia."

"Yugoslavia? But that's a communist country!" I respond. The consequences of my loose-lipped reply start to sink in. Oddly enough, my deeply embedded American fear of communism does not force me to retract my immediate "Yes!" to Jan's question.

Matko's phone rings—not very insistently, only a few times, but snapping me out of my California dreaming all the same. I awake to the present moment in Zagreb. Unlike the unknown caller, who capitulates so easily, I am not ready to hang up on my Yugoslavia adventure before it really begins.

"Come on, Matko, where are you?" I mutter. "You did not hire me to sit around waiting for Godot!"

How much time will I have to spend waiting around for people to appear and things to happen? I wonder.

On the other hand, not every Yugoslav is a busy film chief. Had Matko not interrupted his office schedule to take me room viewing?

I feel stuck at a long Yugoslav red light signaling a very clear message. To work successfully in this unhurried society, I will have to stop.

Stop what? Stop becoming annoyed or upset at the waiting and delays? Is there any solution for what I experience as an unbearable Yugoslav slowness of doing? Even I, running in my usual American way with my head more than my feet, was able to catch the departed electric tram at its next stop.

My American habits encourage me to move in a whirlwind of action. The American desire for quick results binds me. I have a surplus of ambition and drive. My accomplishments are based on my own efforts. Contrary to traditional peoples, I have no humble attitude to life derived from the belief that an omniscient Power guides all. As a secular Westerner, I am not dependent on any godlike force to arrange or prearrange the timing of my deeds and misdeeds. Using solely my own power, I have to keep on doing, going, and making things happen.

Plodding Yugoslavia is, quite ironically, very quickly confronting me with me. The unexpected encounter is speedily yielding some instant insights. Not only do I have to learn to be patient, I have to understand when to wait, when to watch, and when to act. This triple whammy of a new behavioral requirement will not be easily achievable for a person prone to swift thinking and sometimes-impulsive actions. I assure myself: "Patience is not passivity." I will have to find a balance between patience and acceptance on the one hand, and energetic efforts and assertiveness on the other.

4
Living Like the Locals

Pangs of regret overmaster my tiredness as I wait in Matko's congested office. In this alien society I am exiled from everything known to me. Here I have no home, family, friends, or even acquaintances. I feel desperately alone. Not that I never felt alone or lonely before, but Yugoslavia is puzzling and I cannot speak the language. I question myself: *Can I handle the vast differences in attitudes and lifestyle?*

A woman of refined appearance enters the room. She shares no similarly with the Yugoslav women I have seen thus far; she bears no comparison to the blue-uniformed receptionist at the front desk; she looks worlds apart from the travelers at the train station; she presents an agreeable contrast to the Yugoslavs garbed in rough, plain garments.

This woman's exterior reminds me of people back home. I could envision her employed in a New York office. Her blouse, in a light green complementing a dark green, knee-length skirt, displays hand-stitching and carved wooden buttons. The smart outfit is definitely tailor-made. Beige suede shoes featuring broad high heels and a strap across the instep give the impression she has stepped away from a tango dance.

Large and inquisitive eyes brighten the woman's attractive face. She parts her straight brown hair on the side, letting short, wispy strands cavort on her forehead. She introduces herself in very good English. I hear scarcely an accent when she announces: "I am Svetlana. I work here. Comrade Matko told me of your plight."

"I am so glad to meet you!" I say. "Will we be working together? What's your job?"

Svetlana smiles and tells that she translates for Zagreb Film. "Only sometimes," she adds. "Usually I teach foreign languages at the University of Zagreb."

Some years my senior, Svetlana is one of Yugoslavia's modern career women: university-educated, single, independent. She does not seem to be bragging but simply stating fact when she mentions that, besides her native Serbo-Croatian, she speaks fluent German, Russian, French, and English. "Why didn't you like the room Comrade Matko showed you?" she asks.

A bit embarrassed, I repeat the reasons I gave Matko. Thinking she might dismiss me as a spoiled or fussy Westerner, I do not cite the apartment's lack of all civilized amenities.

"I have been in the West," comments Svetlana, implying that she catches my unspoken words. "I imagine your standards are different from ours." Before I can explain further, she invites me to stay at her place.

As spontaneously as I had exclaimed "Yes!" to the film job offer, so immediately do I accept Svetlana's proposal. My requirements for hot water and a fridge dissolve in the warmth of her invitation.

"All set?" queries Matko, returning to the office. Giving a pleased tilt of his head to Svetlana, he says he will instruct someone to drop off my baggage. "Take a few days to rest up," he advises. "Then be ready to dive in!"

Svetlana says we can walk to her apartment. She lives nearby. My ears savor the click-click-click of her Spanish-dancer shoes on the cobblestoned streets as well as the historical information she imparts on our route.

"Constructed in the previous century," says Svetlana, pointing out certain buildings that are handsome but decidedly rundown. She wants me to know that Zagreb contains spots of bygone architectural beauty. Her own apartment building also predates the socialist period. Reflecting a faded elegance, the building emanates a classical Old World dignity. Carved stone figures and large potted plants grace the spacious entrance hall. Svetlana guides me to an elevator with a notable sliding gate of black wrought iron in a swirling design.

"The electricity sometimes fails, and we have to be prepared to walk up," cautions Svetlana as she opens the elevator gate. "I'm on the fifth, the top floor, allowing access to the roof. My own private roof terrace!"

The elevator ascends very slowly. Like the tram passengers, she takes inconveniences in stride. I was right not to speak of hot water or a fridge.

Stepping across the threshold into Svetlana's apartment, I detect the enchanting scent of fresh flowers, or is that her balmy perfume filling the rooms? The charming ambiance helps me forget the July heat. Svetlana's well-appointed flat possesses the grandeur of high ceilings and fine parquet floors. Antique hand-carved wood furniture provides a quiet chic against sturdy walls in the color of Svetlana's shoes. Cupboards and side tables boast large and small ornamental bric-a-brac.

"The furniture and the objets d'art are of Germanic and Austrian origin," states Svetlana. "Wonderfully unlike the furniture and styling of Yugoslav socialism, so plain and drab." She inherited the apartment and its tasteful contents from her late parents. They served in the diplomatic corps.

"A gift from a friend," she notes, positioning me in front of a large canvas in grays, blues, and greens. A lone figure faces the horizon on a windswept beach. "I love the seaside," says Svetlana. "How does this painting make you feel?"

"Lonely, in a big space."

"Well, I hope you won't feel lonely here. I have to warn you, though, I am away a lot visiting my boyfriend. And, yes, we are in a big space here, at least by Yugoslav norms."

The spaciousness of her apartment "is good and not good." Bitterly she explains, "Some people resent my living in the apartment alone. Because of the housing shortage."

But there is only one bedroom, though generously sized. A cotton duvet and throw pillows cover the bed. Books stand carefully aligned on the wooden night table. Family photos, pieces of costume jewelry, and a radio sit atop the chest of drawers.

"You will sleep here," conveys Svetlana in a tone assuring me I have no decision in the matter.

"And you?" I ask.

"I will use the cot."

I suggest that I sleep on the cot. "Not open to discussion," declares Svetlana in a friendly but firm tone. "We Yugoslavs are a hardy people. I myself can sleep on the floor if required. We are Yugoslavs. We are tough."

Her casual remark, certainly not intended to hurt me, inflicts a wound. I see I have much to learn about being flexible and adaptable.

"When we Yugoslavs travel, we usually stay with people," she goes on. "Most Yugoslavs do not have money for hotels."

Svetlana does not attempt to benefit financially from my extreme fatigue, which might have me consent to any rental price. Like her friends, I can stay for free. She refuses to consider any other arrangement. Before friends arrive in a month or so, we will search through rental ads in the local newspapers and she will accompany me to view possibilities.

"Now we will drink tea," says Svetlana. "Earl Grey from England. You like it?"

Svetlana adores tea. When friends travel abroad, they bring her back English tea. Proudly she shows me the tin. She empties it, using the last leaves of the precious foreign tea for me.

Unexpectedly soon, a Studio worker drops off my luggage. Revived by the tea, I start unpacking. Svetlana and I sit together on her bed as if we are teenagers relishing a weekend sleepover. "May I?" she asks, stroking my scarves and wanting to try them on. She is clearly a clothes lover. Tenderly she drapes her neck with my burgundy-red silk scarf, decorated by tiny silvery appliqués, letting one end float artistically across her chest. She "oohs" and "aahs" over my outfits bought in upscale Manhattan department stores and boutiques. My Chinese-style sheath dress of emerald green silk elicits her criticism of the mass-produced Yugoslav clothing.

"Yugoslav garments lack imagination, both in materials and styling," she comments. "No chic." She gets around this deficiency by collecting design ideas from German magazines and entrusting them to her seamstress. Labor costs are extremely low, but the unavailability of suitable fabrics forms a constant problem.

"Our fabrics are rough and heavy," she clarifies, "made to last a lifetime." Indeed, some of the clothing I saw at the train station might formerly have been burlap bags.

My garments receive Svetlana's critical acclaim, all except the mini-skirt dress I am wearing. I bought the dress, with short sleeves and a skirt ending well above my knees, on sale at Saks Fifth Avenue. The material, a soft cotton jersey, clings pretty much to my bodily contours.

"Too short and too tight," concludes Svetlana. Her conservative opinion indicates she is not as modern as she fancies.

"Women in America are fighting for their equal rights," I say. "That also means wearing what we like, when and where we like, and how."

"Wear a pantsuit," she replies simply. Svetlana is well read and informed. American women are starting to wear pantsuits to work as casually as they would dresses or skirts.

"Some conservative offices do not approve pants for women," I remark. "And some restaurants are in a quandary about whether to allow women in pantsuits to enter."

"The pantsuit, rather than the miniskirt, makes the female a more serious competitor with the male in the workplace," states Svetlana.

The fashion talk travels a different route when we speak of cleaning my clothes. Most Yugoslavs do not have a washing machine.

"We have shops that wash laundry by machine," she tells. "They take a week. Foreign items like yours might get conveniently lost."

Dismissing the laundries, she evaluates Zagreb's dry cleaners: "Poor quality and very expensive by our standards." She adds that the dry cleaners might also "lose" my clothing.

"Or," begins Svetlana, chuckling, "you can carry your soiled clothes in the summer heat to the only self-service laundry in town, reachable from here by only two overcrowded and sweltering trams."

I had already related my adventure in the tram.

"Then you can sit at the laundry and wait, and wait, until everything is washed and dried. Better just follow my example and rely on the power of your own two hands to rub away the dirt using our government's one brand of soapsuds and my hot running water."

Hot water!

"Come," suggests Svetlana, escorting me into her bathroom. More spacious than mine at home, it possesses a tub with a shower-head that is not fixed to the wall and is handheld. Vintage porcelain faucet knobs beautify the sink. Above it, under a large mirror, a white marble shelf holds various beauty care items. The lighting is a bit dim to apply cosmetics easily. Blank areas on the wall call attention to missing tiles.

"Here is my Yugoslav washing machine!" Svetlana exclaims, picking up a galvanized metal sheet. It is reminiscent of the wood-framed washboard of heavy corrugated glass that my mother used when I was a child.

"I rub out my frustrations on this," she says, returning the washboard into an oversized metal bucket sitting on a wooden table near the tub and shower hose. The small wooden wringer my mother turned by hand to squeeze out wet laundry in my childhood might be a bit of a luxury here. I had fancied I wanted to live Yugoslav-style, but I had not realized the hardships entailed.

Svetlana's spontaneous kindness and generosity remove doubts concerning my immediate welfare. Suddenly I feel lucky, blessed by good fortune. Although I am not a religious person, from time to time I feel "blessed"—by whom and for what I do not know. Whenever the "blessed feeling" surges, it reminds me of something, though I can never remember what. A pesky sensation intimates that I have forgotten something important about myself that I truly need to remember. But I do not have the time to sit and concentrate on trying to remember just what that forgotten something might be. Nevertheless, the very sensation that something important to my life has slipped my memory makes me wonder: *Is there more to me than I know?*

Two days later, in my jersey-miniskirt dress—which I washed by hand and dried on a wooden rack in Svetlana's bathroom—and wearing beige fishnet stockings, another new fashion hit at home, I go to a *Trgopromet* (trading company), a state-run grocery store. Despite closely following Svetlana's directions to the store, I almost pass it by. Lacking display windows or any kind of sign advertising its existence, the shop is just another gray building on another street of gray buildings. The man at the cashier's desk squints and strains in his inspection of me when I enter.

As I walk the few aisles to survey the store's scanty merchandise, the wooden floors creak and shoppers turn their heads to observe me. Their garments are colorless and their faces reflect reserve. They do not allow their eyes to meet mine in a greeting. My clothes single me out, again, announcing I am a foreigner. My minidress hugs my body in the way their loose-fitting attire does not embrace them, and my fishnets provocatively reveal skin, but am I staring at their lack of fashion styling? To avoid their furtive glances, I focus on shopping, feigning exaggerated interest in the few items on the shelves. Never have I seen a store so sparsely supplied. I gape in disbelief. How does anyone survive here? Some of the wooden shelves are literally empty.

Exiting the store, carrying foodstuffs in a string shopping bag supplied by Svetlana, I walk to the street corner. There is no traffic light. Small-size Yugoslav cars whiz by, often rounding the corner at breakneck speed. Apparently the Yugoslavs compensate for general societal slowness once they get behind the wheel of a vehicle. In contrast to the locals, who skillfully cross the street with no hesitation, I venture from the curb several times, and as many times I dash back. Finally comes a brief lull in the traffic, and I sprint to the other side.

As soon as I reach the opposite sidewalk, a small elderly woman runs over to me. She is clad in a black *marama*, black top, long black skirt, and the black oxford shoes. Shouting in Serbo-Croatian, she pulls at my minidress, lifting it to expose my underwear. In my shock, my arm automatically swings out to push her away. The bag of groceries slips, my purchases tumbling to the ground. Passersby look on amused. No one offers to help. The woman spits at me before rushing out of sight.

Arriving at Svetlana's apartment building my heart a-racing, I climb the stairs rather than wait for the slow-moving elevator. If the minidress incident is so minor and silly, why am I trembling? Western thinking maintains we have a natural right to be ourselves, including how we clothe or do not clothe our bodies.

But have I not already experienced incidents in regard to my way of dressing?

My freshman year of college I spent at the University of Missouri, in the farmlands of the American Midwest, attracted by the university's well-known journalism school. My dorm mates, in their white bobby socks and pastel-tinted skirts and sweaters, lost no opportunity to mock the bohemian-style dark outfits and black stockings I preferred in those years. Not because of the clothing issues but for academic challenge, I left "Mizzou" after one year. I preferred to spend my college days in Manhattan, at the top-rated Barnard College of Columbia University.

In my junior year, a minor crisis erupted. The exclusively women's school formulated a dress code banning Bermuda shorts and slacks to class. A national TV news team spotted me walking across campus. When the interviewer asked me, camera rolling, why I defied the edict by wearing slacks to school, I replied something to the effect that I had come to Barnard so I "could be free to be me." My response, well practiced, came immediately; since my college years, I had uttered variations of that phase many times while defending my clothing style to my parents. Apparently my mother thought I should still dress like her or in her choices for my clothing; such was an American mother's expectation in the late 1950s and early 1960s. Now the elderly woman in Zagreb dramatically vented her disapproval of my appearance by cursing and spitting.

Svetlana listens to my account of the minidress incident with both sisterly and cultural understanding. Her comments are few: "The woman was a peasant, literally. From the village. Old-fashioned. Your tight and very short skirt shocked her sense of propriety."

This attitude of the local social fabric is not complicated to fathom. Matko used the term "social adjustment" to describe problems of the poor peasantry flooding into the cities. Although my gigantic ignorance of Yugoslav customs makes me a blank slate in Zagreb, I can recognize the error of my own social adjustment. Dressing in a short skirt here demonstrates that I am either ignorant of the conservative culture or needlessly defiant of it.

Instead of "I told you so," Svetlana cheers me: "Forget this. You and I are modern."

I cannot release the incident so easily. "The old woman is not modern," I say. "She is from a village. Is that why she wears all black? Or is the all-black a religious thing? So many women totally in black."

"As in your country," Svetlana explains, "people in Yugoslavia wear black to show grief for someone's death. In the rural, traditional context, when someone in a family dies, the women wear black for mourning. Older women often never get out of the black. But you and I are not in mourning," so Svetlana exclaims, "and we are modern!" She goes to her liquor cabinet. "Let's drink to leaving this clash behind." Becoming lightheaded and lighthearted from a dry Croatian wine, we laugh and click glasses. "Here's to Western decadence!"

"The next time you wear the minidress, I'll have to come along to give a running translation of the shouts and curses directed at you!" Svetlana declares, and yet in the undertone of her remark I hear: "But don't put it on again."

That night, I review the collision with the cursing elderly woman who was so disgusted by what she considered my immodesty. The transparent blouses, the bare midriffs, and the wide, plunging necklines currently the trend at home would also send her into a rage. Our clash takes me back to the train station's waiting room. Vividly I recall the stares, the "tsks," the giggles, my discomfort.

In the morning, over breakfast tea, Svetlana assumes a changed position. She advises, "It is important to show respect for the local customs." I welcome her guidance in this strange society. My jersey minidress is clearly too short and too tight. The issue does not require deliberation. "Try to see yourself through the people's eyes," she adds.

Svetlana encourages me to accept the slogan, "When in Zagreb, do as the Zagrebians do." I understand this as no prescription for uniformity; it is a means for moving closer to the Yugoslav people. I will not pretend to be what I am not, but I can appreciate that the more my appearance upsets the locals, the harder it will be to associate with them.

"Fine to let the minidress remain in the closet," Svetlana emphasizes.

"You are so right," I concur.

5
Getting to Know Zagreb Film

I wake up early on my first day of work. An irresistible urge draws me to the clothes closet. As I assess my dresses, skirts, and tops brought from home, one item jumps out, asking to be worn. My hand reaches for it.

When I enter the kitchen, Svetlana looks amazed. A wave of disappointment flits over her face. "Tea is prepared," she mutters, pouring two cups.

She drinks her tea quickly before excusing herself to put on her powder and lipstick. I sip my tea and think about the Barnard administration telling us independent Barnard girls what to wear and what not. *Not wear my jersey minidress in Zagreb? I am not a Yu-go-slave!* I affirm to myself. *Am I not an American, free to choose what I want?*

Cleaning the breakfast table and washing the dishes, my morning task, I wonder: *How to adapt to the local lifestyle while holding on to my personal principles and staying myself?* I do not have the answers, but I sense I am asking the right questions.

Just as I am ready to leave for the Studio, an impulse propels me to the bedroom. Quickly searching, I pick a flowing cotton skirt, knee-length. Slipping into it, I spy my high-necked, long sleeved blouse. My hands cannot re-dress me fast enough. "Hey, what's going on?"

Svetlana looks happily surprised, and pleased, also a bit relieved, when I reemerge. "Good girl," says her smile.

She will accompany me to the Studio, permitted to arrive later than usual so she can show me the best walking route. Summery green trees enliven the drab streets lined by buildings of dull gray stone.

As on a first day joining an American office, my stomach is nervously a-fluttering. I hear the thumping of my heart, the clicking of Svetlana's heels on the wooden floors, and typewriters clacking away. Remembering the breakneck sounds in my high school typing class during exams, I hardly think that the typists I now hear would have met the course's minimum requirement to type fifty words per minute.

"Ah, good morning Miss Green," exclaims Matko as we enter his office. He extends his large hand for his hearty shake. "Well done," he says to Svetlana in English before dismissing her with additional words in Serbo-Croatian.

Matko leans back in his chair and summarizes our duties. He handles the Studio's foreign business deals and sells the Studio's documentaries and animated films abroad. My main task is to polish and rewrite English narrations and subtitles for the films intended for distribution to English-language countries and to record voice-overs. I will oversee Matko's foreign correspondence. I will greet and orient Zagreb Film's English-speaking foreign visitors and show them around the Studio and the town.

"We have many foreign visitors," proclaims Matko with an air of contentment. "Such days may last until midnight."

He informs me: "In America, most offices start at nine, but we are a developing country. Your official hours will run from eight in the morning to around three in the afternoon. Most of us are at our desks by seven."

Undoubtedly he notes my astonishment, since he continues: "Some workplaces begin at six. We start early, end early, and enjoy the rest of the day. Because you are a foreigner and outside our system, you may arrive at the Studio later."

He leads me down the hall into a cluttered room a bit larger than an oversized closet. There are no windows. Behind one lone desk, submerged under papers in the Matkovian manner, sits a middle-aged woman whose blonde hair exposes dark roots. She wears the usual blue smock. The woman smiles apologetically as Matko sheepishly points to a plain wooden table and says to me, "There is your desk." Equality obviously reigns in the assigning of my work spot.

On my "desk" sits an old portable typewriter. It is a year one model that an American office would have discarded decades earlier. No American employer would have dared offer me such poor working conditions. Yet the Yugoslavs cannot give me what they do not have. Matko addresses my unspoken thoughts: "Our hard efforts and ingenuity compensate for our antiquated equipment, Miss Green."

Still, after depositing me at the improvised office, he remarks: "Sorry I have to put you here. We are short of space." Nodding toward the blonde woman, he adds, "Well, you'll learn *Hrvatski* ('Croatian')."

"I hope so," I respond. "I feel so locked out."

"Just the opposite of how we feel."

Then he tours me around the Studio.

"Zagreb Film is a production company engaged in diverse film activities," he states. "We produce and distribute short and feature-length documentary films. Our animated cartoons have earned the Studio a worldwide reputation."

The Studio is an informal place staffed by many more men than women. The people dress similarly to people outside the studio except that there are no women clad head-to-toe in black. Most of the women wear skirts of knee-length. The men wear open-collared polo shirts or cotton sweaters and loose trousers. I spot no suits or ties. Several of the animators sport long hair. They speak no English besides a few rudimentary expressions as "hallo" and "pleasure to meet."

From what I grasp of Matko's abbreviated account of filmmaking in Yugoslavia, no one can make a film or other cultural product privately, even if possessing the financial means. Everything is directly or indirectly in the hands of the state. The country's cultural institutions minimize commercial criteria. The state partially supports Zagreb Film but the Studio pays its own way, so to speak, by winning festival prizes. Film awards raise national prestige. International recognition for Zagreb's animated films enhances Yugoslavia's film image abroad. In the socialist film industry, box office receipts signify less than contributing to the national ideology and culture.

Matko explains that once an idea for a film is developed, the Studio presents it to a governmental committee. If the committee approves the film, it votes on the amount of government funding. The amount depends on the merit of the idea. Any extra costs have to be raised by the Studio from its own sources.

If a film wins prizes either in Yugoslavia or abroad, the Studio earns the equivalent of Yugoslavian "brownie points" of one type or another. Brownie points are a valuable social currency in a system of financing where commercial success is no criterion for an artist's subsequent projects. Gaining good will and favor with government officials and the board of censors may help future productions come to fruition.

As the Zagreb Film letterhead memorializes, the Studio achieved its international breakthrough and great triumph in 1961. In that year, the cartoon *Ersatz,* also known by its Croatian title, *Surogat,* "Substitute," became the first non-American entry to win Hollywood's Academy Award for best animated short film. Dušan Vukotić, a forerunner in the Yugoslav animation field and one of Zagreb Film's chief artists, directed the film.

In 1949, the twenty-two year old Vukotić, trained as an architect, worked as a cartoonist for the satirical magazine *Kerempuh,* led by Fadil Hadžić, an early pioneer of animated film in Croatia. When Hadžić secured Croatian government funding to open Duga Film, a studio for animated films, Vukotić was assigned his own unit under Hadžić. Since Yugoslavia was pretty much cut off from the rest of the world, the Duga Film artists had to learn animation on their own by trial and error. The experimentation lasted only one year. In a period of economic crisis in 1952, the government decided that building schools was a better use of limited funds than making animated films. But the love for animation had been established.

Vukotić and others formed an animation company for advertising films, distributing them through Zagreb Film, a film production and distribution house newly founded by the Croatian Union of Film Workers. In 1956, Zagreb Film formed a unit for animated film. Vukotić directed the Studio's initial attempt at story animation, *The Playful Robot*. He and his fellow artists explored new, non-Disney animation techniques. By 1958, Zagreb Film had received international recognition at the Oberhausen, Cannes, and Venice film festivals. At Cannes, the sophisticated technique and the audacious themes of Zagreb cartoons impressed the gathered film professionals. Film historian Georges Sadoul coined the label: "Zagreb School of Animated Film."

Early in the Studio's history, Dušan Vukotić, with six of the artists, issued a collective statement on animation:

> Animation is protesting against rigid forms. Animation, which only conveys natural movements, cannot be creative animation. Animation is a technical process, the result of which has to be creative. Animation means breathing spirit and life into a drawing, not by simply copying reality but by giving it a design. Life is warmth. Warmth is movement. Movement is life. Animation can be lukewarm or boiling. Cold animation isn't animation; it is like a stillborn child. Making animated cartoons means rubbing tree trunks against each other until there is a spark perhaps or just a little bit of smoke. Take a kilogram of ideas (if possible not too confused), fifty kilograms of talent, and a few thousand drawings. Stir it well and then with a bit of luck you won't get the right answer to your question.[6]

---

[6] Collective statement of Zagreb Film animators Borivoj Dovniković, Ante Zaninović, Zlatko Grgić, Vladimir Jutriša, Aleksandar Marks, Dušan Vukotić, and Nedeljko Dragić, as reprinted in *Z is for Zagreb*, by Ronald Holloway, Tantivy Press, London, 1972, p. 9.

Soon after my arrival, Matko announces he has set up a screening for me of Zagreb Film's best cartoons of the decade.

"You need to know the films for our work. We'll have to go to a *kinoteka,* a cinema, because we don't have screening facilities here."

"No screening room in a film studio?" I blurt out.

Matko smiles. He seems accustomed to this reaction from foreigners. "Lack of resources has actually benefited Zagreb Film," Matko remarks when we recline into the worn, red-velvet seats at the *kinoteka.* "The Studio owes its international reputation to its material deficiencies."

He explains that in the Studio's early days, in the 1950s, materials were scarce, as everywhere in Europe after World War II. The artists faced shortages of celluloid drawing sheets, the transparent "cels" used to make a hand-drawn animated film. Rather than simply adjust to an already existing film method, they experimented to uncover the secrets of animation. Their ingenuity compensated for what they missed materially.

"Necessity is the mother of invention," I cannot help but say.

"Material shortages led the artists to develop a unique animation technique, earning them recognition as 'The Zagreb School.' Well, not really a school in the sense of 'one style.' The term signifies a community of creative artists, each with an original signature.

"Zagreb Film produced a new style of animation based on 'reduction,'" he continues. "Drawings are limited to the absolute minimum, one-third the usual number. Nevertheless, the finished cartoon displays a dynamic movement and a visually rich whole."

As head of marketing and sales, Matko has apparently developed a sales talk to persuade the potential buyers of the Studio's films and cartoons. Zagreb Film's animation style "liberates the depiction of a 'definite reality,' thereby giving its artists enhanced creative freedom."

He maintains that in a field dominated by Disney, "reduced animation" is no less than revolutionary. "Unlike a general house style established by Disney, each Zagreb Film animator is distinctly unique. International film professionals noticed our pioneering technique and themes in 1958. That's when we won our first international film prize, at the documentary film festival in Oberhausen."

Quite predictably, Matko begins the show with Vukotić's Oscar-winning *Surogat,* which is fast becoming a classic in its genre. Considered a masterpiece, the ten-minute film attracted Westerners to East European animation and placed Zagreb Film on the international film map.

"Observe the simple lines," Matko whispers to me as if we are not alone at the special screening. "Such imagination and whimsy!"

A strange little man, composed of triangular lines, goes to the beach, bringing a collection of simple and stylized geometric shapes. He inflates the shapes into beach items including a chair, air mattress, tent, and barbecue grill. After enjoying a fried fish lunch and a drink, he pumps up a female figure. He tries to romance her and is spurned. He next inflates a sharklike creature that follows the female form into the ocean. Using a fishing line, the little man rescues her from the shark and is rewarded with a kiss. Immediately she abandons him for another inflatable figure, a male, that suddenly appears and absorbs her in passion until they both disappear by deflation. The little man is consumed by jealousy and revenge. At the film's end, a small nail destroys the make-believe world, a reminder of the artificiality created.

"So, what do you think?" Matko asks enthusiastically when the lights come on. During the screening, he laughed often.

"Lively, amusing. I kept wondering what would happen next, though the ending deflated me a bit, too. Isn't the ending a bit obvious?"

"Maybe there is more to the film than you see," suggests Matko. "What is real and what is artificial? Does our obsession with certain aspects of life lead to our destruction?"

Matko is correct. The film is less important for its ending than for the unanswered questions it stimulates. Or, as the Zagreb artists might say, "With a bit of luck you won't get the right answer to your question."[7]

Waiting for the next cartoon, I ask myself: *Yes, what is this world really all about? What is true? What is false? What in this world leads to our destruction and what to our betterment?*

---

[7] Collective statement of Zagreb Film animators, ibid.

The Ceremony, by Borivoj Dovniković, presents the next challenge. Five men stand in front of a wall. A sixth man arranges and rearranges the men in a straight line, as if for a group photo. He checks his wristwatch while choreographing the obedient men into different positions. Finally satisfied, he shouts a command. Onto the scene march uniformed men wearing helmets and carrying rifles. They aim at the five men. The ostensible photo shoot is, instead, an execution by firing squad.

"That was a surprise!" I exclaim to Matko. I had not expected such black humor. "No predictable ending."

"Life is like that, don't you think?" he asks. "Can we always believe what we see?"

Distinct from the Bugs Bunny and Mickey Mouse cartoons that colored my film palette as a child, these cartoons are not simple entertainment films for the young. Their probing adult themes project solely through image, music, and sound effects. Like music, or silent films, the wordless Zagreb cartoons transcend language boundaries. They exert universal appeal. I look forward to extracting the message of the next film. The lights dim and on comes *Elegy*, a cartoon by Nedeljko Dragić.

A man of sorrowful mien peers out from behind the bars of a prison window. Snow falls on the ground below. The snow stops and the season changes. A single red flower springs to life; a large smile brightens the man's face. He kicks up his heels, and attempts to reach down to touch the flower as it grows taller, almost as high as the prison window. He waters the flower. He waves away a bee. He tries to protect the flower from heavy rains. Winter returns and the flower disappears under a new snowfall. The man grimaces angrily and retreats into his prison cell. When spring comes again, the flower blossoms. The prisoner rejoices. The clatter of keys and a turning lock signal the cause for his elation—his release. He reappears on the sidewalk below the prison window, now a free man carrying a briefcase. He lets the briefcase fall on the flower, which he passes by unnoticed.

In scarcely four minutes, filmmaker Dragić guides the viewer through a wide range of emotions. After a few more films, I turn to

Matko and say, "I see what you mean. The artists handle confrontational themes using satire and zany amusement."

His sales pitch creeps into the question: "Did you detect how the artists step from worldly reality to the reality they create with their cartoons?"

That reality, I conclude, is no people's or workers' paradise. The cartoons depict an environment in which Sun barely shines. Although each animator has his own inventive style, the films seemingly express a common philosophy. The cartoons bring me into the human conditions described in the books of Franz Kafka, Jean-Paul Sartre, and Albert Camus. Like those literary giants, the Zagreb Film animators often portray people alone and afraid, frustrated and helpless, trapped in existential dilemmas and artificial constructions. Society's legal and bureaucratic structures imprison and entangle them.

How to interpret *The Fly*, directed by Aleksandar Marks and Vladimir Jutriša? A man in a field hears the persistent buzzing of a fly. The man's large blue eyes follow the fly's movements. The fly lands near his feet; he tries to trample it; he misses. The fly swells to a monstrous size, zooming in and out the film frame. There is a loud droning noise. Dazed by fear as the gigantic fly towers over him, trying to crush him, the man falls to the ground in apparent defeat. The monster's colossal form surrounds him. The man is on his knees in submission. The fly swoops him up, transporting him through space. Then the man is back in the field and the huge insect flies to him. They are now of equal size and height. The redheaded fly places an arm around the frightened man. The two embrace.

Informational materials for *The Fly* speak of "a Kafkalike tale about a man and a fly butting heads but ending as equals." The film won an impressive array of awards in New York, London, and several European countries, including Yugoslavia.

Layers of meaning infuse *The Fly*. The film surely has social and political implications. Like the Studio's other cartoons that I have already seen, it transmits secret messages for decoding. The animators apparently weave political statements indirectly and ambiguously into the moral and psychological dilemmas portrayed by the cartoon characters. They hide criticism within allegory, parody, and whimsy.

Thus the Zagreb artists present audiences and government officials a puzzle: decipher what is, or what is not, being said critically about the Yugoslav system and society. When criticism does not please Big Brother or a ruling elite, fear may stifle the citizen's tongue, the writer's pen, and the individual's urge to march to a different drummer. Through the special language of cartoon, much can be said while not being said. The Zagreb Film cartoons, I learn, are less daring than some animated films being made in some Soviet satellite countries of the Eastern Bloc, notably Czechoslovakia.

The Yugoslav cartoons of cryptic political content make me think of American TV commercials and advertising films. Advertising employs psychology and concealed or subliminal messages to activate consumers to buy and keep buying. The Western ad makers and the Zagreb animators share a strong affinity. Both use a secret language to influence the mindset of their audiences.

Betty Friedan's well-researched 1963 book, *The Feminine Mystique*, showed that American advertisers promoted the image of the American stay-at-home-housewife-mom for commercial purposes. The fewer women who pursued professional careers, the more housewives would be available to buy all kinds of needed, and unneeded, household products. When I was growing up, American advertisers tried to convince me to want all that belonged to the successful and happy good life termed the American Dream: a husband (with a well-paying job), children (at least two), a good home that I owned (preferably in the suburbs), two cars (the newer the better), and all of life's material comforts.

In my case, a stronger message-giver overrode the commercial indoctrination. Since early childhood I had heard, from inside myself, that my future and its rewards were connected with my creativity, most likely my writing.

Betty Friedan advised women not to seek total fulfillment through marriage and motherhood alone, but also to pursue work outside the home. Such work required the full mental capacity that could generate the same kind of self-actualization men attain.

Unknowingly I am a feminist, a young woman searching for her fulfillment via a path that includes a professional career in a male-dominated world.

At Zagreb Film, there are no female artists and never have been. I enter Zagreb Film's all-male territory after pounding for a while on the old typewriter in the oversize closet. My fingers, slowed from hammering the heavy keys that often got stuck, let me experience why the Studio's typists cannot meet the beat of my remembered high school typing class.

A cartoonist is gone for the summer, so Matko relocates me to a vacated desk in a large room where the younger animators sit together. A walkway separates two identical rows of desks, each desk lined up directly behind the one in front. On one side of the room are many windows surprisingly unobstructed by papers.

Glancing around at the men, Matko says to me, grinning broadly: "You can pick up even more *Hrvatski* here!" He installs a hefty pile of papers on my desk before sauntering out, exchanging comments with the animators as he leaves. Animation cels, drawing utensils, and cigarette stubs in ashtrays cover the artists' desks. The men are passing around a bottle of *šljivovica*.

"*Gut!* [Good]" one of the artists calls to me in German, downing a small glassful. I smile one of my smiles, that supplements my meager Serbo-Croatian vocabulary, and shake my head to say, "Thank you, but no." The men laugh heartily and return to their drawings.

"No other East European communist country possesses as much artistic and intellectual freedom as Yugoslavia," Matko tells me one day. Receiving governmental financial support, the Studio is free from the market forces driving capitalism's profit-dependent enterprises to pander to the widest public. He explains that the Zagreb Film animators enjoy creative expression in all phases of production, from the initial inspirational idea to the final cinematic result. As one of Zagreb Film's several pioneering distinctions, the animators write, design, and direct their own films.

My colleagues generally work in a slow, carefree rhythm. Their relaxed approach, banishing stress, cannot be attributed only to the plum brandy. Most days they joke with each other even before taking their first drink. They have a good sense of humor, less dark in everyday life than their films imply.

The Studio artists use all the timeless Yugoslav minutes they want to make a film, yet they do have their exciting peculiarities. Being around them on a daily basis, I interpret information from their body language. Suddenly they decide something needs doing and flutter their arms rapidly and speak excitedly. Then ensues an intense period during which they whip that something into shape. If the task remains unfinished, they become lackadaisical until the next, furious, "must-be-done" or "supposed-to-be-done" spurt of energy propels them into another creative frenzy.

Having seen their films, and observing them every day at their desks in the open common work space, I get the idea that these artists are not striving against each other to create the best film individually. I sense that they are working together within a common goal to make pertinent statements as part of a national cinema. Even so, the animators do not capitulate to a standardized societal thought. Each expresses his own artistically free thought, as veiled as it sometimes may be.

But, I observe, their constant improvisation is not always creative. The lackadaisical style, simultaneously exasperating and charmingly Old World, also leads to disorganization and energy loss. Nonetheless, interacting in the take-it-easy, no-pressure–no-stress atmosphere gives naturalness to my days, even when I work overtime shifts. I have no option except to adapt to their flexible, improvisational style. I slow to their pace. Still, habit dies hard.

The first time Matko hands me a film synopsis to rewrite into good English, I polish it up in a nonstop blitz, keen to establish my American efficiency.

"Oh," he says, raising his eyebrows when I return the improved text to him in a quick tempo. He mutters under his breath and nonchalantly places the sheet on his stack of papers. "I'm just a lazy Yu-go-*slave*," he laughs, speaking to my perplexed look.

Tired of waiting for the text's return, I forget about it. One morning I find the scenario on my desk, none of my text changed but with new sentences added for me to improve.

My Zagreb Film colleagues act like strangers to the Western work ethic that is geared to speed, efficiency, productivity, lower costs, and higher profits. They labor in sync with the timeless Yugoslav time clock, where "back in a minute" can mean hours, and decision-making travels a leisurely route. Assured of their job security, my colleagues follow the pulse of their personal inclinations.

While Matko refers to his country as "Yu-go-*slave*-ia," he and his colleagues do not act like slaves, neither to their work nor to their society. No slave master, not even a faceless Big Brother trying to impose collective prosperity, and certainly not a corporate boss striving for increased personal profit, stands above my Studio colleagues wielding a mental whip demanding they work harder, faster, longer. They reflect the attitude of "Can-do-it-tomorrow—or not."

One day Matko delivers a pile of papers to me. "Here are scripts to polish."

I flip through the texts, so literally translated from the original Serbo-Croatian that I cannot grasp the meaning of the resulting poor English.

"You know, I think it might help if I see the films," I suggest to Matko.

"Oh, all right," Matko responds, as if I have made an unreasonable request. "I'll arrange a screening at the *kinoteka*."

When necessary, I consult a film's writer or director. For one script-polishing assignment, a Zagreb University student translates each Serbo-Croatian word one by one into English as I write down the meanings for recasting into new sentences. I miss an American grammar book. Not even the student can locate one for me in Zagreb.

Early in my stay Matko says: "Oh, by the way, can I ask a favor of you? I have a letter to send to an important firm in America. Could you look it over and fix it up a bit?"

"Sure," I reply, not realizing that I have agreed to a challenging exercise indeed.

"Then," he adds, "could you type it for me before you leave? I'd really appreciate it."

After a while, Matko does not ask before depositing correspondence on my table. He trusts that my work style, grounded in the American work ethic, will result in the best and earliest completion of his business letters. Soon he stops preparing rough drafts and simply dictates thoughts for me to form into good letters.

Everything at Zagreb Film hinges on the management meetings Matko attends. Yugoslavia is a showcase country for "Workers' Self-Management." WSM, workplace decision-making by employees, is one of the experimental features of Yugoslavia's Third Way.

The Law on Self-Management, passed by the National Assembly in 1950, forms the basis of the Yugoslav economic and social order. WSM demonstrates Tito's intention to experiment with a nonstate type of socialism to create a socialist democracy of equality, freedoms, and other departures from the Soviet model of a socialist state. Collective ownership in Tito's independent Yugoslav socialism means that workers in state-run enterprises own a factory or company. The state does not act as intermediary. The workers themselves run their own affairs through workplace management councils. In a form of direct democracy, the workers reach decisions through consultation and consensus. They influence policies and share any surplus revenue equally.

WSM contrasts definitively with the bureaucratic centralism of the socialism in the USSR and its satellites. In the Soviet style, the state owns the means of production and workers take orders from a government-appointed manager. A power elite of communist party members from the central bureaucracy makes policy decisions. The state is supreme.

Nor does WSM follow Western capitalism's hierarchical system, in which, similarly, a small elite usually runs a company and there is little, if any, worker input. Even in companies encouraging people to be engaged and make autonomous decisions relevant to their jobs, ultimately the management or board makes the decisions.

WSM sticks to a middle way between the monopoly of power wielded by communist central bureaucracy and capitalist management.

The basic idea of Yugoslavia's WSM is decentralization, meaning autonomous management by workers.

Yugoslav workers have great independence in business operations and production. Workers in every company, factory, or enterprise elect from among themselves representatives to serve on a company council. Composed of workers each possessing one vote, the council has full decision-making power. The councils choose and supervise their company's manager or CEO. There is no managerial-class authority figure or "boss" ordering what to do and where and when and how. The council decides all matters such as general production methods, the division of labor, scheduling, salaries, and vacations. Decisions on large issues are made at meetings attended by all workers coming together to question, discuss, and vote.

WSM, management-by-committee, entails a slow process allotting endless meetings to the discussion of issues and decision-making. A Western executive manager can formulate a shrewd and productive business decision in a fraction of the time it takes a self-management team to reach consensus. In Yugoslavia, speed is less a priority than practicing worker democracy. Teamwork forms the core of the Yugoslav approach.

Governing workers' councils exist not only in business and industry, but also in all service organizations in the public sector, such as the post office, railways, the telephone network, universities, and cultural institutions, including museums and theaters. Businesses consisting of five or fewer employees—for example, construction firms, personal services, restaurants, trucking companies, and farms—can operate as private enterprises.

I discuss the functioning of workers' councils with a scientist from Serbia whom I meet only once and do not see again. She elaborates on self-management by mentioning her husband. The workers' council of a factory in Bosnia with eight hundred workers appointed him, an economist, its CEO.

"My husband is trained to lead, but he never makes decisions alone. He proposes policies that he discusses and defends at council meetings, but the workers' council decides. You have to remember," she stresses, "that the factory is owned by all the workers. My husband is the director, but everyone has an equal share."

"Does everyone have the same salary?"

"No. Some workers have a salary larger than my husband's even though he is theoretically the boss."

"If every worker has an equal share in the profits, why doesn't every worker have an equal salary?" I ask.

"I can tell you from my own experience," she responds. "My job is in a hospital lab, where I earn four times more than the worker getting the lowest salary. Because the workers' council decides on the amount of salary workers get, I explained at the hiring meeting that I had studied ten years to finish my training. During those ten years, the other workers were building their pensions. To compensate for those ten years' of lost pension, I receive a higher salary now."

"I have heard that the workers vote for their own pay increases."

"Yes," she confirms. "Most people think workers' involvement in management and company decisions is theoretically excellent. Still, not everyone likes all the measures workers take. Sometimes pay increases are decided at the expense of productivity."

She describes the pension system: "Any worker can retire at age sixty and receive a state pension. The pension is quite adequate and lets us live well, also because we have low rents and free health care and medicines. Alternatively, a man can retire after thirty-five years on the job and a woman after thirty years. Or, we can go on to age sixty."

"Workers' Self-Management sounds very democratic," I say, "but don't both WSM and private enterprises operate under the strict guidance and watchful eye of the Party?"

She laughs. "Most of the workers in the workers' councils are Party members!"

The decentralized system of Workers' Self-Management makes good political sense in Yugoslavia, I gather, where each of the six republics has its own ethnic and regional diversities and nationalistic aspirations. Decentralization apparently lessens the conflicts and rivalries existing among the culturally varied republics. Unfortunately, though, the very decentralization itself influences the individual republics to create protectionist barriers that waste money in unnecessary practices and prevent cooperation. To illustrate, there is the costly requirement that every Yugoslav train crossing into another Yugoslav republic has to switch to an engine that meets the specifications of that particular republic.

Engine-switching is a light-hearted illustration among more serious examples. Even though decentralized and independent, the republics often have interdependent economies. Natural resources and labor from the southern part of the country are habitually directed to northern factories; exports go through the country's western area. The west of Yugoslavia consequently blossoms at the expense of the southern republics, including Macedonia, Montenegro, and Bosnia. The standard of living and degree of economic development varies substantially between the republics. This disparity intensifies friction between the republics already dealing with ethnic differences and conflicts. Sometimes the richer republics resent the investment funds apportioned to less-developed republics.

"Workers' Self-Management has helped our economy rise at unprecedented high rates," Matko says one afternoon as we prepare drafts for letters to Western film distributors. "Our per capita yearly income has been doubling." He wishes Yugoslavia would catch up to the Western countries economically while continuing to offer universal health care, universal access to education, and secure employment.

"Everyone in Yugoslavia has a job for life," he remarks. "It is nearly impossible to get fired."

I press him and he concedes: "There is some unemployment. Work stoppages in some plants. But our country gives unemployment benefits, Western style," he adds, exhibiting a touch of nationalistic pride. "No other East European country dares admit any unemployment exists."

"Does full employment guarantee meaningful jobs, or do some people count paper clips and number and renumber the same pages?"

"At least everyone has work, Miss Green. We give everyone a task to do for the country, in company with other people. That has meaning. And they get paid."

The Yugoslav attitudes to time, teamwork, and participation in society for a common goal raise questions for me about my American upbringing and my own behavior. I like the idea of a participatory horizontal democracy, especially in the workplace, but not the debit side of worker democracy in Yugoslavia. WSM must ultimately answer to a dictatorial regime with a long record of stifling criticism and independent initiatives.

The Studio's consensual management structure catches me when I work days (and nights) on a documentary narrating the manufacture of a medical drug. I redo into good American English the poorly translated voice-over text to save the writer of the original Serbo-Croatian commentary from undeserved embarrassment. The polished script needs to receive the management committee's stamp of approval. My patience is repeatedly tested while the committee holds meeting after meeting and I wait, and wait, and wait . . . and keep on waiting for the news of the final decision. At last, I get the green light to record the narration.

One day Matko says, "We would like you to record the voice-over for a bug spray commercial. The Yugoslav version has appeared on Yugoslav TV. We will go across town to Jadran Film to make the recording."

Made by a state enterprise, the commercial is a clever animated cartoon demonstrating the virtues of an insecticide called Piretoks. In Titoist Yugoslavia, I am beyond the reach of my own country's commercialized system based on turning human beings into avid buyers. Now I will lend my voice to promoting a Yugoslav consumer product, and one based on killing? As an employee hired to perform what the Studio stipulates, I think I cannot refuse.

Several weeks after my arrival, Matko announces: "The quality of your work is getting us contracts from other Yugoslav studios. They want us to do the English dialogue continuity and subtitling of films they will enter in international film festivals." He mentions the feature film *Podne* (Noon), showing how the lives of people in a Serbian town change after the Yugoslavia-Soviet split. Then there is *Tri Sata Za Ljubav* (Three Hours for Love), the amorous adventures of a pretty, domestic maid whose thoughts eventually turn away from sexual cravings to the subject of worker exploitation. I am chuckling to myself as Matko tells me most seriously: "You will have to make the Yugoslavian political references clear for Americans."

In contrast with my previous assignments, this time Matko has not waited until the last minute to place a text on my desk and declare, "Put it into good American; we'll record tomorrow." I cannot imagine any of the Studio's Yugoslav workers meeting such tight deadlines, but Matko knows he can depend on me.

The compliment about my work pleases me until I realize: my workload is getting heavier while my salary remains the same. Even while laboring in a business enterprise based on worker democracy, I myself enjoy no fruits of that democracy. Partly writer, partly secretary, I have a job that also requires me to follow orders. I am expected to accept, with no complaints, a heavier workload for the same pay.

My associates seemingly accept their conditions. All but two of the workers, Matko tells me, earn much less than I do. No discontent is discernible among them. Do they speak out their grievances at the workers' council meetings? Do they count as part of their salary the fulfilling opportunity to toil for their country's collective ideological goals?

Undeterred by the long hours and low pay, I enjoy my work at Zagreb Film immensely, and it does not occur to me to request additional compensation. Besides, regardless of the steady stream of papers Matko deposits on my desk, I feel no real pressure to meet any deadlines. Matko relies on my American haste even as I have somewhat slowed to the Yugoslav pace. The unhurried tempo, I notice, has a calming effect. Compared to my work experiences in America, in Zagreb I am more relaxed at my desk. I stop thinking about time as something to "lose" or to "find." Time is acquiring a timeless quality. Am I developing new attitudes simply from being in the company of the people around me?

6
Comparing Lifestyles

New ideas about food and eating come my way naturally in Yugoslavia. I am accustomed to American breakfasts of toast, butter, and jam, eggs, or cereal, along with orange juice, as well as coffee or tea. The skimpiness of Svetlana's morning meals astounds me. Breakfast consists of the same bland and strong black tea poured into elegant bone china cups from a delicate white porcelain teapot, toast biscuits the size of small hotel soaps, and locally made butter and fruit jam. Appreciating Svetlana's generous hospitality, I consider it rude to comment on the sparse fare. I simply bring extra foodstuffs sufficient for two, and insist she accept dinar contributions for the general costs of my stay.

Sharing breakfast ripens into more than merely putting food into my belly. Svetlana's meals go first to my heart. I relish watching her present the breakfast on a fine cotton tablecloth with matching napkins, as if I am a very special guest. The morning ritual expands my thankfulness for her kindness. Observing her also grants me the luxury of receiving private lessons in European graciousness. Not needing to rush out the door and get quickly to the Studio, where there is no time clock to punch and the workers stroll in casually, I emulate Svetlana's slow dining.

She begins by using a silver-handled butter spreader, another inheritance from her parents, to smooth butter neatly onto the fragile toast-biscuits. It takes finesse to spread the butter without crumbling the biscuit that melts in the mouth. Using a matching demitasse spoon, she lifts jam from a porcelain pot and gracefully pats the fruity mix atop the butter. She limits her biscuit ration to two. I follow her example. Despite initial hunger pangs, after a while whatever I eat in Svetlana's company proves to be enough, neither too little nor too much. Our conversations supply the most plentiful morning nutrition.

Svetlana never throws food into the garbage; she finishes everything on her plate. That is my habit, too, established in my childhood. At P.S. 56 elementary school in Brooklyn, I joined the "Clean Your Plate Club." The membership encouraged me to put on my plate only as much food as I thought I could eat, or to eat all that my mother served, even when I had to smother the horrendous fried liver under a blanket of ketchup to get it down. My mother herself did not belong to the Clean Your Plate Club officially. Having weathered the economic depression of the 1930s, she cleaned her plate "because we can't afford to waste food." Often she added, "There are starving children in India."

Svetlana knows the Western habits of waste. She has traveled widely in Western Europe, where an overflowing abundance of "beautiful, unique, and wonderful things" confronted her in fashionable shops. She still hankers for items her lack of hard currency prevents her from acquiring.

Svetlana confides details of her sufferings in England, desiring the foreign products she could not obtain. Once, while she toyed endlessly with a top brand fountain pen in the stationery section of a High Street department store in London, a man literally wearing a "Customer Service" badge asked what she was doing and loudly requested her to buy or to leave. "Shocking and humiliating!" Svetlana declares, screwing up her face in remembered pain.

By Yugoslav criteria, Svetlana enjoys good quality housing, clothing, and food. Her country's policy of free health care, education, and full employment satisfies her. "We are comfortable," she states. "Socialism takes care of our basic needs."

Having encountered the Western horn of plenty, her country's insufficiencies disgruntle her. "The economy needs to be run better." Her society has failed to raise the material standard of living. Svetlana's semiconsumer mindset contests her homeland's bare lifestyle. She wishes to go shopping and have choice in her purchases.

Svetlana is as intrigued to know about my American life of plenty and comfort as I am to comprehend her existence of scarcity and hardship. She wants to hear my experiences of living in the racing heart of the world's most exciting hometown. She listens intently as I relate my love of my Manhattan neighborhood and my apartment, situated in an old building on the Upper East Side.

To counteract another possible cycle of Svetlana's frustrated yearning for the Western good life, I speak of the street violence and crime in New York and other large American cities.

"Being out alone late at night can be risky for a woman. Arriving home after dark, I rush quickly from the bus stop to the entrance door of my building. When it is really late, I take a taxi. Quickly I walk to my building, keys already in hand, unlock the entrance door, and dash in. Carefully I ascend the three flights of winding stairs, attentive to any movements or sounds. You never know if someone may be lurking in wait."

"No way to live," mutters Svetlana.

"Once inside my apartment, immediately I triple lock my door and place a safety bar across it." To make the ritual sound less hair-raising, I add, with a laugh, "I am not interested in receiving uninvited visitors!"

Svetlana shakes her head in disbelief.

"My bedroom windows open to fire escape stairs extending the length of my building. That's why my windows have iron bars." To demonstrate the need for the bars, I narrate an incident that occurred in a previous apartment, in Greenwich Village.

"An unknown man climbed the stairs next to my third floor window and sat on the fire escape peering in. I noticed him, screamed, and he hurried away. I stopped opening the windows," I admit. "A short time afterward, I relocated."

This talk evokes the fears I knew in Manhattan before going to Stanford. "Some New Yorkers have been mugged several times."

"Mugged?"

"Attacked or robbed at gunpoint."

To pacify Svetlana's alarm, I assure her that I myself never underwent such a frightening incident. I do say, though, that I was accosted one spring afternoon in Midtown Manhattan.

"I had just left my accountant's office. Had my income tax papers in my attaché case. Walking to the bus stop, I passed a group of five or six teenage boys. They directed boisterous remarks at me. I felt a tap on my left shoulder. I turned around and one boy grabbed the case from my right hand and ran off. Sensing no physical danger, I raced after the boy who was gaily tossing the case like a football between himself and his friends. My awkward pursuit in heels greatly amused the boys, who laughed heartily and rallied each other, howling and yelping as they sprinted in front of me. Then one boy unfastened the case and saw it contained only papers. 'Shit!' he snapped, throwing it down. 'Take it and run!' a passerby yelled to me."

"And?" asks Svetlana, absorbed by the story.

"On the street corner was a candy store. I burst in, huffing and puffing, causing the shopkeeper to shout: 'Again? Don't tell me! Those street bullies are constantly bothering passersby. The police do nothing. Not serious enough, they claim.'"

"Yes," I answer Svetlana's next question, "I did phone the police. They came and, no, they did not do a thing." Again she shakes her head in disbelief.

"They called it bullying, and dismissed it as minor. But such incidents can escalate. Still, I do not let fear keep me from living my good life. It's not that I deny fear. Maybe a bit of fear keeps me alert. For some reason, I feel protected. That gives me a sense of fearlessness."

The origin of my fearlessness is a mystery to me. Perhaps it derives from the same place as the occasional blessedness. The blessed feeling makes me feel loved and protected, by whom or what I do not know.

"My sense of fearlessness is no protection if someone wants to hit me on the head," I continue, "but it does make me more aware of possible dangers. I will walk out of my way to bypass a suspect situation not because I am afraid, but because I am intelligent. I am not going to hug a bear!"

"In Zagreb, as in the other socialist countries, criminal violence is no issue," comments Svetlana. "We feel safe. Most people don't even lock their apartment doors. Our women walk on the streets day or night without attack. Our children play on the streets without molestation."

"Yes, I am astonished by the sense of overall safety I experience here. I could not have imagined a society free of the fear of crime."

"Oh, don't get the wrong impression," responds Svetlana. "We have fear and crime, but of a different sort than yours. We have a low rate of violent crime, possibly also because our police are very strict and powerful. We have crimes of corruption. Our indoctrination into sharing has, ironically, given some of us selfish thinking. People pay off officials and store clerks to obtain items in limited supply, or to jump the long lines formed when shipments of scarce items arrive. Some people steal the scarce items."

"Corruption, an age-old problem."

"We promote our national slogan of *Bratstvo i jedinstvo*, 'Brotherhood and Unity,' in every conceivable manner. Most towns have a street or a bridge, sometimes both, named Brotherhood and Unity. And still we steal from each other and cheat."

Apparently not all Yugoslavs embrace the "We-ideology." The self-centered side of human nature persists. Old habits usually die a slow death.

"Don't get a mistaken idea," Svetlana adds. "Every system has bad apples. We do strive for brotherhood and unity. We have a collective goal; we want to build our country. Both children and adults volunteer to help in community projects."

"Volunteer, or forced?"

"You may not believe it. We have waiting lists for volunteers who want to help build roads and tunnels, fix train rails, plant trees, and the like. Community service is very popular. We believe in solidarity, helping each other."

At one point in our discussion, I mention: "New York lacks clean air." I describe that no matter how often I dust my apartment, I find heavy black soot on my windowsills. "The soot even comes through the air conditioner."

"At least you have an air conditioner," Svetlana utters dryly.

Ignoring the sourness her words convey, and pursuing my own one-track thought, I grumble: "And the soot-laden air is the same air I breathe in!"

"At least it is *free* air," remarks Svetlana.

The term "free air" reminds me of Matko's reference to "Yu-go-*slave*-ia" and "Yu-go-*slaves*."

In an acrimonious tone, Svetlana sums up: "Your complaints are petty compared to the various deficiencies we have to endure."

"Deficiencies fit into my stereotype of life in a communist country," is all I can manage to respond.

Svetlana corrects me when I use the word "communist." As she contends, "The communist party rules Yugoslavia, but we are socialists." She clarifies that Yugoslavia, and the East European countries that I consider communist are, in fact, socialist.

"Calling us communists shows ignorance of political theories and systems," says Svetlana. "Since you have come here, don't you have an obligation to know what the words 'communist' and 'socialist' really mean? And whether 'communist' is an accurate label to apply to us? Look at the tragedies people in your country went through from unclear conceptions of communism."

"Whether or not I understand what communism and socialism and even capitalism fully mean and intend," I parry, "all political isms make us ask what values we hold and what values we wish to see upheld in our society."

"At the very least, you can clear your misunderstanding," she responds. "To refresh your memory of courses you had in school, I'll use very simple, if simplistic, definitions. Both socialism and communism are based on the principle that the goods and services produced in an economy should be owned publicly and controlled and planned by a centralized organization. However, socialism asserts that the distribution should take place according to the amount of the individual's production efforts, while communism asserts that goods and services should be distributed among the populace according to the individual's needs."

"From each according to his ability. . . ."

". . . to each according to his deeds is socialism, and to each according to his needs is communism. In other words, socialism says we're responsible for each other, while communism says government is responsible for you."

"And capitalism says we are responsible for ourselves."

"Communism is an ideal," she continues. "Communism is a goal of a future social organization that has changed from the economic system of competitive private ownership into a cooperative governing system."

Svetlana elaborates that citizens in the idealized communist state hold collectively, and share in common, all resources such as property, wealth, and the means and products of production. The rule of the few expands to include the many. Egalitarianism reigns. There is no exploitation.

"We and the other East European socialist countries are in a stage of social and economic development that is very far from the goal of the classless, equalitarian society," she admits. "Comrade Tito is taking us on our own unique socialistic path to the goal of communism. Our country is forging a free and independent way in a totally Yugoslav system we ourselves have created," she professes, emphasizing the "we."

Her nationalistic spirit intensifies.

"Already in 1948, our country declared its independence and freedom from the Eastern Bloc of socialist nations led by Stalin. Tito rejected the role of Soviet satellite. Socialist Yugoslavia is not part of the Eastern Bloc. Never has been, never will be. Soviet socialism has nothing to do with us. We never followed the dictates of Moscow. We never imported a Stalinist form of socialism."

I can only listen.

"Tito leads the Yugoslav Federation by the principle that to attain the ultimate goal of communism, Yugoslavia has to conform to the situation existing in Yugoslavia. The idea is not to adopt a pattern set by another nation. Our country has to walk its own distinct path."

"Isn't that the ideal of every nation? No other country tells you what to do and how?"

"Tell that to the superpowers!" says Svetlana, going on to explain the Soviets' reaction to Tito's independent stance. Tito's choice for Yugoslav nationalism and national economic self-interest led to the expulsion of the Communist Party of Yugoslavia[8] from Cominform, the Communist Information Bureau of the Communist and Workers' Parties. Nine Eastern European communist parties founded Cominform in September 1947 for mutual advice and coordinated activity. The organization became the center of propaganda efforts directed by the Soviet Union against the West. Because Tito resisted Soviet control and Soviet Marxism, Cominform expelled the Communist Party of Yugoslavia in June 1948.

"We are no other country's puppet," proclaims Svetlana. "Tito pulls our strings."

"He certainly has a strong presence," I state.

Before I left for Zagreb, I read an article about Yugoslavia that my mother clipped from an old issue of *Reader's Digest* magazine. An arresting quote introduced the article: "'Tito!' Stalin once snarled. 'I will shake my little finger, and there will be no more Tito!'"[9]

The threat did not manifest itself. Now, at seventy-six, Tito is Eastern Europe's most dynamic leader and Stalin is fifteen years dead.

"One reason the Communist Party of Yugoslavia changed its name to the League of Communists of Yugoslavia was to distance itself from Soviet-style practices," Svetlana explains. "We are free from Soviet ideological, political, and military domination," she emphasizes

---

[8] Known after 1952 as the League of Communists of Yugoslavia.

[9] "Yugoslavia: The Bellwether Keeps Turning Right," by Charles W. Thayer, *Reader's Digest*, New York, September 1967, p. 63.

again, adding that in the Soviet system the Party is the sole repository of political power.

"Two years earlier," she goes on, "Tito removed the ruling power of the League of Communists. Gave it more of an advisory role."

Although Tito was once a dedicated Stalinist, wanting to bring Stalinist-style communism to Yugoslavia, he discovered in practice the weaknesses of hardline Soviet Marxist economics. As one example, Svetlana relates the changes Tito brought to the Marxist principle of nationalizing all means of production, including land.

In the beginning, the Yugoslav government partially nationalized the land and redistributed it to the citizens, and partially collectivized the land. Some landowners were required to surrender land for redistribution; small farmers had to give a portion of their crops to the state or face severe penalties. Svetlana recounts that during the first years of implementation, on seeing the system's imperfections and its unpopularity with farmers, "Tito liberalized agricultural policy, dropping forced collectivization. Tito gave farmers the choice of choosing for socialist collective farming or private enterprise farming."

"Was it really a choice?" I counter. "Doesn't the state favor socialist farms by granting subsidies and supplies and higher prices and other benefits that private farmers do not get?" This information was also in the *Reader's Digest* article. "And aren't many farmers obliged to work with cooperatives because they lack farm machinery and other services?"

"Well, we are free from the ideological course dictated by the Soviet Union," Svetlana rejoins.

"Free from, but not free," I comment, alluding to her "free air" remark.

Svetlana nods in agreement. "All too true, yet we Yugoslavs are freer than the citizens of the East European socialist countries."

"What about you as an individual? What does it mean not to have free air?"

Svetlana sucks in her breath and is on the verge of answering. She stops, becomes pensive, and takes another extended moment before replying: "Even in Yugoslavia, the freest of the socialist lands, we do not have real personal freedom."

I am stunned when she discloses "the risks of having an interest in foreign things," a risk applicable to herself. She gives an example. "It is not wise for Yugoslavs to go into a music shop and ask for Western phonograph records. Your name can wind up on a list." She no longer dares enter a certain shop in Zagreb.

"Incredible!" I exclaim. There is no comparing this bizarre situation to my innocent Manhattan precautionary routine of stepping from a bus or taxi at night, house keys already in hand. "Does the list-making imply that an interest in foreign art or cultural products can divert one off the nation's ideological path?"

"In a manner of speaking, yes. So you see, all the East European countries may boast a degree of equality and justice in social life, but not real personal freedom."

"Is it worth limiting freedom to achieve some amount of equality and fairness?"

Svetlana ignores my question. Although we sit alone in her apartment, she explains in a lowered tone that the League of Communists is organized in cells of three members, and no one knows where the headquarters is located. "Much about the Party is cloaked in mystery," she whispers. "The police are very powerful and feared."

Svetlana refers to a scandal two years earlier, involving Yugoslav Vice President Aleksandar Ranković. He was the chief Party organizer and head of the dreaded *Uprava državne bezbednosti* (UDBA), "State Security Administration," Yugoslavia's intelligence service, the secret police system of the Tito regime. Ranković, seventeen years younger than Tito and considered his heir apparent, had the police secretly watch everyone, including high government and Party officials. "Faithful correspondents" were planted in firms. Tito found listening devices hidden in his own office and in his home. Ranković lost his positions and was expelled from the Party. Ranković disagreed with Tito's reforms to Marxist ideology, suggests Svetlana.

In the wake of the upheaval, Svetlana assures me, Tito downgraded the secret police, and a political culture of reform is developing. As one example, she says, the country has abolished exit visas for Yugoslav citizens.

"Allowing people to leave the country without needing official permission signals a liberalized police system," she asserts. "All of the East European communist countries require exit visas, and they are not always easy to get."

Svetlana's understatement confronts me with a situation I do not know as an American: the lack of the right to leave one's home country and travel to another. As an American, I have the right to travel freely, except to those countries on the government's travel ban list.

A bit overwhelmed by the murky police state information, I wonder aloud if any "faithful correspondents" walk the halls at Zagreb Film. I have noticed mysterious-looking men wandering around. "Or has the public exposure stopped the practice?"

Svetlana does not know the answer, except to say: "You never know who is on the payroll of the secret police."

Her attitude changes, as if she has revealed too much about the functioning hidden behind Yugoslavia's dark curtains.

"You in the West may enjoy some amount of personal freedom, but little equality and justice. Your society may be more free; ours is more fair. Your system of economic battle and unbridled competition creates a huge obstruction to social order and peace. Competition is not good for society."

"Competition brings out the best in people, pushes us beyond our limits," I counter, repeating an American truism learned as a child.

"No," objects Svetlana. "Competition is self-destructive, encouraging selfishness and egocentric behavior. If I want to win, the other person has to lose. My needs and wishes count most. When we compete, the result is much more important than the means. Competition implies working separately; there is no fundamental sense of brotherhood. Here we strive to work together, in cooperation, toward the end goal of a better society."

"This sounds very good, Svetlana, but we both know that most people are selfish. We care for ourselves first. How much coercion does your government use to attain the cooperative ideal?"

"Individuals do tend to be selfish. In our system we work together for something greater than our own little lives."

"How much force is involved?"

"It is true. We do enforce regimentation for the collectivist ideal. We sacrifice individual liberty to the principle of equality. Equality of opportunity and status for all."

"What about the individual's need for freedom?" I ask. "Are you condoning limitations on freedom for the sake of equality and fairness in society?"

"I admit that people will endure, for only a limited time, excessive regulation of their lives in exchange for collective order and equality," responds Svetlana. "Look at Czechoslovakia. Czechoslovakia is forging democratic reforms, compromising between a forced communal life and freedom of the individual. If this lasts, we may see a socialist democracy combining freedom, equality, and justice."

Svetlana is apparently referring to the Prague Spring, the political liberalization that is taking place in the Soviet satellite.

"In Czechoslovakia a new government is in power. The people want enhanced personal freedom, but I am not familiar with what exactly is going on there," she says.

"The UN designated 1968 the International Year for Human Rights," I mention.

"Let us hope it is prophetic!" she declares. "Tito's reforms of de-Stalinization, de-centralization, de-collectivity, workers' self-management, private enterprise, and other innovations to Marxist ideology are observed by our East European neighbor countries." She bursts into a smile and remarks, "By the way, people in Czechoslovakia are now getting clothes of better design!"

Svetlana narrates again her visits to Western Europe. She neglects the sore subject of shopping to acknowledge the exhilarating atmosphere of personal liberty she had savored. "Mostly I said and did what

I wanted, where I wanted. I did not feel watched—well, except in that department store."

By the end of the sometimes-spiky discussion, we conclude that without personal freedom, there can be no equality and justice. Similarly, without social equality and social justice, there is no freedom. The means used by Tito's government to reach the desired Third Way between Western capitalism and Soviet communism oppose the nation's originally stated ideals. "Free air," says it all.

"Do you long, as I do, for a society based on economic and social justice as well as personal and political freedom?" she asks.

Before I climb into bed, Svetlana knocks on the bedroom door. There is an air of conspiracy as she hands me a piece of folded paper. Baffled, I open it to see the name of a phonograph record and the address of a local music shop. Will I go to the shop and request the record? The phonograph record was manufactured in the West. "No suspicion will come to you," she assures me. "You are free."

One evening, as a token of thanks for her hospitality, I present Svetlana a bottle of French cognac I bought at the state-run grocery store for a hefty price. When I bring her foods and drinks I think she might like, or would be too expensive for her to buy, especially imported foreign items, invariably she poses the question: "Why do you do it?" In turn I respond, "Why do you do this?" when she insists on sharing the gift with me rather than her boyfriend, as I suggest. Svetlana's translating job for Zagreb Film allows her to work in the office or at home. This flexibility gives her many opportunities to visit her boyfriend at a beach resort town in Dalmatia, on the picturesque eastern coast of the Adriatic Sea some hours away, where he has a full-time job.

"Opening tourism is another crucial thing Tito did after breaking with Stalin," notes Svetlana. "Tito built all kinds of tourism facilities, especially in Dalmatia, to attract foreign tourists who pump hard currency into our economy."

While Svetlana gets the cognac glasses from her liquor cabinet, I flash back to my lifestyle at home. Rarely do I drink alcohol except at a party or on a date. Yugoslavs seem to imbibe alcohol as a daily habit.

At Svetlana's, after the working day, I may drink a glass of wine at her prompting. Now I hold a low, spherical cognac glass in my hand. I warm it the way she does, then put my nose to the glass edge and inhale the fruity scent.

My very first sip encourages me to divulge: "Our conversations make me think more deeply about the freedoms I take for granted. If I interpret the word *free* solely in political and sociological terms, by such reckoning my country is a very free land. I grew up proud to be an American, citizen of the nation with the most freedoms in the world, as they taught us in school. Freedom of this, freedom of that."

"America has a good constitution," interjects Svetlana, well informed on many subjects.

"Yes, the privileges of my American nationality are guaranteed in our Constitution and the Bill of Rights that helped establish our great nation," I affirm, exposing my own touch of national pride. "In the Declaration of Independence, the great founders of my country asserted certain truths to be self-evident. The phrasing is very beautiful. They said that all people are created equal and endowed by their Creator with certain inalienable rights, including life, liberty, and the pursuit of happiness."

"Happiness signifies different things to different people," comments Svetlana. "As a Yugoslav, I maintain that happiness means everyone has enough food to eat, a home to live in, paid work, sufficient money, free education, free health care, and an adequate pension upon retirement.

"We have no huge economic divisions between people, though there are some low incomes in the southern part of the country." She addresses the people's right to the basic necessities of life. "Our system of free education is producing a generation of young people much better educated and more capable than those now in power."

As Svetlana speaks, again I imagine her lecturing at Zagreb University, not on language but on social issues. Her social passions, and another sip of the cognac, have her trumpet: "I do not approve the policies of the rich capitalist countries that produce citizens who have nowhere else to live than on the streets! Morally indefensible!

"How degrading, to be dependent on the charity and spare change of passersby. You will never see our people living on our streets because they have no home. Capitalists may find our living conditions substandard, but at least all our citizens have a roof over their heads!"

"This may be so, but even if I were to become homeless and fated to sleep on the streets of an American city, I would possess a personal freedom to choose and follow my preferred lifestyle. Few Yugoslavs are allowed such choice," I counter.

"Really? Do you really think you would choose to live on the street?"

I take another sip of cognac.

"The purpose of government is to represent all the people and not just the rich," she declares. She accuses America of worshipping a religion of greed. "Capitalism convinces people who are victimized by the system to support the system, manipulating them as if to demand their own victimization."

Svetlana presents so much for me to defend! Her view is so politically biased. She is indoctrinated by her country's propaganda. I definitely have to correct her wrong perception. "People live on the streets in poor countries too," is all I can retort. The cognac is fuzzing up my thinking process. "Look at India."

"A totally different set of circumstances," she says, dismissing my remark as irrelevant to the subject at hand.

Once in a while I cannot escape the feeling that the Cold War conflict enters into our conversations even though Yugoslavia is a founding member of the Non-Aligned Movement (NAM). Tito helped develop a "Third Force," giving Third World countries a way to cooperate and act globally and have more leverage with the superpowers while avoiding participation in the Cold War. In Belgrade in 1961, some thirty-five Mediterranean and Afro-Asian Third World countries agreed on a policy of nonaligning militarily or politically with the Cold War's opposing power blocs of the US and the USSR and also not with the People's Republic of China.

In my now cognac-wobbly brain, I rummage around for a calm response to Svetlana's prickly remarks. Another sip of the brandy has

me grant that our esteemed American Constitution is not always inter-
preted from the most generous, caring, and compassionate perspective.
I admit, "It was a bitter pill to swallow when I learned that America's
Founding Fathers designed a system preventing females from voting
in government elections. Of course, thoughts concerning the woman's
role in society were different then, but . . ." Again I take a sip of the
cognac. "Not until the early twentieth century did American women
step out of the shadows of male citizens and receive the right to vote."

Carelessly, I have given Svetlana an opening for her to proclaim:
"The Socialist Federal Republic of Yugoslavia made a good beginning by
establishing itself on values of gender, ethnic, religious, and class equality.
From the very first elections, in 1945, Yugoslavian women easily got the
vote that women in other countries had to struggle to receive." Her
slightly sing-song manner indicates she may be repeating government
propaganda memorized as a child. "To get the vote, you American
women had to wait more than one hundred and thirty years after the
adoption of the United States Constitution in 1787."

"The second-class citizenship of women is changing," I shoot
back. "Taking guidelines from the Civil Rights Movement, women are
demanding full and equal legal rights and social privileges." I tell her that
American women now publicly confront traditional patriarchal authority and attitudes; women are standing up to men in new ways.

"Maybe some influence will rub off on us," she says as if conced-
ing a point. "Men dominate our one-party system and we don't have a
women's rights movement."

Svetlana follows the women's rights activities on the rise in America
and other Western countries and stays abreast of international current
events. She has a good schooling in history, her country's and mine,
knowledge unsurprising for the daughter of international diplomats.
Svetlana grasps American history better than many Americans.

Discoursing on "equal rights for women and everyone," she
mentions that the signers of America's freedom documents owned
African slaves. "They fought a war against England for national freedom while allowing some people to remain the legal slaves of others?"

she questions. "Surely your founders knew slavery was wrong. They did nothing to stop it as a reprehensible institution."

I have to concur. It is a source of hurt to me that even our venerated American genius, Benjamin Franklin, passionate lover of freedom and signer of both the Declaration of Independence and the Constitution, owned five African slaves.

"Repair and reform are in process," I say apologetically, but I bristle when Svetlana challenges: "Don't you see the connection between using humans as a commodity subject to buying and selling, and the system you have today? If a country is carved out of land grabbing and genocide of the aboriginal population, and built up on slave labor, can it last?"

Ouch—the truths relating to the early American settlers yield a mean slap. My face is red from a kind of nationalistic embarrassment. I try to stay composed. Unprepared for the assaults, I realize that, for all her worldliness, Svetlana is a product of her Third Way political system wanting to prove itself superior to either communism or capitalism. Mentally I formulate an all-inclusive reply defending my country. Before I can speak, Svetlana comments, in a conciliatory tone: "Hypocrisy exists here too. That's why it is easy to become cynical. How else to protest in a monitored society?"

In my own attempt to smooth ripples, I ask: "How about protesting through the whimsy of the cartoon?" Still, I am not completely won back. "Doesn't the financial support your government gives Zagreb Film automatically mean that the Studio has to adhere to governmental guidelines? Films, in some way, have to benefit Yugoslav socialism?"

She answers: "We are aware that in a monitored society the human tendency for self-preservation brings on self-censorship."

We are both relieved when the Bach playing on her phonograph reaches a dynamic section overwhelming our talk.

One day, glancing through the English language books stacked on Svetlana's bookshelves, I spot a large book simply titled *Yugoslavia*. Printed the previous year by the Workers' Council of Zagreb, it has black-and-white photos. There is no page numbering. I read that Yugoslavia's economy has grown in the past years at unprecedented high rates; the national per capita income is now around five hundred dollars. The low figure, so many times below America's per capita income, sets me to wondering. I have not observed any dire poverty in Yugoslavia, at least not in the Zagreb area. The people in the gray and materially deprived Croatian capital appear well fed and healthy.

In Yugoslavia's developing economy, the people are neither very rich nor very poor. By my American yardstick, they are very poor. Yet their basic subsistence needs are met—except, of course, the essential need for personal liberty and freedom. There is no hunger or starvation, and no one lives on the streets. Free health care, free education, and secure employment are available to every citizen, as Matko and Svetlana lose no opportunity to repeat.

In my own, rich country, a large minority of the populace lives below the poverty line in dismal circumstances. During a one-year job as a "social investigator," or social worker, for the New York City Department of Welfare, predating my graduate studies at Stanford, I helped poor and disadvantaged Americans living at the low end of the American economic spectrum.

One of the families on my caseload comprised an unwed black mother and her three children, from three absent fathers. They lived crowded together in one shabby room in a low-rental tenement hotel serving poor transients in Manhattan's Spanish Harlem. My introductory visit I cut short, unable to tolerate the dwelling's stench. The walls literally stank. Cockroaches marched boldly across the floor, and mice tried to get their share of the family's limited food supply. The old and deteriorated building obviously received neither long-term maintenance nor daily upkeep.

I thought of this family when the Department asked the social workers to nominate one household as "most deserving" of a special Christmas. My essay won. Just before the twenty-fifth of December, I presented the prize, an overflowing gift basket containing festively wrapped holiday foods, toys, and clothing. "Mommy, mommy! Oranges!

Oranges!" shrieked the four-year-old son, jumping up and down. "Slippers!" screeched the six-year old. "Slippers!" His very first pair. The mother shed tears and exclaimed, "Best Christmas ever!" Personal contact with the desperate poverty existing in my wealthy country exposed me to a reality that I had, until then, known only intellectually.

The conversations with Svetlana bring up significant contrasts between the American Way and Tito's Third Way. I become more conscious of my country's discrepancies, the disconnects between some stated principles and practices. The vast differences in rights, rewards, and responsibilities between white and black, rich and poor, powerful and weak, and male and female in American society make me ask myself: *Is there a more fair and balanced way to live together as human beings?* I am impressed that nearly all citizens in a "poor" country like Yugoslavia are secured of their basic subsistence needs.

But I do not envy the Yugoslavs; I deplore their loss of freedom, liberty, and privacy. Communist Eastern Europe has a reputation for its limitations and repressions. Now I am encountering these limitations and restrictions.

It is clear that both Svetlana and I have some fundamental criticisms of our respective societies. Equally obvious, neither Svetlana nor I can quite follow each other's objections except intellectually.

Unlike Svetlana, I do not long for personal freedom and liberty because I already have them. Like most of my compatriots, I take American freedoms for granted, as if they always existed and will always endure.

The talk about political and personal freedom, and Svetlana's longing for both, makes me aware of a deep longing of my own that seems connected with freedom. I think of the mysterious blessed feeling I get from time to time. I sense there exists a freedom I do not know. Specifics elude me. This yearning reminds me again of the "something" I have forgotten and need to remember. Every flower bud has its own right moment for blossoming.

7

Exercising a New Simplicity

My colleagues respect my "American," as they term my language, but no one except Matko and Svetlana can carry on a substantial conversation with me. American, as other varieties of English, is out of their grasp, just as I cannot converse in Serbo-Croatian. Yugoslav society has thrown me into a dark dungeon of nonverbal communication. Through an opening in the stonework of this mute prison, a thin stream of light carries Serbo-Croatian words into my field of perception. Words come to me by osmosis.

My initial vocabulary of "Matko" and *druže, marama* and *živeli* builds to steadily more words, starting with simple *molim* (please), *hvala* (thank you), and various forms of *dobro* (good). Crucial phrases embed themselves quickly: "I don't understand"; "Please speak slowly"; "Please repeat." My comprehension grows, but my attempts to train my tongue into the correct placement for the *tz*, *dz*, and *ch* Slavic sounds prove tough going. My tongue needs to practice Yugoslav cooperation! A language mispronounced is a poor transporter of thought. Not even my fervor "to be one of the team" can break through the language barrier keeping me from extensive social exchange in the workroom.

Every morning, the beloved plum brandy warms the animators to their drawing pens and their friendly camaraderie. "*Dobro jutro!*" (Good morning!) they call to me, often simultaneously raising on high their *šljivovica* glasses. Although water is the only colorless liquid in my glass, sometimes I join my colleagues as they slowly drift into their workday. Back and forth flies their morning chatter. Unable to jump into the conversations, I remain silent in their midst though pleasant, unspoken feelings pass between us. My "I am here but not here" smile burns lines into my face.

A pity, I conclude, to be in the close company of extremely creative artists and be unable to enter their thought worlds to any significant extent. I would like to get insight into their ways of looking at life. Their cartoons project the animators as intelligent, sensitive, and caring men. Watching them lunch cordially together in the Studio canteen, I sense the humanism that infuses their art. Their unpredictable alternation of work pace from the slow to the temporarily fast, and back again, may exasperate me, but their style undeniably has its charm.

My smile and the unavoidable silence accompany me to the workers' canteen. Usually I lunch alone, watching my colleagues engage in animated discussion. "Hello, how are you?" is my chief form of address; further into conversation I can barely limp. My Serbo-Croatian vocabulary keeps increasing, yet I am unable to communicate beyond an elementary level. With nothing to do except bite, chew, and swallow, and study the graining in the lunchroom table, I become a close observer of the canteen scene.

The co-workers mingle at wooden tables, lunching from generously filled plates they always empty, Svetlana-style. Truly I enjoy watching them chat together like good friends or family even while I sit alone. At home in America, the law of social gathering requires streaming exchange of knowledgeable opinions, humor, and witty repartee; stone silence might nominate one for a "dull person" award. Although I do not consider myself dull, I am only a shell of my vivacious American self as I lunch mutely in the Studio canteen, where loud talk and laughter boom merrily.

Nonetheless, I am not invisible to my colleagues. Occasionally an animator waves a shot glass of *šljivovica* in my direction and grins or winks. My nondrinker status has become the butt of a running joke. Is the dark and lethargic energy I generally experience in Zagreb of too slow a vibration for some people to bear without the aid of alcohol, notably plum brandy? Primarily to be less apart and more like them, I adopt the Studio's other characteristic drink. The first sip of their thick, sweet, and strong Turkish coffee gives a kick, unsettling me as could a quick gulp of neat Scotch. The liquid jolts from both the Turkish coffee and the *šljivovica* undoubtedly help my colleagues endure the sameness of the Studio's luncheon menu and, perhaps, the very grayness of Yugoslav life itself.

In the canteen, I get accustomed to a simple procedure. I walk along the food bar and point to items that the blue-smocked woman on the other side of the counter puts on my plate. Besides serving the food, she prepares the tea and Turkish coffee. The Studio buffet presents an unchanging pallet of thin, pickled peppers, cold sandwich meat resembling salami and bologna, slabs of locally made cheese, heaps of coarse bread, mountains of tomatoes, yogurt, and fresh fruit juices.

Just as I usually eat the same breakfast foods at Svetlana's every day, I resign myself to the set luncheon fare. But resignation does not mean enjoyment. My American food habits are entrenched; I miss my varied diet. New York City offers a lavishness of foods from nearly everywhere. My rich society allows me to eat pretty much what I desire, according to the sensory wishes of my taste buds and the fullness of my pocketbook. My tongue's pleasure decides the content of my meals.

In Tito's Yugoslavia, food limitations force me into an abrupt cold turkey from my American dietary pattern based on abundance. I have lost my freedom of choice, the great privilege of an American. Occasionally, grinding away on a chunk of coarse Yugoslav bread, about which my mother might say, "It's good for your teeth," I daydream of a smooth, New York white-flour bagel smothered in creamy cream cheese. Oh, how I miss American brownies and New York pizza and baked Idaho potatoes dripping with salted butter. Shopping for food or other articles in the Croatian capital is a torturous exercise in accepting the given circumstances and not grumbling. What option do I have? The stores, all state-run, mirror the opposite of a Western shopping paradise. Often the shelves are quite bare.

Zagreb offers scanty fare at low prices inside unadorned stores lacking even display windows. Not that I really miss displays projecting seductive merchandise arranged according to psychological marketing strategies. Here no advertising aims at enticing me to want and then to buy from among a large assortment of similar items. Here I simply buy what I need, if available. If I need soap powder, and only one brand exists, I have no choice but to accept it, no matter how inferior I may think it to be. Otherwise I end up empty-handed. Rare are alternatives to choose between. Such a situation robs me of my freedom to take something or leave it. Yugoslavia downgrades me as a shopper, and the demotion does not please me.

I am not seeking the familiar. I am not trying to find Yugoslav replacements for the consumer products I left behind in America, although certain vital items are simply not to be found. Even resourceful Svetlana does not know of a store selling tampons and sanitary pads. These articles of feminine hygiene probably fall into the category of "unnecessary luxury goods."

"The women here use a primitive form of cotton batting, sold in long strips," I write to my mother after resorting to this only solution. "You pull off pieces as needed."

When Matko was to travel briefly on Studio business to Trieste, Italy, boldly I asked if he would bring me back the foreign-made tampons unavailable in Yugoslavia. I gave him American dollars for the purchase. Handing the boxes to me upon his return, he said that he bought some for his wife too. Mrs. Matko had never before heard of tampons.

My letter to my mother detailing the failure of the local hygienic and beauty-care products to meet my quality standard prompts her to send me personal care items. While waiting for the parcel to arrive in typical Yugoslav slow motion, I learn once again that deprivation has its benefits. Observing Svetlana, I pick up do-it-yourself beauty tips.

After soaking a small cucumber in cold water, Svetlana cuts two thick slices and places them over her eyes for about fifteen minutes, telling me, "This is for relaxation and to reduce puffiness." She beats the yoke of an egg and applies it to her face, leaving it on until nearly dry.

"For nourishment and softness." Massaging vegetable oil into her hair gives it a great shine, especially when she keeps a hot wet towel around her head for about an hour before washing out the oil. "You can also do this with milk," she says, "or use milk as a last rinse." Several times I join her at the beauty salon where she has her hair groomed on a regular basis. The equipment is decidedly old, but a cut, wash, hair set, and drying cost me ridiculously less than at my Manhattan beauty parlor. Svetlana clips pictures of up-to-date hairstyles from German magazines and shows them to her beautician to duplicate.

Although I welcome my mother's beauty-care parcel, I do not ask her to send me the American foods for which I long. As in the Studio canteen, I have to accept the food locally available. On Saturdays, I visit the outdoor food market off Trg Republike (Republic Square), the main shopping and business hub in city center. The market, combining state-owned stalls and private stands run by farmers from the surrounding countryside, relieves Zagreb's tedious grayness. Under oversize umbrellas, the vendors offer colorful piles of fresh fruits and vegetables.

These farmers cultivate their produce in gardens and on small farms without large machinery, in places like the simple farms I saw as the train chugged through the Balkan countryside. Large-scale farming and the encroachments of modern civilization have not yet driven small farmers from rural areas. The farmers seemingly pursue farming as agri-culture rather than agri-business. Their vegetables and fruits are of limited variety and lack the perfect beauty of produce in American supermarkets, but the taste is better. In contrast to the fixed prices of the state stalls, the private farmers challenge me to bargain. Playing their game, I haggle for fruits and vegetables in my broken Serbo-Croatian. The private farmers call out very low numbers to make a sale.

When I compare the prices for similar items at home, I am flabbergasted at the huge differences. This low-income country has catapulted me into the high-income bracket in terms of my ability to buy. Not only do I earn more than most Zagrebians, I also have in my suitcase a supply of American dollar traveler's checks. My hard currency converts into piles of the soft dinar that is virtually worthless outside Yugoslavia. Although of middle-class American means, in the eyes of the Yugoslavs I am a rich foreigner. Above all else, they may consider me wealthy because I possess an American passport.

As well-heeled as I am in Yugoslav society, I become a local in that I, too, lack choice and have no access to a refrigerator. The absence of a fridge and an air-conditioner during the hot Zagreb summer requires me to buy food almost daily. Svetlana and I rarely have dinner together. She has a busy social life and is often away.

The loss of time caused by frequent food shopping annoys me until I notice that no food gets wasted, since I buy only as much as I need for a day or two. Additionally, I observe the physical benefits of habitually eating fresh foods. The lack of "convenience food" or "take out" forces me to cook meals from fresh produce from scratch. Sometimes as I leave the Studio, there flashes the thought: "I'll save time today by grabbing a fast meal out of the freezer." I laugh. I can enjoy the joke my mind is playing, trying to make me think I am back in New York.

In the consumer paradise of America, I can obtain just about anything I want from just about anywhere. Only the boundaries determined by my budget can restrict my purchases. In Zagreb, there is little to attract my dinars. Visiting a shop for tourists, I buy hand-carved wooden folkloric items of appealing naïve simplicity to give as gifts. Very reasonably priced, decorative cut glass bowls, plates, and vases are too difficult to ship or carry home.

When I can put aside my complaining attitude, I recognize that Yugoslavia's lifestyle of scarcity has its advantages. I go to the state-owned grocery for a bar of soap or a box of soapsuds, and one-two-three I find the shelf, select the only brand—the state brand—and pay; if, that is, the item is not sold out. Shopping in this simplified manner saves me time and energy. I do not lose precious minutes or mental energy deliberating what to choose from a vast display of merchandise packaged and arranged to convince: "Buy me!"

Shopping in Zagreb is quite the opposite when foreign goods arrive.

One day I hear that a special store, which occasionally offers imported items, expects a shipment of English breakfast tea the coming Saturday. I decide to buy a box for Svetlana. Unsurprisingly, she has a low opinion of the black tea ordinarily available in the shops, including a brand imported from America. After waiting in line nearly six hours for the shipment to be shelved, as I later write to my parents, I happily secure a "one-to-a-person" package of the coveted Twining's Earl Grey. As usual, Svetlana says on receiving my gift, "You shouldn't have." Immediately she sets the teakettle on the stove and, anticipating a delicious brew, gets out her best bone-china cups.

Even the restaurants present a limited fare, normally simple combinations of meat with potatoes and potatoes with meat. Meat appears in various forms as roasted, cooked on a spit, or grilled. I do not develop a lasting taste for the traditional dishes of *ražnjiči*, shish kebab of grilled pork or veal, and *ćevapčiči*, a grilled or pan-fried minced meat mixture of beef, lamb, and sometimes pork shaped into skinless sausages. Yugoslavs apparently love *ražnjiči* and *ćevapčiči* the way Americans go for hot dogs, hamburgers, and French fries.

On the plus side, Zagreb's restaurants serve everything fresh, never from a can. I suspect that the Zagrebians abhor canned foods. Simple raw salads are popular, especially vinegar-soaked tossed raw cabbage. Salads complement most main dishes. I do not push the salads to one side as I do the finely chopped raw onions accompanying every plate of *ražniči* and *ćevapčiči*. The fresh foods and salads served in abundance encourage my growing habit of eating more fresh and raw foods. I sense that fresh foods serve my health better than my taking fruits and vegetables from cans, bottles, and frozen food boxes, as has been my American wont.

Then there is the wine, everywhere. Wine seems an indispensable part of Croatian culture. I mention to Svetlana the presence of wine at most meals.

"Grapes are plentiful in our Croatia, and so we have many wineries and wine," she responds. "You Americans have your Coke or Pepsi, do you not?" she asks, adding that wine is better for one's health than soda pop.

The tedious sameness of foodstuffs evokes boredom. Yet every day I am hungry, and hunger leads me to eat what is available. Hunger overrides the fatigue of a repetitious diet. More than once I remember my mother's statement about "children starving in India." I begin to see how spoiled I have become by my native Land of Plenty.

One morning, helping Svetlana lay out the breakfast, I ask about her country's scarcities.

"Our scarcities are real," Svetlana assures me. "Our government does not create shortages or perceived shortages to achieve or keep prices high, as sometimes your stock market speculators do. And unlike your shops operating on the competitive economic principle of supply and demand, our state-run stores have fixed prices."

"A Westerner can save much money here by nonshopping," I quip. "There are no consumer allurements to tempt me."

"Well, your marketplace usually extends to the entirety of New York City."

In the defensive tone I sometimes hear when we speak of our respective countries, Svetlana informs me that the sparsely filled shops of Yugoslavia appear heavenly to tourists from Bulgaria, Romania, and other East Bloc nations. "It may be hard for you to imagine, but consumer items in those countries are even more scarce than here. Women from those countries regard our fashions as elegant, though compared to Westerners we look like peasants."

We proceed into the pattern of Svetlana describing the Yugoslavian governing system that confronts me with endless unknowns.

"Yugoslav socialism puts the spending priority for its limited national funds on state projects rather than the production of consumer items," she begins in her professorial tone.

"You mean," I interject, "that your country asks its citizens to subordinate their personal comfort, convenience, and prosperity to the common good. This is a fine ideal. Do your people accept this?"

Svetlana hems and haws, asserting that the embrace of this ideal by all people would help humankind immeasurably.

"I understand what you're saying, or not saying," I comment.

"Let's face it," she finally states. "Unless people are induced by patriotic propaganda, or forced by laws or circumstances, they do not usually feel disposed to put the welfare of a larger whole ahead of their own self-centered interests. Our citizens are no exception to this basic instinct of human survival."

As if to escape the topic, Svetlana asks, "Does the breakfast please you?" If she had asked this during the first week or possibly the second, I might have blurted out, "Well, it does lack choice." Instead, nearly one month in Zagreb behind me, I astound myself by answering: "I am content."

Nonetheless, sometimes I desire change. Then I splurge and order a meal of "wild game bird," wild berry sauce on the side, at Zagreb's luxurious Esplanade Intercontinental Hotel dating from the presocialist era. This tendency I acquire after inviting Svetlana for dinner in her favorite place; she chooses the Esplanade, with its posh interior of Carrara marble and Art Deco. If I find the location next to the train station odd for a top-end hotel, that is before Svetlana explains, "Built in 1925 as a luxury stop along the route of the Orient Express."

A meal of wild bird at the Esplanade Intercontinental Hotel — Zagreb's hotel intended for the foreign tourist and prohibitive for the ordinary Yugoslav—represents the epitome of splurging, since it gobbles up a huge chunk of my Studio salary. I justify the expense by rationalizing that my diet lacks a variety of protein.

Exceeding my budget to dine at the Esplanade Intercontinental exposes me to a different clientele than frequents the local coffeehouses. Once I meet a bureaucrat dining alone in grand style. Drinking after-dinner coffee together at his invitation, he mentions that government business often requires his absence from his Belgrade desk. He travels around Yugoslavia lodging and dining in the country's best hotels, those providing comforts for international visitors (at international rates as well). My coffee companion hints that he is a Party member. I could have guessed that he belongs to the privileged minority of the League of Communists. He enjoys a Yugoslav good life unknown to the ordinary citizen. I think of George Orwell's oft-quoted maxim in *Animal Farm*, his novel satirizing the rise of an elitist "new class" in a supposedly classless communist society: "All animals are equal, but some are more equal than others."

Taking special privileges for itself, the Yugoslav communist party elite is in this respect no different from the ruling political elites in other countries. I sense I will get no response if I question this bureaucrat about those comrades who have left the Party disgusted by the bureaucracy and petty politics; also I do not inquire whether he himself joined because membership gave him the best chance for job advancement, just as personal connections help in a democratic country.

When in Zagreb, he visits the Esplanade. Four years earlier, he tells me, it became the first socialist hotel to enter into business with a Western hotel firm.

"The venture between capitalism and socialism proved successful, bringing American standards to the Croatian hotel world," he states proudly. "Yugoslavia is open to integrate into its Third Way the best aspects of American capitalism." Unfortunately, I neglect to ask him what he, as a Yugoslav bureaucrat, considers those best aspects to be. Our conversation shifts to my loneliness in Zagreb and his antidote: the glories, beauties, and mysteries of Belgrade.

"You must visit *Beograd*," he declares in a commanding tone I identify as "governmental." Arrive when he is in town; he will show me around. He writes down the name of a small hotel he is sure I will enjoy. "Ask the Studio to make the booking."

He advises: "Forget shopping, except for folk crafts. Our shops in Beograd are not much different from here, offering items geared mainly to essential needs. Discover one of Europe's oldest cities. Seven-thousand-year-old history!"

While I sip my coffee, he draws up a list of "must sees" in "unforgettable Beograd" and declares, "You must go."

8

Stretching Mind's Boundaries

Zagreb is forcing me to look at my old ideas afresh. Caught between my American priorities and new concerns beginning to form, I am almost desperate to find someone who might understand my struggle between West and East. Interestingly enough, the person I find, while being found, is someone I would have ignored as a conversation partner had I any choice.

One morning, Matko calls me into his office and introduces me to "*Herr* Stern." He emphasizes the "Herr" in the same way he lays stress on the third syllable of "Yu-go-*slave*-ia." As he pronounces the German word for "Mister," a chill shudders my body. Perhaps, like me, anything German reminds Matko of Nazi atrocities. Is Matko viewing *Herr* Stern through an anti-German bias?

On March 25, 1941, one and a half years after the start of World War II, the Kingdom of Yugoslavia joined the Tripartite Pact of the Axis Powers, the military alignment of Nazi Germany, fascist Italy, and imperial Japan. Preferring to join the countries opposed to fascist expansion, the Yugoslav people protested violently, provoking a coup d'état in Belgrade. Yugoslav Air Force General Dušan Simović led the bloodless coup, threw out the Pact-signing government, and rejected the Pact.

In early April 1941, an outraged Adolph Hitler sent Nazi planes into Yugoslavia during a revengeful "Operation Punishment." At night, while people were sleeping, the Nazis dropped bombs on important Yugoslav towns. Roughly ten thousand people were killed or injured, and nearly ten thousand houses and public buildings were destroyed or badly damaged. The Axis forces of Germany, Italy, and their ally, Hungary, invaded Yugoslavia, aided later by the Bulgarians and Romanians. Yugoslavia quickly capitulated. The Yugoslav government and the reigning king, Peter II, fled abroad. Although Yugoslavia was partitioned among the Axis allies, the German military assumed virtual rule.

Yugoslav troops retreated to mountain strongholds where they separated into two rival resistance groups. The Chetniks remained loyal to the Yugoslav monarch, who set up a government-in-exile in England, as did other European countries under Axis occupation. The Partisans, made up of workers and peasants, followed the military command of Josip Broz Tito, an experienced communist warrior.

Josip Broz had, during World War I, fought for the Austro-Hungarian Empire. He distinguished himself to become the youngest sergeant major in the service. Sent to the Russian front, he was seriously wounded and captured by the Imperial Russian Army. In a prisoner-of-war camp, his fellow prisoners appointed him camp leader. Broz became a Bolshevik, joining the communist organization founded by Vladimir Lenin and Alexander Bogdanov to effect a workers' revolution against the Tsarist autocracy. In 1917, Broz participated in the October Revolution, which brought the Bolsheviks to power during the several revolutions making up the Russian Revolution. Eventually the Bolshevik Party was renamed the Communist Party of the Soviet Union.

Three years after the overthrow of the repressive Tsarist regime, Josip Broz returned to his native Croatia. Before World War I, Croatia had belonged to the old Kingdom of Hungary within the Austro-Hungarian Empire. Postwar Croatia was taken up in the newly formed *Jugoslavija* (Yugoslavia), a kingdom of Croats, Slovenes, and Serbs ruled by the Serbian king, Peter I.

Broz became an active member of the illegal Communist Party of Yugoslavia, founded in 1920. For his activities as a prominent union organizer and political agitator, he was arrested in 1928 and jailed for six years. In 1934, he adopted his code name "Tito" for underground Party tasks. He also used the code name "Walter." In 1935, the Party sent him to the Soviet Union where he worked as a member of the Soviet Communist Party and the Soviet secret police (NKVD). The following year, "Comrade Walter" was sent home to purge disloyal members from the Communist Party of Yugoslavia. After the Nazis invaded Yugoslavia in 1941, Walter-Tito emerged as a military leader in the Communist Party of Yugoslavia.

In June 1941, the Central Committee of the Communist Party of Yugoslavia appointed Tito as Commander-in-Chief of the Yugoslav National Liberation Army. In 1943, his troops gave Tito the title "Marshal of Yugoslavia." Despite the Nazi occupation, before the end of the year Marshal Tito declared a provisional democratic Yugoslav government based on a federation of the diverse Yugoslav peoples.

Under the difficult conditions imposed by the Occupation, Partisan acts of sabotage occurred daily. In retaliation, the German occupiers, with the collusion of Italian, Hungarian, and Bulgarian forces and the collaborationist, profascist puppet governments in Zagreb and Belgrade, conducted the burning of villages, mass executions of the population, forced labor, and transport to concentration camps. Tito led the Partisans, the National Liberation Army, using insurgent activity to oppose the Axis occupation.

In the liberated areas, People's Liberation Committees collected arms, food, and clothing, recruited new Partisans, and organized economic, social, and cultural life. Developing over the course of the war into permanent bodies, the committees became the foundations of the postwar socialist system.[10]

In 1945, the Partisan Army totaled over eight hundred thousand men and women. Yugoslavia had largely liberated itself by its own armed

---

[10] As reported in *Yugoslavia*, a hard cover, coffee table–size book compiled by the editorial board of the Yugoslav illustrated magazine *REVIEW* and published by Grafički Zavod Hrvatske, Zagreb, Yugoslavia, 1966. The book has no page numbering.

forces. At war's end, many non-Yugoslavs acknowledged the Partisans to have been Europe's most effective anti-Nazi resistance movement.

As in any war, where even one fatality is one too much, World War II took the lives of up to one million seven hundred thousand Yugoslavs. This toll included over sixty thousand Jewish Yugoslavs who were rounded up and perished in accord with lethal Nazi thinking, as well as local Serbs and Roma (Gypsies) murdered by the *Ustaše* (Ustasha) fascist Croatian puppet regime, and Croats and Muslims killed by the Chetniks pursuing ethnic cleansing. Three and a half million people were left homeless; the country's infrastructure was destroyed.

The new Yugoslav government purged noncommunists and held an election limited to only one party, the Communist Party–dominated National Liberation Front. War hero Tito was elected the governing chief. His postwar government faced the mammoth work of rebuilding the devastated country.

Matko is old enough to remember the wartime sufferings caused the Croatians by the Nazi Germany and fascist Italy occupiers and the Croatian collaborationist Ustaše government, all despised as ruthless. From 1941 to 1945, the "Independent State of Croatia" (NDH), set up after the Axis invasion, was an unimaginably cruel Nazi puppet regime that sent hundreds of thousands of "Enemies of the State" to their deaths in German concentration camps or in Jasenovac, the infamous Yugoslav concentration camp.

In my case, a dislike of the dominant Axis Power at the root of the wartime horror had inscribed itself on my tabula rasa as a child. Born into an American Jewish family that lost its East European members to the Nazi Holocaust, I inherited an anti-German attitude. Growing up, the more I learned about Nazi Germany's diabolical strategy leading to the murder of minority peoples on an industrial scale, the stronger became my predisposition to react negatively to things Germanic.

"*Herr* Stern is a distributor of East European films in Western Europe," Matko tells me. The German businessman arrived unannounced in Zagreb to view the Studio's latest films. "My packed schedule prevents my hosting *Herr* Stern during the screening," Matko pronounces. "You will sit in for me."

"Certainly," I reply, by now accustomed to my lack of choice in Yu-go-*slave*-ia.

The chill I experienced at Matko's crisp articulation of the German word "Herr" evidenced my anti-Germany attitude. And yet, when I booked the journey to Yugoslavia, I accepted an itinerary at odds with my prejudicial thinking.

"No airline flies direct from New York to Zagreb," the travel agent says. Sudflug International can fly me to Frankfurt, Germany, I am told. Arriving in the morning, I can get a flight to Zagreb the next day. The alternative, catching a late afternoon train to Zagreb, seems to me a better option than staying in Germany, albeit only overnight.

Landing at Frankfurt Airport, I say to myself: "It is twenty-three years after the war. The past is the past." But traveling into my future through Germany calls up my past, at least that past stemming from my heritage as a second-generation American of Jewish ancestry.

I go straight into the center of Frankfurt, to the railroad station. Buying a ticket goes smoothly. Helpful Germans point me in the right direction to the train. Once on board, sitting at the window in the close quarters of the train compartment, three people to my left and four across, I converse with two young German passengers who speak English. The subject of my religion does not arise, and I do not bring it up. We part in Munich, where I have a two-hour stopover. "Success in Tito's Yugoslavia!" they say. I avoided mention of my Jewish background quite purposely. This is no novel behavior. For similar reasons, I do not speak of my Jewish heritage in certain situations or among certain people in America.

During the travel pause in Munich, I explore the shopping area outside the train station. A new thirst to know about Germans and their customs pulls me into a *Bierstube*, a traditional German beer hall. Finding a picture postcard of this particular Bierstube on a table, I read that it is one of sixteen such establishments in the city. Each has four thousand seats and serves nearly fifty thousand liters of beer every day.

The people gathered around the wooden tables imbibe the foamy brew from exceedingly tall steins. A band of musicians, wearing lederhosen, the leather shorts with suspenders that are traditional men's wear in southern Germany, play bouncy tunes and sing in German. Many drinkers sway to the oompah-pah music, waving their steins in the air. I cannot avoid assuming that the older people in the beer hall crowd had supported, or at least had not resisted, Nazi tyrant Adolf Hitler. In this very city, Hitler's adopted hometown, and in a beer hall no less, the Nazi Party held its first meetings, in 1923.

My mind takes me on a disastrous tour, leading my thoughts to the Nazi concept of Aryan superiority. Based on a theory claiming the supremacy of an Aryan race of white-skinned people of German or Nordic descent, and to protect the purity of this "Master Race," the Nazi government instituted its infamous "Final Solution" plan. More than ten million "racial inferiors" and "undesirables" were exterminated, including six million Jewish people plus political dissidents, the physically disabled, the mentally ill, Roma, homosexuals, communists, and other minorities.

In the Munich Bierstube, it is difficult to associate the Nazi atrocities with these Germans who look so harmless while merrily enjoying their beer and the music. A stein-swinging man waves to me. "Come on, sing," he gestures. "No, no thanks," I motion. There is a barrier between us caused less by language and culture than by my German antipathy.

To lighten my reflections and tune to the sing-a-long, I order a beer. The beer brings up thoughts of my maternal grandfather, Noah. He was named for the Old Testament flood-and-ark patriarch, representing righteousness, regeneration, and the continuity of life. The biblical Noah indulged in the intoxicating grape; my grandfather Noah also had a penchant for beer. His favored beverage he bought at a local brewery near his residence in Ridgewood, a German neighborhood in the Queens borough of New York City. When Prohibition became American law from 1919 to 1933, and alcoholic drinks were illegal except for permitted small amounts that folks could make for home consumption, Noah turned his basement laundry room into his own private brewery and winery. Grandpa Noah's first name actually was Abraham, after the biblical patriarch, but he always called himself Noah.

Abraham Noah Silberberg was born in 1871 in Latvia when it was part of the Russian Empire. He first came to America as a young man with his wife Ernestine, most likely at the end of the nineteenth century, exact date unknown. For some reason, they returned to Russia where their first daughter, Rebecca (Betty), was born. In 1904, they reentered the US at Ellis Island. They took up residence in Biloxi, Mississippi, in the heart of the Deep South, where Ernestine's father had a retail store. Ernestine died of malaria, and Noah returned to New York with their children, by then numbering two.

Quite soon Noah met my maternal grandmother, Mary Fischer. Born in Warsaw—Poland was, at the time, part of the Russian Empire—Mary entered America with her parents in 1872, at six months of age. When she and Noah married in 1907 or early 1908, she was a widow raising five young children. The couple opened a women's clothing store and brought six more children into the world.

Knowledgeable in the Talmud, a central text of Judaism, Grandpa Noah helped found a synagogue. Simultaneously, he participated in neighborhood civic affairs. He also joined the Free Masons, the mystical international brotherhood of ancient origin, rising to the thirty-second degree, the next to highest rank. Alas, I never had the chance to know him. He breathed his last when I was eight months old.

My travels down an ancestral memory lane continue after I re-board the train. We ride past the outskirts of the Dachau concentration camp, the first of the Nazi extermination camps opened in Germany. I think of my Hungarian family, perished in the Holocaust.

My paternal great-grandparents were potato farmers born in Hungary in the old Austro-Hungarian Empire. Whether they were "large potatoes" or "small potatoes" as potato farmers I have no idea, but they apparently provided the funds for three of their teenage children to migrate to America. At the very beginning of a mass exodus of Central and East

Europeans to America between 1900 and the 1914 outbreak of World War I, an older son of the potato farmers crossed the Atlantic Ocean all alone. At age seventeen, in 1901, my grandfather-to-be, Schmuelhersh (later Americanized to Samuel) Eisner left behind his parents and siblings in his quest for religious safety and a better life in America. A brother, Joseph, and a sister, Esther, followed later on.

Dvorah Braun (later Dora Brown), the eldest daughter of twelve or thirteen children in a Jewish shoemaker family, also dared to leave the Hungarian homeland for the unknown. At age sixteen, traveling alone, my future grandmother endured the seven or eight days' voyage across the sometimes perilous Atlantic Ocean. As her ship entered New York harbor in 1903, I can only imagine her joyous awe at beholding the magnificent Statue of Liberty. Always an inspiring sight, the colossus represents the Roman goddess of freedom extending aloft the torch of liberty.

My paternal grandparents would not see their Hungarian relatives again. It pains me to imagine the horrors my Holocaust-murdered East European relatives must have suffered. This explains my visceral reaction, my antipathy, to Germans, despite my intellectual awareness that a minority of non-Jewish Germans actively opposed Nazism. The Nazis, and those whose silence allowed them to thrive, robbed me almost entirely of my European family heritage and traditions. Nazi anti-Semitism prevented that inheritance from being passed to me. I feel uneasy in Germany. Despite America's own touches of anti-Semitism, I do not fear that my government will torture, shoot, or gas me because of my ancestry or religious background.

As my Zagreb-bound train approaches Yugoslavia, the German passengers depart, leaving me on my own for the last stretch of the trip. I have to admit that in Frankfurt, in Munich, and during the train ride through Germany, I appreciated the agreeable exchanges I had with German people. Inexplicably, I muse: "The only thing worse than any lingering anti-Semitism by the German people will be my prolonged dislike of them and their country." My mind knows it is unfair to consider all Germans collectively guilty for Nazi crimes.

"Miss Green, are you ready?" Matko asks, breaking my reverie. My attention returns to today's distasteful assignment, navigating the German businessman through the Studio's films. Despite my aversion, I try to give this task a positive spin. Helping Herr Stern offers me another chance to work toward the goal of releasing old and negative thoughts.

I face a full day in the company of Herr Stern. A middle-aged man of slight build, he is smartly attired in a finely tailored gray suit of shiny material. Svetlana would value his care for stylistic detail. A black silk handkerchief emerges daintily from his breast pocket, matching his tie; small golden cufflinks of a circular design close the sleeves of his blue and white, thin-striped cotton shirt, and he wears black leather loafers enlivened by perky tassels.

Stern and I take our seats at the *kinoteka*. "Zagreb Film lacks screening facilities of its own, and . . ."

"I know the Yugoslavs and their limitations," states Stern, cutting me off. He pronounces English with the characteristic German accent. "I know their sense of timing, too," he adds as we wait, and wait, for the film showing to begin. The lights finally dim and on the screen appear 35 mm color slides that are—upside down.

Resigned to the unpredictable Yugoslav ways, Stern simply utters, "I wonder if they are upside down, or are we upside down?"

"Beg pardon?" I have been attentive to his Germanic delivery rather than to what he is saying.

"It is only by habit that we see images as we do. I know people who have stood on their head for fourteen days. When they turned right side up, their images were upside down."

The topsy-turvy remark shatters my fixation on the rise and fall of his vocal pitch.

"Images upside down? Would that induce in someone a new kind of thinking?" I ask. "Just because you look at something from a different angle doesn't mean anything changes."

"Correct," replies Stern. "An image does not change because one's perspective changes, yet a changed perspective can alter one's quality of life."

Strange. He speaks to my present concerns. This German man's ability to tap into my thoughts, and instantly, completely surprises me. I return the conversation to Stern's original comment.

"You know people who have stood on their heads for fourteen days?"

"Indian friends," clarifies Stern. "Yogis."

"Oh, I've heard of yoga."

What an unusual start to a business meeting!

"Stanford is a half-hour drive to San Francisco's Haight-Ashbury neighborhood, the center of America's flower power, hippie counter-culture," I say to Stern. "People are trying out yoga and various self-knowledge techniques as part of a nonviolence ideology."

"And you?" asks Stern.

Confide my personal matters to a German? Still, he is a Westerner.

"Once a week I attended a non-Stanford encounter group. We were students and nonstudents in our twenties, except for the group leader. He was an older flower-power hippie type, very open-minded as we spoke of our experiences. Probably I could have benefited from the sessions had I been really honest."

"Meaning?"

"In the spirit of progressive California, one women related going to bed with her brother. She quoted his off-color praise that she was his best lover ever. Slang words interspersed her otherwise intellectually rich vocabulary. Her story shocked me, her actions disturbed me, but I admired her frankness. Why am I telling you this?"

"Because you are being honest."

"So I kept a straight face. I did not want to reveal my upset; I did not want to be labeled uncool by these California free thinkers. I did not mean to be a hypocrite. My views were not as broad as theirs. I wanted to be accepted by them."

"Dishonesty is always a misbehavior, especially when the one you are being untrue to is yourself," asserts Stern.

His simulating thoughts compel me to listen intently.

"A shame," he declares. "Missed opportunity. Being really honest in the encounter group could have helped you uncover hidden things in yourself."

"I know. Guess I was not ready. I dropped out of the group the night the leader announced our next session would be a nude encounter on the beach."

Stern laughs. As if on cue, the room goes dark and Zagreb Film's recent cartoons and a few documentaries pass Stern's review. His filmic comments segue into questions probing my life at the Studio and in Zagreb itself.

"I work long days from eight in the morning, and they keep giving me new tasks and longer hours." Narrating a typical day, I mention my increasingly heavy workload.

"All that for thirty-two dollars a week!" exclaims Stern. "You, an educated American woman, willing to work for slave wages in Yugoslavia?"

"I am not a slave. I am here voluntarily," I reply defensively. "And my salary is considerably high. That's what Matko told me. He said workers don't earn much. They live well because they enjoy social benefits of personal welfare and security."

Stern raises his eyebrows and smiles skeptically.

I repeat Matko's avowal: "Your salary may be low compared to American standards but, because you are American, we have given you the third highest salary in the company."

"Back home, you could earn many times that amount."

"I didn't come here to get rich," I make clear. "Moneymaking has never been my main goal," I emphasize.

"What about your work on the scripts and the voiceovers you have recorded? Are you at least earning screen credits?"

"I did not ask."

"And they did not offer," interjects Stern.

"I am carrying out an experiment, investigating a lifestyle," I explain. "Although I would not want to earn less, I feel a little uncomfortable at the inequity my salary represents. Third highest salary for what is essentially an internship?"

From the time of my first paying job, at age thirteen shelving books in a local public library after school, I relate, I never reckoned my payment solely by the wages received. I point out: "I go by the popular proverb, 'Experience is the best teacher.' Really, always I care less for economic gain than for the richness of 'another experience,' as if my experiences are the provider of my life's education and prosperity."

"Well and good," states Stern, "if you can really take the timely benefit."

This talk has become prickly. Stern's remarks suggest that the Studio is mistreating me. Stern falls silent. Reaching into his jacket, he removes a pack of top-brand American cigarettes. Undaunted by his failure to light the cigarette using Yugoslav matches, he asks me: "Wouldn't you rather have matches that strike?"

He refers to the creature comforts unavailable in a communist economy.

"I wound up here without matches," he says, "and had no choice but to buy this substandard product. Few consumer items are imported, and Yugoslav national production is of limited range and unreliable quality."

Stern is describing what I have already experienced.

"At least the shoddy products made by the nationalized enterprises are no longer subsidized," he adds. "The incentives of profit and loss are replacing state subsidies and supports. Tito abolished the subsidy practice a few years ago to increase efficiency and better product quality. So, if people can buy an alternative to this company's matches, the factory will go out of business, just as in the competitive West. Tito has introduced elements of capitalism. Perhaps a balance between the two systems could work better than the one or the other alone."

"Curiously," I observe, "the less I have here, the less I seem to want."

"It's 1968. Rejecting materialism is politically correct among some people."

"I'm not hostile to materialism," I clarify. "Wealth and material possessions constitute a great achievement."

Do Stern's statements on consumer niceties suggest I go on treading the given path of consumer abundance? Thoughts coming to me in Yugoslavia intimate the opposite advice. The Western economy promoting the excessively consumptive lifestyle is based on the acquisition of a wide array of things deemed necessary but, I find myself asking, "Are they really indispensible?" Circumstances in Zagreb compel me to buy from my needs rather than my wishes or wants. Despite initially loathing Yugoslavia's scarcities, I am starting to accept this unaccustomed simplicity. Then again, what choice do I have?

A silence descends. Stern's vibrantly intelligent eyes gaze inward. He surprises me again by declaring: "Love one another with compassion and charity."

This assertion is certainly a non sequitur. In a New York instant I follow him into the next area of conversation.

"Your Christian-based homeland rightly honors Jesus," Stern says. "The majority of your country's elected or appointed leaders are Christians. Yet they run the country as if Jesus transmitted moral, ethical, and righteous principles to be studied, not practiced. Do you ever ask what happened to values and norms based on truth, goodness, and love?

"The situation is the same in my country," he continues. "Many people give persuasive lip service to Christ's commandment, 'Do unto others as you would have them do unto you.' Still, often we take actions that go against this noble principle. In our self-absorption and social apathy, sometimes we take no actions at all. How many of us really follow Christ's teachings? In fact, what religion does not espouse the Golden Rule? And what applies to us as individuals, applies to us when we are in governing positions. A society that professes one thing and does another is not moral."

After this unexpected outpouring, and before I can respond, Stern goes on: "And what about, 'Blessed are the poor?' Don't you think Jesus favored the basic necessities of life for all? The essentially socialistic instructions of Jesus are as little practiced in socialistic Yugoslavia as in the capitalistic Christian countries."

"If Jesus was a socialist, why do the modern churches and most Christians follow the path of capitalism?"

"Imperfect people cannot make a perfect world," Stern sums up. "Institutions and governments cannot create the future society of higher ideals. We individuals have to believe in, and strive to realize, our highest human possibilities. We have to initiate the changes we yearn for. The ideals of understanding and friendship between peoples and nations demand to be brought into practice."

Stern glances at his watch. Another silence ensues. I imagine an America where more of the Christians, and other people of faith, and nonfaith, really practice the noble qualities exemplified by the loving, simple, and truthful Jesus. What kind of a world could we have if more of us walked, and not mainly talked, the values preached by the great spiritual leaders? If we integrated into our own lives the nonkilling mindset of visionary trailblazers like Jesus, Buddha, Mahatma Gandhi, and all the peace pioneers unknown and unproclaimed? Speaking with Stern has an inspirational effect.

"I also consider this stay in Zagreb as a way of learning about myself."

"What have you learned so far?"

To answer requires thought, and Stern does not press me for an instant response. Finally I say, "Being out of my comfort zone has forced me into different behavior."

I explain that in America I have a habit of comparing myself to others. In the strange Yugoslavian society are no people to whom to compare myself. I cannot look at Yugoslavs and judge my success and myself by their accomplishments. Too many differences exist. "Their lives are no yardstick by which to measure my own life."

"How is your way inside?" asks Stern. "How are you on the inner planes?"

"I am looking into that too." Intuitively I decipher his language.

"Tell me, do you know your limitation?"

"What do you mean? Intellectually? Emotionally? As a worker, an American, a woman, or what?"

"I mean," says Stern, "if there is a circle, and at the core are all the things and layers that make up you, what is the outer definition of the circle?"

"I don't know," I respond.

"You see," he goes on, "if the core is strong and all your energies are radiating from it, the circle is endless. It has no outer boundary. You can really do whatever you wish to do, anywhere."

"But. . . ."

"Yes," says Stern, cutting me off. "You must know what you want."

"Easy," I immediately respond. I relate that, since childhood, I have loved writing words on paper through my pencil, pen, and, later, my typewriter. Still, something is missing. Not yet have I discovered the purpose and content of my communication skills, much less of my very existence itself. It bothers me that I do not know what is really worth doing. Where am I going? What is my direction, my highest goal?

"Is it not ironic that Yugoslavia's material scarcity and deprivation have caused me to brood over my abundant American good life?" I say aloud.

"You are starting to walk on the path of sandals," proclaims Stern cryptically. He stands and announces his departure.

I catch my breath. "Will I meet you again?"

"If you want to enough, you will. Wait and see if there's a need. My plane leaves tonight and I must be on it. I've accomplished what I had to here."

"It's really quite a coincidence, isn't it?" I reflect. "I've been crying inside for a right person to talk to, and you just happen to pass through on a business trip you had put off and off."

"There is no such thing as coincidence," replies Stern. "I had a feeling to come here now. Maybe you did too."

Like most people, I am familiar with the phenomenon of coincidence. Inner and outer events meet in a significant way that cannot be explained. A good number of times I have experienced instances of meaningful coincidence, the amazing conjunction of seemingly unrelated, unexplainable but purposeful, inner and outer events or circumstances. Although the events or occurrences appeared to be taking place by mere chance, all worked out as if planned or arranged.

"People will consider something a coincidence because they don't know the future," declares Stern. "What will happen, will happen. Some people call this God's grace."

"Isn't this what Carl Gustav Jung spoke of?[11] Life is not just a series of random events. Life is, rather, the expression of a deeper order?"

"True. He believed that coincidence, or synchronicity, shifted a person's egocentric conscious thinking to greater wholeness."

"Are you suggesting that behind coincidence a cosmic cause could be operating?"

"This is something for you to seriously consider."

"I feel confused," I admit.

"A sign of growth," concludes Stern.

---

[11] Carl Gustav Jung (1875–1961) was the Swiss psychiatrist and psychotherapist who founded analytical psychology.

9
Detaching from Conditioning

Reflecting on the insightful conversation with Herr Stern, I note that his English, flavored by the distinct accent, straightaway revealed his roots. Curiously, the more we spoke, the less I heard his Germanic intonation. His English pronunciation improved and his delivery became less stiff and didactic. During our talk I was very aware: "He is German." While attracted to his mode of thinking, and stimulated by his comments, my attention often shifted to his Germanness. Could he have been a Nazi? Had he served the Nazi war machine? The name "Stern"—could he be Jewish? A concentration camp survivor?

The coincidence tied to the arrival of Stern, fulfilling my wish for a meaningful contact with a Westerner, assumes enhanced import when linked to his German background. My family in principle boycotted German products, places, and people. As an adult, I myself followed looser guidelines. Occasionally I stopped in for Black Forest cake at the German *konditorei* (confectionary shop), in the Little Germany neighborhood a short walk from my Manhattan apartment. In Ideal Restaurant, a simple German eatery on East 86th Street, sometimes I savored a meal of *sauerbraten*, pickled German pot roast. And had I not traveled to Zagreb via Germany? Regardless, I still tend to uphold the family custom of shunning things Germanic. This habit I have, until now, not given a second thought. Meeting Stern sets me to ponder further my negative feelings toward his native country.

I first encountered religious bigotry at age six. Wednesday afternoons I attended an after-school children's class in the Jewish religion held in the local synagogue. One day, class over, outside the synagogue in our mixed Christian-Jewish neighborhood in Brooklyn, I spotted a classmate from my public school.

"Hi Siegfried," I said, smiling. I did not question why Siegfried, a German Christian boy, was waiting by the synagogue. I began walking home. In those years, child abuse or abduction were not general sources of fear. Children could go to and from school alone, if considered able to cross the streets safely.

"Dirty Jew! Dirty Jew!" suddenly I heard. Turning around, I saw Siegfried running in my direction, waving a long metal tube in his hand. "Dirty Jew! Dirty Jew!" His shouts launched me into running too, propelling my legs faster and faster. I reached home uninjured, at least physically. Dashing into our brownstone walkup, I left Siegfried behind on the street, slashing the air with the metal tube.

"What is it?" asked my mother as I rushed into our apartment, the door in those days ordinarily left unlocked. I blurted out what happened. She sighed and said: "There are some things you have to know." She enumerated a child-comprehensible list of the discriminatory treatment one may receive as a member of a minority group. The "Dirty Jew incident" she reported to the school principal, who invited Siegfried's parents for a talk. From then onward Siegfried totally ignored me, to my relief. As I grew older, I learned the public secret that in America, even on the liberal East Coast, some residential buildings, schools, clubs, and social and work establishments maintained a "No Jews" policy or, at least, a Jewish quota.

After interacting with Stern, I recognize that my behaving as a reverse Siegfried is foreign to my character and natural inclinations. I had, after all, at age nine penned: "Hand in hand to make this land a better world to live in." Those words won the first prize out of ten thousand entries in the New York City National Brotherhood Week slogan-writing contest sponsored by the National Conference of Christians and Jews. The judges supported my childhood idealism that a "better" world called for human unity. I believed what I wrote. My inborn instinct for friendship and cooperation obviously clashed with the anti-German attitude I absorbed in my family.

Stern helped widen my perspective. Our exchange underscores that prejudice impedes one's inner freedom. The seeds of prejudice develop roots very hard to extricate as they twist and twine, clogging our mind and squeezing our heart. My anti-German attitude imprisons me in narrow thinking. Preconceptions restrict me from stretching my limitations. Holding on to prejudice makes me tight and unloving. I want to unshackle myself from the clutter of obstructive opinions. I vow to dissolve my German antipathy. Releasing negative thoughts will create space in my mind, allowing new thoughts to enter. I want to open to the German people of today, to know what kind of people they are.

Stern encourages me to look from my core. His hints at mysteries concealed in everyday matters suggest that my European adventure is unavoidable. I sense something "predestined" about the journey of discovery starting to move me past the boundaries of my circle. As if to bolster my intuition, I remember an incident in my nineteenth year.

During summer vacation, I am swimming in the Atlantic Ocean at Jones Beach on New York's Long Island. Certified in high school as a junior lifeguard, I usually venture beyond the waves. On this particular day, so etched in my memory, I swim far from shore. When I attempt to swim back, the strong current battles my strokes. I thrash my arms and legs to keep my head above the water.

Scenes of my life flash before me as photographs in a book whose pages flip quickly in front of my eyes. The book covers my life up to the point where I am floundering in the ocean, and then it continues further. It moves so speedily there is only whirling color. I cannot distinguish any specifics. Watching the pages of my future zip along, I glimpse an existential truth: my life has a definite and ongoing story line. I have no details, but I know I will not drown. I am not to take my last breath in this ocean. The process takes barely a few seconds as my head bobs under the water several times.

Suddenly a reassuring arm surrounds my chest. The strong grip of an unknown savior pulls me horizontally above the water. Closer to shore, I can swim again on my own.

Remembering my survival encounter with the mighty power of the ocean, the picture book unrolling my past, present, and future, and the arrival of a rescuer, urges me to wonder: "Is everything happening for a reason?" The memory of my life looking like photos in a book or images in a film calls up Matko's words in the screening room: "What is real and what is artificial?" I recollect Stern's forceful assertion: "There is no such thing as coincidence." Stern supports my unexplainable thought that the stay in Zagreb is directing me in a predetermined way. If this applies to individuals, does it apply to groups of people and nations as well? If so, are wars and violence also part of a "predesign"?

Suppose that our lives indeed guide us toward a predestined end? Why bother to make any efforts? Will not all unfold according to the will of the "Predesigner"? Hmm, this seems a recipe to become passive, lazy, and fatalistic. My best approach, I decide, is to persist in making my best efforts. The word "trust" arises, although in what or whom to trust I do not know. Simply trust in myself and my thoughts, ideas, and intuitions?

Accepting the possibility of an existential predesign, I resolve to stop complaining about the circumstances of my life. The Yugoslavs do not openly complain, at least not in public, and rarely to me, a foreigner. They have to be careful to whom they speak. Who knows who could be listening in? Not complaining gives them a strength I lack. I aspire to adopt the noncomplaining attitude. If my living situation in Zagreb constitutes an immediate testing of my well-meant intention, I do not score high.

10

Seesawing between Emotions

My first month in Zagreb is drawing to a close. Svetlana's friends will soon arrive. She and I study newspaper "To Rent" ads. We place a "Room Wanted" notice. The search makes tangible for me the serious housing shortage.

"Caused by the government's inability to meet this essential need of the citizens," says Svetlana. She elaborates that because people cannot find housing, middle-aged people may still live with their parents or grandparents. Two or three generations of a family may squeeze into a small apartment. Couples sometimes remain engaged for years; young couples may lodge with in-laws or other relatives; divorced couples may have to continue living together with all the inherent emotional stress.

"And don't think a rented room will supply a fine area rug or soft cotton sheets on the bed," she warns. In socialist Yugoslavia everyone, except perchance the elite of the League of Communists, lacks consumer niceties of the type I consider fundamental. Stripped of expectations, in a Yugoslav rented room I do not anticipate having a proper reading lamp and certainly not a radio.

Of the rental rooms Svetlana and I visit, one emerges as the best of a poor lot. The kitchen has no fridge, and cooking is done on a two-burner hotplate, but there is hot water and the apartment is neat and clean. The Yugoslav lack of choice is leading me to a room I would have rejected at the beginning of my stay. Perhaps Svetlana's example of flexibility is rubbing off on me.

On my moving day, I hug Svetlana goodbye. The taxi driver turns on the motor. "We will stay in touch," affirms Svetlana.

"We'd better!" I respond. Svetlana has become a friend. I will miss our closeness. At the Studio we will not see each other. Her short-term contract has ended. As the taxi drives off, I turn to wave goodbye. Already gone, she has not witnessed my moist eyes.

The faded apartment building of the landlady, Ana, has no potted plants in its tiny entrance hallway and no elevator by which to ascend the three flights to her door. The taxi driver carries up my luggage as Svetlana requested. After he leaves, I stand for a few long moments outside the apartment. Painful loneliness, absent during my stay at Svetlana's, assails me again. With various misgivings, I knock on the door. Almost immediately, it opens.

"*Dobro jutro* [Good morning]," says the landlady cordially.

Ana is a middle-aged woman whose clothing, a bit too snug for conservative Zagreb, discloses that she has gained weight and perhaps cannot afford to buy roomier clothes. She holds a full time job as an accounting clerk in a government office.

Ana ushers me into the apartment. An attractive man wearing tapered sports shirt and tight trousers, carrying a battered duffle bag, saunters out. He does not acknowledge my presence.

"Wait!" shouts Ana in Serbo-Croatian. She rushes into an adjoining room and returns waving a handful of passport-size photos angrily in the air. She throws them at the departing man's back. He utters not one word, does not turn around, and does not stop to pick up the photos. A flood of tears washes over Ana's full round face.

Ana shows me the photos, of young pretty women, when we sit for a get-acquainted talk. She knows basic English and we carry on a simple conversation helped by my *rečnik*, my English-Serbo-Croatian / Serbo-Croatian-English dictionary. Ana had not given Svetlana a full picture of her home situation. The exiting man is the woman's philandering ex-husband. They divorced six years earlier. He refused to leave, claiming he had nowhere to go. Because the apartment belongs to the state, she could not evict him. The housing shortage forced them to carry on living together. He brought his girlfriends to stay overnight in the bedroom across from Ana's. She never knew which woman, sometimes half-dressed, might be sitting in the kitchen in the morning.

"My life was a hell," she grumbles, describing her ex by pointing to words my *rečnik* translates as "devil" and "worthless."

"Did he ever go room-hunting?" I ask. Ana shrugs.

For my room, clean and bare except for a few pieces of the styleless furniture of Yugoslav socialism that Svetlana abhors, I am paying a "foreigner's price." The fee for my room exceeds many times the monthly rent for Ana's entire apartment. The first night in my overpriced room I stretch out on the plain wood-frame bed and survey my surroundings. The walls are undecorated. There is a wooden table, one chair, and a modest-size cupboard for hanging my clothes. No mirror. Everything is dark colored. I feel cooped up. I have trouble reconciling this Spartan room with its exorbitant cost.

To establish their happiness individually, my landlady and her ex took advantage of the city's housing shortage to get the maximum rent from a foreigner. They calculated the monthly rent by applying the supply and demand principle of a market-based capitalist economy. I did not expect Yugoslav socialists to exploit me, especially while I am struggling to know their way of life. Are not Ana and her ex educated in the principle of sharing that idealistically underpins any form of socialism?

Yugoslavs surely learn in history class that the socialist system originally grew out of the excesses of human greed. Socialism arose in the West in the late-eighteenth century as a reaction to the Industrial Revolution and the arrival of machines and the factory system. Instead of the new inventions and approaches bringing benefit to all the people, factory owners became very rich at the expense of their workers whom they exploited. The workers suffered abominable conditions and extremely long days for proportionately low wages while enjoying none of the economic prosperity.

"Social-ists" called for reform of the economic system. As a political theory, early socialism proposed a socioeconomic system structured to create some equality of wealth between the members of a society. The ultimate goal was a just society of social welfare based on cooperation, communal property, and sharing. Classical socialism allowed private property. Social change was envisioned through a free and fair democratic process reflecting the will of the people and their interests.

Now here I am in socialist Yugoslavia, where a divorced couple acts like a high-profit seeking landlord in a housing market where demand outruns supply. These two people exploit my ability to pay, snatching exaggerated revenue for their pitiful rental room. Of course, the inflated rent gives the alienated couple the financial push to live apart after six miserable years under one roof. A share of my excessive rental payment in his pocket, Stef packed up, not to return, heading for his village in the countryside.

Compared to Ana and Stef, I possess financial abundance. Even though the overblown rent eats up a disproportionate portion of my Yugoslav wages, my supplementary American traveler's checks allow me to pay the steep, foreigner's price. Examining the situation from more angles than simply a linear position of what I see as "right" or "wrong," I understand better the anxiety and desperation of vulnerable people in difficult housing straits.

One evening, as I sit in the silence of the overpriced room, a strange emotion comes up, nestling between my heart and my head. To my astonishment, I feel great satisfaction that my rent money lets Ana and Stef live separately at last. Although they gave me no choice in deciding whether to support the cause they represent, their own well-being, my rental payment served to extricate them from their hell.

Yet the exploitation of foreigners in a land proclaiming "brotherhood" is inexcusable. This is not the first evidence I receive in Yugoslavia that the dream of socialistic equality remains only a dream. There was no possibility that I would stay in Ana's apartment as a friend, as at Svetlana's, but to be considered an American dollar cow to be milked for maximal profit?

My own participation in the disagreeable process I view less harshly. Am I not the victim of a system I cannot change? Do I have any alternative to paying the exorbitant rental fee? I struggle internally. Once I handed the milked money to Ana, I assisted in the continuance of an abusive economic practice I deplore. I legitimized exploitation. Why had I not resisted, and searched further to find a room at a fair price? Perhaps I could have contributed a small defense of fairness and truth to Yugoslav society? My satisfaction with helping the unhappy couple turns into disgust for my own hypocrisy.

I contrast the behavior of Ana and Svetlana. Ana's background is unknown to me. Svetlana's parents were active in the Yugoslav Resistance movement against the Nazis, and later they were officials in the new Yugoslav government. Svetlana was early on indoctrinated into her country's socialistic ideology. She opened her home to me not asking one cent in return. Is she an example of socialist sharing, or rather of a finely developed quality of personal caring independent from political thought?

Soon I settle into a daily routine at Ana's. In the evenings, returning from our jobs, we greet each other and exchange simple comments about our day. Increasingly she glides through the rooms buoyed by a lighter step. She appears taller, as if her body is stretching toward a place just discovered and still unfamiliar.

While the spirits of my landlady soar in her newfound freedom, my own inner state spirals in the downhill direction. On the job, I yearn to know my Studio coworkers, but I feel no connection with them. Except for the interchange necessitated by the Studio work, I do not seem to exist for my colleagues. This conclusion proves true during a one-day Studio excursion.

A busload of coworkers, all in exuberant spirits, leaves Zagreb on a great adventure to Vienna, in nearby Austria. I am one of the party. The ostensible purpose is to visit historic sites. The bus parks smack in the middle of a busy shopping street lined by colorful and fully stocked Austrian stores. My colleagues literally race to the shop windows displaying the latest European fashion in clothes, shoes, accessories, and cosmetics. They stare and gasp at the wondrous products conjuring up a perfection of beautiful things they can only dream of owning. Have they not learned their school lesson that indulging in the appetites of capitalistic society will not lead to equality and justice?

I join my colleagues staring into the window of an elegantly appointed *konditorei,* creamy fine pastries and delectable desserts temptingly visible. As if at a workers' council meeting, they huddle and discuss whether to enter. One of them examines the price list attached to the window. Again discussion. They back away, embarrassed. Yugoslavs may officially visit and shop in neighboring Western countries such as Austria, Italy, and Germany, but lack of funds generally blocks the possibility. Most people live from hand to mouth, Svetlana had told me. They have no money left at the end of the month. They are unable to save. However, she proudly related, the Yugoslav social system allows even the lowest paid worker to vacation at the Croatian seaside.

Now my colleagues and I have landed in high-priced Austria. I, too, gape at the marvels of abundance in large and elegant Vienna. The roads are wide and well paved, lighting is bright, shops carry up-to-date clothing, and restaurants offer refined dining in sophisticated surroundings. I would love to rush into the shops but a feeling of solidarity with my colleagues holds me back.

We reach a museum. The group spontaneously breaks apart into smaller units. My colleagues gather in twos and threes to explore the monumental building. I am left alone. Slowly I stroll through the rooms, admiring the elegant furnishings and paintings in old, Austro-Hungarian classical style. An unwelcome surprise awaits me outside the building. A photographer has just finished photographing our group. Everyone is included in the portrait, except me. The group assembled for the photo and no one informed me, not even Matko.

Weeks later, a colleague passes around the printed photo. My wound of abandonment still hurts. The workers at Zagreb Film form a closely knit family, and I am not even treated as a visiting distant relative. Being an outsider causes me to think about the fabric of family between people. I daydream: *What would life be like if all human beings considered themselves relatives in one big (and harmonious) family?* It occurs to me that for all of humanity's advancements in the arts, science, and technology, as a race we have failed miserably in developing our minds and hearts in ways naturally encouraging us to live in friendship and peace.

On the job, tackling Matko's assignments, I forget the aching, extraordinary loneliness that surges up in me after I exit the Studio's large wooden doors. Then I am utterly on my own. The invisible band of friendship's protective energy links me nowhere. Since leaving Svetlana's apartment, she and I see each other much less. The verbal barrier restricts my social contact with other Yugoslavs. During extreme bouts of homesickness, I may visit the American Embassy. Besides the Embassy staff, consisting of both Americans and local Yugoslavs, I have not met any really good English-speakers. Lacking meaningful personal relations in Zagreb, I become isolated.

Television is not available to me, the radio programs are in Slavic languages, and the cinemas screen feature films predominantly in Yugoslav tongues. I hunger for news from outside. Even the international magazine *Time*, banned in the USSR and its satellite countries, may also be off-limits in Yugoslavia. I cannot find a copy except at the Embassy.

Loneliness, driving me as a motor, propels me after work to explore Zagreb's cultural offerings. Since the government subsidizes and controls the cultural life, ticket prices are kept low so that anyone can afford a ticket for a concert, play, or film. Zagreb, Croatia's cultural center, boasts three concert halls, the Croatian National Theatre, and many museums and galleries.

To break out of my solitude and assuage my melancholy, occasionally I attend classical music concerts by Yugoslav musicians and other East European artists visiting Zagreb. Opening my ears and closing my eyes, not listening to the thoughts in my head but concentrating on the outer sounds, breathing in the music through my ears as well as through my every pore, I flow with the instruments and their universal messages. Perhaps loneliness has burned holes in me, giving extra space to receive the music's positive energy. At a concert by a symphony orchestra from the DDR, the German Democratic Republic—East Germany, that is—I keep my amazed eyes open. The musicians do not sit on chairs. They stand for the entire performance! I respect their discipline and strength, qualities East Germans surely need to survive in their harshly repressive society.

Also occasionally I attend performances of traditional Yugoslav folk music. The folk music provides relief from the linguistic limitations pestering me. My mind does not need to comprehend words; it has only to vibrate with the power of sound. Approaching the performances as more than entertainment, I plunge into the regional music to know the people behind it. I try tuning in to the Croats, Serbs, Montenegrins, and other Yugoslav ethnic groups. Transcending the language barrier to some tiny extent, I discover the Balkan peoples to be basically cheerful folk carrying sadness and wistful longing in their hearts. Every July, Zagreb's main square serves as the venue for the International Folklore Festival, drawing villagers from all over Yugoslavia to perform their regional songs and dances in traditional costumes.

Always I exit a musical performance refreshed by the invisible magical nourishment of solace and inspiration. But the cultural events deliver only temporary comfort. The salubrious effect lasts only briefly. The cultural explorations represent only small interludes in my solitary circumstances. Then it is back to my bare Yugoslav reality in my plain room.

The majority of evenings I spend in my room. When I tire of writing letters to family and friends, or making notations in my logbook, I do nothing much more than sit and stare at the room's unadorned walls. Doing something by "doing nothing" is for me, in itself, an accomplishment. The forced retreat of my mind from outer activities prompts a mental quietness.

Often I climb into my bed accompanied by an unhappy emptiness. I may sob myself to sleep. Many a tear have I previously shed, for many a reason, and in Zagreb I am again crying rivers into my pillow. Or I may fall into a well of sadness. On my lonely island, I am a Robinson Crusoe desiring companionship.

Nonetheless, I am not prepared to share my existence with the domestic animals that come to me seeking food and shelter.

Suddenly an unexplainable itching of my scalp intensifies and demands an investigation. Combing my hair, I discover gray things that resemble dandruff—but move! In a whirl of American-style action I dash from Ana's apartment, find a taxi, press the driver to rush me to the nearest hospital, and hold on for dear life as he races through Zagreb perhaps thinking I am having a heart attack or have gone crazy for all my distraught cries of "Are we there yet?"

Depositing me before a large white building, he drives quickly off after I, in a frenzied state, drop too many dinars into his hand. I enter the hospital and wander the corridor. In this instance, my foreign look serves me well. Two uniformed young men appear, secure me under my arms, and hurry me into the emergency room. A nurse escorts me into an office where a middle-aged doctor asks, in good English: "What is your trouble?" I blurt out the story of the gray itching things in my hair that move.

The doctor asks what I am doing in Zagreb—where, why, and so forth. Never once does he glance at the clock. Inspecting my scalp, he remarks calmly, the trace of a smile on his lips, "Pets. It's not such a tragedy. It's very common here. You told me you are trying to adapt to our local ways, isn't that correct? Now you have Yugoslav pets. We call them our domestic animals."

Without any haste, he discusses my uninvited and unwanted domestic pets. Not for a moment does he imply I am overreacting ridiculously. If he is amused at my fear of the head louse so common in Yugoslavia, he listens seriously before imparting his medical advice. To kill the head lice, he advises: "Get yourself DDT. Keep it on your hair all night. Dust it on all your clothes. Better boil everything too. The things you can't boil, dry clean."

Having addressed my health issue, in a cherry tone the doctor wishes me a swift goodbye to my unwanted pets. Although relieved to know my affliction will soon be in the past, and against the strongest effort of my will, I cannot prevent a few tears of my upset from spilling down my cheeks.

The doctor puts his arm around my shoulder and says reassuringly: "Come now, one week and you'll forget all about this. I think you'd better have a mild sedative and rest here for a bit."

He hands me two pills. I ingest the nameless pills, fully trusting in the doctor's expertise.

"I will write you a note for the apothecary," he says, leading me into a small adjoining room containing two cots. "Lie down here and sleep for a while. You'll feel better." He goes to the door and locks it.

"What are you doing?" I ask.

"I have a break now," he says, lighting up a cigarette with the patience of a practiced smoker accustomed to the unpredictable Yugoslav matches. "I'll keep you company."

Thanking the doctor for his kindness, I relax on the cot. He stubs out his cigarette, comes over to me, sits, and takes my hand. "You're very lonely here, aren't you?" he asks.

"I suppose so," I answer, retrieving my hand.

"Well, you're not alone anymore."

"I'm not?"

"No," he declares, leaning over to kiss me.

"Hey! I thought you were a doctor!" I snap, sliding out of his reach and sitting up. Until then I had a good opinion of the moral and ethical criteria of doctors. "Is this your idea of professional behavior?" I ask indignantly.

"I think it's the medicine you need."

Although I did swallow the nameless pills compliantly, the Rx this doctor now wants to prescribe is not on my list of appropriate medications.

"Yes, doctor, I am very lonely here in Zagreb, but not lonely enough to spend my time with a pet who is a beast like you," I *could* have said. Instead, I explode in a burst of my hot Hungarian temper (which has since been tempered) and shout: "No, doctor, it is *you* who must calm down!

"Besides," I add, "I'd much rather have the bugs I have than the ones itching you!"

The doctor does not press his home remedy, and I demonstrably slam his office door shut as I leave.

Yugoslavia's policy of universal health care covers everyone, including me, and the hospital does not charge me for either the consultation or the medications. But the irregular (foreigner's?) fee this doctor tried to impose, under the guise of giving, dismays me. I have to confess I did not report the doctor's improper behavior to the hospital management. The doctor, to me a louse worse than any parasite crawling around in my hair, would most certainly have denied my accusation of his sexual pathology.

Back in my room, having extensive time on my hands for the self-reflection sessions that are becoming habitual, I puzzle over the doctor's attempt to misuse my vulnerability. I wonder if it is my loneliness that is causing me to see the Yugoslavian society as so dismally gray. Or are the colorless buildings, the shops deprived of display windows, the people's drab clothing, and the substandard facilities transmitting an energy I feel to be depressingly lethargic? No Yugoslav I have seen lacks the basic material necessities of life, but still I experience only a grim society of scarcities. Are they, or am I, stuck in a summer holiday gone wrong?

The Yugoslavs work long and hard for low wages, and I sense they are displeased with their society's material lacks. This discontent I do not pick up from their words, Svetlana excepted, because they do not complain to me. Their attitudes do the complaining, as if they are weighed down by a pent-up dissatisfaction. I too am weighed down. Just as my Serbo-Croatian vocabulary continues to expand by osmosis, so do I absorb in Zagreb a dark, undermining energy. In my despairing frame of mind, I act a bit recklessly.

Since my very first week at the Studio, when I pass a certain office in the business division, a man who appears to be in his thirties makes sure to catch my eye and smile at me. Never do we speak a word to each other. To myself I call him "Mr. Turtleneck," as that is the only type of shirt he wears. When he locks his dark brown eyes with mine, or winks, my face turns one or another shade of red and crimson. His oiled black hair, his totally black outfit, and especially his thick sensuous lips bring on tingles rising up from my toes. The man exudes a vital animal power. One day, Turtleneck Man asks me: "*Veceras?*" (Tonight?) His voice is sweeter than his smile. "*Da*" (Yes), I reply. The rendezvous is scheduled for Trg Republike.

He is waiting in the designated spot and smiles broadly when I walk up to him. His warm lips brush my cheek softly with a welcome kiss. I step back to make space between us. We stroll in silence to his favorite café. Film posters, mainly of old American film stars, decorate the small locale. Laurel and Hardy, Mae West, Jane Harlow, and Count Dracula dominate. On one wall flash projections of old *Tom and Jerry* or *Farmer Gray* cartoons.[12]

His knowledge of English turns out to be skimpy. As we converse, in a combination of his broken English and my minimal Serbo-Croatian, his spell over me weakens. Between sips of Turkish coffee, Turtleneck Man tells that he lost his parents in the war. He lives alone. He, too, is lonely. "You like Yugoslavia?" he asks in Serbo-Croatian. Searching through my *rečnik* and pointing at words, I try to express my difficulty to answer him properly. Lifting my hand and kissing it gallantly, Mr. Turtleneck declares that he and the *rečnik* will teach me Serbo-Croatian.

"You like Yugoslavia?" I ask him.

"I want go Amerika," Turtleneck replies in English. I get the impression he has carefully practiced this sentence.

"Why?"

"Amerika . . . mucho mucho dollar," he replies. He holds a clichéd view that all Americans are millionaires.

I try to explain that money is not everything: "You do not have mucho mucho money, but you also do not have any worries about meeting your basic needs." He does not grasp my meaning and I cannot find the right words in the *rečnik*.

---

[12] *Tom* (the cat) *and Jerry* (the mouse) was an Academy Award–winning American animated series of short films created between 1940 and 1957 by William Hanna and Joseph Barbera.

Changing the subject, Turtleneck Man asks cheerily, "*Musique?*"

He guides us on cobblestoned streets to an alley leading into an outdoor area. Graceful green trees form a lovely setting in which simply dressed townsfolk enjoy food, drinks, and merriment at rough wooden tables on a floor of soil and gravel. Is this a communal picnic or a restaurant? The strong smell of roasting meat and wine hangs in the air as musicians enthusiastically play Yugoslav folk tunes. Over the lively music, Turtleneck Man orders meat dishes and wine, mucho mucho wine.

"*Gut!*" he exclaims, filling our glasses with an experienced hand. He clinks my glass and toasts gaily: "*Amerika!*"

Encouraged by the wine that he pours extravagantly, our tongues loosen and our spirits soar even as we strain to understand each other's comments about the restaurant, the food, the music . . . and his favorite topic, *Amerika.*

After a short while, he flips through the pages of my *rečnik*. He removes a pen from his pocket and marks the entries for *veriti se* (to engage, to betroth) and *veridba* (engagement). At the top of the page, he writes: *vjenčati*. Immediately he opens another page to *oženiti* (to marry, to wed).

"Are you kidding?" I exclaim.

Slanting his chair closer, and fixing his dark hypnotic eyes on me, he proclaims, "I lof you!" He mimics the placing of a ring on my finger. "*Kinder* [children]," he says in German, sweeping his hand across himself to me. He smiles his magnetic smile, and I appreciate his friendly face, but my anger is mounting, anger at myself. I should have known that dating someone at work would end up badly. Loneliness is a poor matchmaker.

"*Ne* [not] *oženiti, ne Amerika,*" I make clear.

Emptying his wine glass, Mr. Turtleneck avoids my eyes. He suggests we leave. His tone is flat. As we walk to Ana's apartment building, now the silence is stony rather than anticipatory, cold and without sizzle. Mr. Turtleneck coolly bids me goodnight. Disappointed sadness hangs over both of us. I will very much miss his smiles and winks at the Studio and the sense of inclusion his attentions gave.

Mr. Turtleneck's motivation seems obvious. A voice inside him apparently prompts: "Why do you stay here and endure this mean life when a brighter future awaits everyone in the people's paradise of *Amerika*?" He yearns for a better material existence with personal freedoms, including the freedom of choice. Who can blame him?

Being among the Yugoslavs not as a tourist or curiosity seeker but as a person sincerely trying to know their lifestyle by living it, I comprehend the Yugoslavs' desire for a better life. Their personal wishes and wants turn their view to the prosperous Free West. My grandparents had a similar vision when they emigrated to America. If the streets in the Golden Land of America were not literally paved with gold, at least the immigrants found religious freedom, improved living conditions, and possibilities for social advancement.

Thanks in part to my European ancestors, the American Dream automatically became mine. America offers me endless opportunities for attaining success. America's dominant values determine my future, and will move me toward my life's victory, or so I have accepted. Caught up in my society's patterns, zealously I follow our ethic of competition, hard work, and upward mobility.

Now I, a second-generation American and the first of my paternal family line holding a college degree, have returned to the general area of the "Old Country" from which my father's heritage descends. Unlike my grandparents, I cherish no plan to establish a life abroad. I am no emigrant; I neither need nor want a new homeland or way of life elsewhere. I love America despite its imperfections. Yet within me stirs an urge beckoning me to something beyond the American Dream of personal prosperity and success.

Mr. Turtleneck and the people in his struggling nation will never have the chances and choices afforded me. He knows this and I know this. I feel sorry for his plight. He burns to live elsewhere for his economic prosperity and enjoyment; he is unable to do so. His marriage proposal prods me to mull over what constitutes a "better life" for me. The surprising, if unsatisfactorily vague answer that comes is, "Be what you are, not what you are not."

What am I? Human being, female, daughter, sister, niece, aunt, cousin, friend, communicator, and? Intelligent-ignorant, sensitive-dense, adventurous-fearful, self-confident-unsure, trusting-doubting, knowing-searching?

Already in my late twenties and I do not know myself? Certainly I am a human being characterized by certain physical, mental, emotional, behavioral, and personality tendencies. Do I have a "deeper identity"? I did not learn about a deeper identity at Mizzou, The Barnyard, or at The Farm, as my University of Missouri, Barnard, and Stanford schools are lightheartedly nicknamed, suggesting absolutely nothing about their intellectual caliber or social outreach. Similarly, my name gives me a persona in society, but my intuition tells me there is something "more" to what I am. From my childhood days, I have had the thought, or actually the sense, as if through the ether, that there is a profundity to being alive. Else why would I think that a fuller dimension is absent from my life? Surely these thoughts have an origin.

11

Missing Freedom

Although I do not adopt the Yugoslav custom of eating the day's main meal around three in the afternoon, I do sometimes follow the example of napping after work. Waking refreshed, in the evening I may head to Trg Republike, where ten streets and the city's blue and white trams, their bells clanging, converge to assert the plaza's social function. Zagreb's three-hundred-year-old central town square is a hub of activity, bustling with restaurants, cafés, and dance halls. After office hours, the area pulsates. The locals, all spruced up for seeing and being seen, stroll the square in an easy-going Mediterranean style. Young men and women eye each other as if mixing at an outdoor cocktail party, one that is more innocent than the sexy cocktail parties I attended in Manhattan. The men here, at most, shout good-natured comments to the women they pass. I, too, may receive appreciation. To my playful responses in English, the men usually make a "we give up" sign of defeat.

When I engage in the square's pastime of leisurely watching the world go by, I find a viewing place in a congenial café. My *rečnik* accompanies me, slumbering in my shoulder bag but always ready for action. Slowly I may sip a small cup of jolting Turkish coffee.

On one occasion, I meet a British university student visiting Yugoslavia on summer holiday. She and her friends arrived from the seaside town of Split in the morning and will leave early the next day. Zagreb does not appeal to them.

"So gray, so grim," remarks Jane, a robust young woman with sparkling blue eyes. "Not warm and friendly like the resort towns on the Adriatic coast. The girls there dress colorfully and modern. Here all looks so drab."

On the plus side, the scarcity of consumer items and the low prices suit Jane's limited student budget. "The contrast between the Yugoslav lifestyle and my own is not that huge," she explains. "I live on a tiny student grant in England and have the same shortage of material wealth."

"Compared to America's abundance and freedom, I am confined here to a barren existence."

Jane and I agree that life in Yugoslavia is hard. Although there seems no shortage of basics, the shops and restaurants offer little choice. Still, she can travel everywhere. Yugoslavia has a liberal travel policy most communist countries lack.

"Yet I miss a certain freedom of movement," says Jane. One night, she explains, she and her friends slept on a beach. The police woke them up.

"We had to go to the police station. They examined our passports. 'This is the rule,' the police said, 'because you are foreigners. Illegal to sleep on the beach.' At home, the police would just have given us a scolding."

I take special interest in Jane's observation: "The Yugoslavs are known for their knowledge of German but, when I begin in German, the people refuse to respond." One Croat gave her a simple explanation in English: "Many of us don't like the Germans because they occupied and partitioned us during World War II. Memories of that hated period linger on. We are still getting over those horrors."

Clearly some Yugoslavs and I hold a negative attitude in common. This particular commonality, being linked to others through dislike, is not the kind of sharing I envision. Talking with Jane again boosts my determination to dissolve my German antipathy.

Jane is keen to narrate her adventures. Instead of waiting for buses, she and her friends hitch car rides. "It never goes easily. We hardly get lifts from truck drivers. Mainly private cars stop for us. Not very often either!"

"Do you think this has anything to do with a lack of hospitality for the stranger?" I ask.

"That isn't my impression. Maybe hitching is hard since there are so few cars compared to Western Europe ? Don't forget the language barrier."

A young girl at the adjoining table leans over to us. "Hope you not mind; I have listen," she says. "I Yugoslav. Me hitch very different."

I am miffed that someone has been eavesdropping. Jane and I were not conversing loudly. Who would have supposed anyone here could understand our English? The girl continues: "Friends and me hitchhike, no problem rides. We go seaside no money, except for buy beer, cigarettes. Stay people house, family or friend, or friend of friend; no need money. People give sleeping, food, free. Good feeling."

Jane suggests that her own experiences are different because she is a foreigner and cannot speak the Yugoslav languages. The girl nods happily, as if she has successfully defended her country from unwarranted accusations. Abruptly she announces that she has to go and hurries away. Jane and I look at each other, perplexed.

Jane resumes her story in a much lower tone. One car driver who stopped for her and her friends was an older Croatian man knowing good English. He expressed satisfaction with the Federation. He agreed with the postwar establishment of a socialist state based on collective ownership. He found it good that the six republics are theoretically in charge of themselves, having autonomy over some of their affairs.

"He said the problem with the Yugoslav setup is the government's centralization in Serbia," relates Jane. "He complained that everything is directed from Serbia and its capital Belgrade, and Tito is the absolute boss. Tito holds the ultimate power and snuffs out all opposition."

"It's hard to talk politics in Yugoslavia. He really trusted you."

The longer the ride, the more he criticized the federal government, verbalizing tensions between Serbia and Croatia, said Jane. "He said the Croatian economy is good. Croatia earns more of the foreign currency income from tourism and exports than the other republics, but pays too much to the poorer ones. Croatia's income is invested in other parts of the Federation. Serbia siphons off the Croatian tax money. Serbia collects the taxes, Serbia directs its use, Serbia has become increasingly prosperous. He thinks Croatia deserves a better deal."

Giving the foreigners a lift allowed the driver to articulate grievances that he dared not air other than in his intimate circle. He told Jane, "Although we Yugoslavs speak of democracy and our right to complain, the complaining or protesting cannot be done loudly or in public. Too dangerous."

"Your car driver was very daring," I comment, mentioning that a few Yugoslavs have told me there is nothing in their society to criticize. "They say they are poor, but live well and have no worries. They don't even complain about the housing shortage and the barren shops."

"My car driver was more honest."

We decide that the Yugoslavs may actually be proclaiming disaffections when they stay silent on touchy issues, their silence caused by the fear to speak. Personal freedoms and liberties are restricted. There are no laws to protect citizens from monitoring and spying.

"It seems the Yugoslavs are waiting patiently for their society to live up to its ideological promises," I remark.

"Or, have they lost hope of the social betterment Titoism promises?"

"Their patience is really apathy?"

"Or acceptance derived from fear."

"I guess we can conclude that Yugoslav socialism requires the hardworking citizens to bear their fate bravely. The Yugoslavs have much pluck," I say.

"They certainly hold in suppressed frustration."

"What choice do they have?" I ask rhetorically. "Can they revolt against their repressive one-party political system allowing no criticism and no possibility to vote in change?"

Jane is amazed to hear that something so harmless as ordering a foreign phonograph record can draw suspicion to one's self, as Svetlana maintains.

"Does the same hold true for reading foreign books?" she wonders. "Are withdrawals from the library monitored?"

Another time in a cafe at Trg Republike, I converse with an older Yugoslav man. Suddenly he pauses and looks cautiously around, checking for an eavesdropper. We are simply exchanging social pleasantries in simplistic English; we are not critiquing the Yugoslav system. Yet according to the power play rules of a dictatorial system, one always fears offending the state. Fragments of talks can be read out of context and distorted. When a political regime disfavors critique, the natural law of self-preservation forces people to conform outwardly to the country's rules or face the repercussions, usually disagreeable.

One day at Zagreb Film, I meet the literary writer Drago, a noncommunist of advanced age who speaks excellent English. Would I like to drive into the countryside? I seize the chance for a change of scenery. During the ride, Drago lectures on Zagreb's literary life. Perhaps because I listen so attentively, he eventually abandons the cultural topic to divulge his personal troubles. Sheer anguish colors his voice as he confides: "I would do almost anything to relocate to Paris."

Bitterly he elaborates: "You can believe all you want about Yugoslavia being the only socialist country to abolish exit visas for its citizens, allowing us to travel freely. The privilege to travel does not apply to all." Drago explains that he has no passport. He cannot get an official travel document because he wrote a critical, antigovernment article. The government keeps a "black book" containing the names of people prohibited from leaving Yugoslavia, no explanations given. Drago has the dubious honor of being listed.

"All is relative," he philosophizes, saying his situation is rosy compared to that of Mihajlo Mihajlov, a former professor of Russian literature at the University of Zagreb who has been in jail several years already for his critical articles.

During the excursion, I think of suggesting we visit Kumrovec, roughly thirty miles from Zagreb. Kumrovec is the small agricultural village where Josip Broz was born into a poor peasant family on the seventh of May in 1892, when Croatia was still part of the Austro-Hungarian Empire. His father was a Croat and his mother a Slovenian, teaching him multiethnicity at a young age. Because of the empire's harsh policies against the peasant class, he grew up amid social and political unrest. His family's financial difficulties forced him, the seventh of fifteen children, to leave school and start working at age thirteen.

Still standing in Kumrovec is Tito's simple birth and childhood house dating from 1860, when agricultural laborers made up at least 75 percent of the population. The house, of wood and with the thatched hay roof typical for a small village farmer, was turned into a museum of Tito's personal artifacts in 1953. That same year, a joint session of the Federal Assembly and the People's Assembly elected Josip Broz Tito the first President of the Republic of Yugoslavia.

I wonder how the peasant child Josip lived in Kumrovec before his escalation to fame and glory, but this is no day for touristic exploration. The landscape of rivers, rolling hills dotted with orchards and vineyards, and picturesque villages cannot retain my eye. My companion's fear-filled energy unnerves me. Passing churches, their beautiful spires reflecting Croatia's old Roman Catholic background, I question the Yugoslavs' freedom of worship.

"We are not forbidden to believe in God, but it is better not to. We don't talk about God or religion at home or at work or anywhere. People don't take believers seriously."

"Are there government laws against believing?"

"There are rules that you can't be a member of the communist party and go to a church or a mosque. People who are religious are thought to distrust the communist system. If people think you are religious, they won't vote for you to become a member of a workers' council, for example."

Drago himself, like the communists, is not drawn to religion. His comments remind me of a slogan I heard during this year of student revolt against authority: "Even if God existed, He would have to be suppressed."

Drago wishes to make a new appointment. We can meet only while we drive in his car. He prefers not to be seen in public in the company of an American. It is not wise for Yugoslavs to interact with a Westerner. They don't know who I am. Any Westerner could be a spy. Aha! Perhaps his attitude sheds some light on the general lack of hospitality to me, though not on the Studio's indifference to my welfare.

Drago's demeanor makes me feel apprehensive. He is a government critic written into the infamous black book. I have to stay alert to possible traps in this puzzling, secretive society that uses practices of which I am ignorant. Be seen in a car driven by a dissident? Exposed to an infected person, have I caught the contagious bug of paranoia?

Tito's Socialist Federal Republic of Yugoslavia is far less a repressive police state than any of the Soviet Bloc countries, and the Yugoslavs have more freedoms, or degrees thereof, than any of their less fortunate comrades in the Soviet-dominated communist nations. Nonetheless, Big Brother is always watching and, perhaps, misinterpreting. The secret police stays alert for dissidents and critics. Daring to fault the Yugoslav regime can be personally endangering. Does the government exercise guilt by association?

Before arriving in Yugoslavia, I knew about the jailing of high-ranking communist official and prominent communist ideologist Milovan Djilas. He had fought alongside Tito in the Partisan Resistance. In the postwar Yugoslav government, he held several positions, including vice president. He was a committed warrior for the classless society expected to follow the famous principle elucidated by Karl Marx, the nineteenth-century German philosopher, radical economist, and revolutionary leader who said: "From each according to his ability, to each according to his need." Every person would have equal rights of access to consumer goods regardless of his or her personal contribution to the process of production.

Djilas staunchly criticized Stalin's attempts to bring Yugoslavia under control of the USSR, which projected itself as the role model for communist states. Djilas, Tito, and the strong-minded Partisans of the Yugoslav Resistance, having fought off the Nazis and having been the Soviets' only wartime ally in Central Europe, refused to hand over their hard-won liberation. Choosing its own distinct "Socialist, but independent" path, Yugoslavia became the sole East European nation to defy joining the Soviet satellite system.

A loyal member of Tito's inner circle and at the time considered his successor, Djilas influenced Tito to pursue the policy of independent Yugoslav Socialism, giving the people the possibility for free enterprise. He and two associates brought Tito the idea for the Workers' Self-Management experiment with decentralized profit-sharing workers' councils in state-run enterprises.

Things changed dramatically for the man who seemed the future of Yugoslavia when he started writing articles demanding more democracy in the Communist Party of Yugoslavia and in the country itself. By 1956, Djilas was convicted and jailed for criticizing Yugoslav policy. Incarcerated, he did not spend his time peering through the bars of his prison cell looking for a flower of hope. He wrote a powerful book that insightfully examined and attacked the ruling establishment.

The New Class: An Analysis of the Communist System had to be smuggled to the West. Published in America in 1957, it caused a sensation. For the first time, a principal communist official publicly attacked East European communism. Just as his denouncement reached Western readers, Djilas received an extended prison term.

Djilas eschewed the emergence of a political bureaucracy dedicated not to the ideology of fulfilling the people's right to a better life, but to suppressing all opposition and keeping itself in power as a ruling elite (of communist party members) possessing special privileges and economic preference. Rather than functioning as an egalitarian and classless society with no exploitation, the communist system generated an advantaged minority enjoying spoils and powers, setting it apart from the people.

Djilas called Yugoslav communism that type of totalitarianism consisting of three basic factors for controlling the people: power, ownership, and ideology. According to him, the ruling class of bureaucrats monopolized all three in Yugoslavia. Completely dominant, step-by-step the party elite abandoned and lost the ideology that had taken it to power.

"By justifying the means because of the end, the end itself becomes increasingly more distant and unrealistic, while the frightful reality of the means becomes increasingly obvious and intolerable," wrote Djilas.[13] He concluded that most people living under the communist system were not opposed to socialism. They were opposed to the way in which socialism was being achieved.[14] The problem was not the ideal of socialism, but the totalitarian imposition of the ideal on the citizens.

In a democratic system, a ruling elite class may emerge when the elected representatives serve their self-interests instead of the larger concerns of the nation, the citizens, and, ideally, the world. A major drawback of a democratic system in a self-indulgent society is the relatively short terms of office the elected representatives hold. To get reelected, candidates usually promise short-term solutions to problems. The citizens also serve their personal interests, often opting for instant relief of their discomforts and the gratification of their wishes above the overall, long-term welfare of society. Short-term thinking does not create enduring solutions. Governments and citizens unwilling to invest in long-term plans help perpetuate the excessively individualistic, self-centered society.

While a student at Barnard College, I wrote a book report on *The New Class*. What made me decide to analyze the Djilas book among the many titles on the reading list for Professor Basil Rauch's course in world government? Did "coincidence" again help prepare me for a specific event years later in my life?

The personal history of Milovan Djilas reminds me that Yugoslavia, presenting itself as a semiliberal socialist society, enforces sharp

---

[13] *The New Class: An Analysis of the Communist System*, by Milovan Djilas, Frederick A. Praeger, Inc., New York, 1957, p. 98.
[14] Ibid, p. 163.

limits on public speech, opinion, and assembly. Watch on the citizens is many times worse in Yugoslavia than the secret domestic surveillance of Vietnam War protestors in the US. In Yugoslavia, at least, citizens know there is a system of personal surveillance and monitoring.

One day, Matko says he might need my assistance at the Festival of Yugoslav Film in Pula. "The high life of Yugoslav cinema," he observes. The annual summertime event is the oldest festival of national films in the world, and its venue is perhaps the world's oldest film theater. Pula, near the southern tip of Croatia's Istrian Peninsula in the Adriatic Sea, is a three-thousand-year-old city dating from Roman times. The Pula festival screens the best of Yugoslavia's national feature films, subtitled into English. "A prize at Pula is a top reward for a Yugoslav film."

Marshal Tito is the patron of the Festival of Yugoslav Film. Close to Pula, on the Brijuni Islands, he spends holidays. Famous international personages, including Hollywood movie stars, visit him there. Tito loves film. Reportedly he views some three hundred movies a year in his villa's private screening room.

Would I attend Pula, even if I have to pay my own expenses? Hearing the festival pitched as an event not to miss, I agree to go and be on tap for Matko. I am willing to dip into my nest egg of traveler's checks for what seems more a vacation than work. "Film professionals from everywhere attend," adds Matko. I will pack my minidress.

For over one week, every caressingly warm Mediterranean evening finds me watching two feature films in Pula's ancient Roman amphitheater. The Arena, open-air site of the film screenings, is as much an attraction as the films. Built in the mid-first century BC, the well-preserved Arena was originally used for gladiator battles.

Current battles in the Arena date mainly from World War II. Many of the screened films are socialist realism propaganda dramas celebrating the Yugoslav Resistance. Immortalizing the Partisans' courage and fearlessness against their enemy occupiers, the films incorporate an officially sanctioned optimism and patriotic education of the masses. After the screenings I am able to understand the joke told by a Yugoslav filmmaker: "Eight men left their village to join the Partisan Resistance movement. Six were killed. Postwar, ten returned."[15]

During the deliciously sunny Pula days, I mix happily in the international film crowd. Speaking English full blast and nonstop proves an absolute delight. How *not* to enjoy lively conversations in my own tongue while relaxing at the sunlit poolside of the hotel where most of the foreign visitors lodge and where much film business takes place? "This could be Hollywood," I think to myself one day. I am sitting at pool's edge, in bikini with notebook and pen, interviewing one of Yugoslavia's film stars for a possible magazine article. My minidress fits in perfectly here.

Western film pros ask how much longer I will stay in Zagreb. Several give me their business cards should I want to try my writing luck in their countries. From the sparkling days of Pula, I return to my shadowed existence in Zagreb.

---

[15] Joke also quoted in an article on Yugoslavia by Jules Chametzky in the *Atlantic*, summer 1968, p. 20.

12

Assisting Film Trailblazer John Grierson

The depth I sense in myself, a "larger identity," is not accessible, as if locked away. I need a key to open my depth. Will I find in there a greater significance to my being alive? I have no coach or guide helping me gain insight. I have only my life itself. The constant gnawing of search motivates me to plunge zealously into my experiences. If my resulting intensity of living has not helped me know life's profundities, it has turned me into a passionate participant in whatever I do.

I consider work the hub of my life's meaning. It is my work, I think, rather than family, friends, relationships, or religion that will connect me with a purpose greater than my own self-interest. Just what is this purpose? What really is my work?

Matko, in his friendly manner, and usually flashing an expansive smile, adds tasks steadily to my portfolio. One day he announces, in the tone of a pleasantly delivered command: "You will help me greet and entertain John Grierson."

"John Grierson!" I exclaim. I know the name from my film studies. John Grierson was born in Scotland. His father was the local school headmaster; his mother an early feminist and labor activist. Starting his career as a PhD-bearing sociologist, Grierson went on to become the founding father of the British and Canadian documentary film. He coined the very word "documentary." When he worked as a film critic in the US in the 1920s, Grierson reviewed the film *Moana* by the American filmmaker Robert Flaherty. *Moana* was a visual account of the daily life in Polynesia of a local boy and his family. Writing in the *New York Sun*, Grierson said that the film had "documentary value." The new word came from the French *documentaire*, referring to "travelogs."

In the 1930s, Grierson pioneered the new medium of film. He recognized film as a valuable social tool waiting to be utilized. Film had potential not merely to entertain but, more crucially, to raise awareness and educate people on social issues. He believed film could serve a social purpose by focusing on the everyday dramas of ordinary people. The documentary film, he emphasized, required a point of view and should be a force for social change. Upon invitation of the Canadian government just before World War II, he inspired and established the National Film Board of Canada (NFB). Leading the NFB in the making of patriotic propaganda films, Grierson became a major figure in the Allied propaganda campaign against Hitler and the Nazis. He served as the first Film Commissioner of the Board. After the War, the NFB focused on producing documentaries that reflected the lives of Canadians, and Grierson moved on to the US. He formed a company to make films for the promotion of international understanding.

At Stanford, in the Department of Communication, we screened documentaries and cartoons made by the National Film Board of Canada. Janet Voelker, who proposed me for the Zagreb job, was a NFB filmmaker on teaching leave. Did Jan mention Grierson? Or did I initially hear Grierson's name in the course taught by film professor Henry Breitrose?

Dr. Henry Breitrose had the reputation for being "brilliant." He established the Stanford graduate program in documentary film and television in his early thirties. Henry was a few years older than I. Compared to him, in America I could be regarded as a failure. Not yet have I attained much of the exalted material success. I, too, had been termed "brilliant," in my youth, for my high IQ and excellent performance in school or at whatever I undertook. But, as an adult, I still have not "made it."

True, I am pursuing an exciting life as an independent and adventurous young career woman. During the years after college graduation and before heading to Stanford, I built up my CV, juggling several freelance jobs while also working as a professional actress-singer. One job, a very well-paid consultant position, allowed me to work from home or at the Midtown Manhattan office of a national TV ratings company. When I tended my resignation, I told the director that Stanford had awarded me a fellowship. He asked me to stay and become manager of the New York office. The position was a plum assignment at a time when women were just progressing up the executive ladder.

By not accepting the TV managerial job offering prestige, fine salary, and perks, I disappointed my parents. They complained I was not achieving my potential. According to their measure of success, I had no big job, no large bank account, and no well-to-do husband; I had no husband at all; I had no children; I did not own my apartment and, at Stanford, I would buy a car second-hand.

But I had diverse interests and talents. That was the problem. Even though writing always called me, I had not been able to concentrate solely on one thing and stick to it—with one exception. Despite the ups and downs in my personal circumstances, I held tightly to my search for the significance of life. The urge to know the profundities of where we come from and where we are going surfaced in my early childhood.

One morning, I awoke hearing in my head the question: *If I were not here, where would I be?* In my mind I saw an expanse of whitish light that was moving, twirling, whirling. I felt myself vibrating, flying. Even to this day, I vividly remember this experience and that sleeping room. Many years later, questioning my mother about that childhood room, I supposed that this experience occurred maybe two years before I learned to read and write at age six. Once I discovered the alphabet, and could put letters into words and sentences, I knew I would be a writer, write a book some day, travel the globe. Yet my first "want" remained paramount. I wanted to know the answer to my expanded question: *If I were not here, where would I be? Who and what am I really?*

By the time I got to Stanford in my late twenties, I still had not found the answer to my most pressing question. To find the answer drove me on. The search was my unspoken obsession, just as Henry Breitrose's love of film motivated and impassioned his life.

One of Henry's personal role models was John Grierson, and Grierson's philosophy of film was a pillar of the Stanford film program. Once Henry said: "At heart I think Grierson is a combination of political philosopher and showman, who believes that complicated ideas, creatively presented on the screen, can change the audience's knowledge and its consciousness."

Now John Grierson is coming to Zagreb and needs an English-speaking assistant. It is my good luck to be the right person in the right place at the right time. Or, as Stern implied, is there a Force at work? Does a mysterious Power use people and events as instruments to lead us into experiences that are part of a Higher Purpose?

My isolation in Zagreb provides an abundance of quiet moments in which to puzzle over being alive. My gut feeling tells me there is a Will in the world that functions with an intention greater than my own individual wish, want, or choice. Is this Will what people call God—by whatever name? I consider the possibility that this greater Will exerts an influence over tiny human me. Is Grierson's arrival and my assignment to be his personal aide a "coincidence" linked to a cosmically prede-signed blueprint for my life? Or is my new task attributable to plain good luck?

I accompany Matko to Zagreb Airport to receive John Grierson. As the flight discharges its passengers, we immediately identify the Scottish filmmaker. His appearance is a refreshing contrast to the general East European men's look. Grierson wears a soft cashmere V-necked sweater over a fine wool tie and a shirt under a well-cut, camel-colored woolen suit. It is the height of summer yet his garments, undoubtedly made of his home country's renowned wool, prepare him for autumn. "He lacks body heat," I conclude, noting his seasoned, elderly face. He has sensitive, rather sad eyes framed by eyeglasses, and thick eyebrows whose hairs erupt wildly in all directions. A mustache completes his I-know-who-I-am presentation of himself.

The filmmaker will be the guest of honor at an evening billed self-evidently as *Griersonova Škola Dokumentarnog Filma*, hosted by the Filmski Klub "Moša Pijade" of Zagreb. The program features ten documentary films Grierson directed, produced, or supervised from 1931 to 1960.

Meeting the flesh and blood person behind the respected film reputation thrills, fascinates, and awes me. As our palms touch during the introductory handshake, a small electric shock races up my arm. Later, in the restaurant of Grierson's hotel, I am astonished when he declares: "I'm only half a man since I gave up drinking and smoking, over a year now."

His forthrightness surprises me.

"Tea?" he asks. Then he explains, like a teacher: "Whiskey is for the women, smoking for the ideas and the work."

Apparently he still possesses the facile tongue that the god of whisky can bestow. "Since I've stopped drinking and smoking, I've become an imbecile," he says. "I'm coming back to my own head again. Last month I gave my first speech in a year."

Aware of John Grierson's reputation for lecturing in universities, at conferences, and to film societies and filmmakers, I am stunned to hear he speaks so rarely in public nowadays. My reaction causes Grierson to exclaim, as if we are old buddies reuniting in Zagreb: "Hey, do you realize I was seventy this year? When you reach that point, you say: 'Why work so hard?'"

Grierson's remarks on his age occupy me in my room, by now my cave for reflection. Material-deprived Zagreb affords me a luxury previously unknown. Shut away in my ascetic room absent of distractions, living almost as a hermit, I can deliberate on my life both backward and forward. In America, I had little time to internalize as I piled up experience after experience in my fast-paced busy existence. In the Croatian capital, where a slower tread overpowers my step, I have ample opportunity to review, absorb, and integrate my daily experiences.

Enthused by the unique chance to assist John Grierson, I wonder about a career in documentary film.

Although I feel myself a writer and not a filmmaker, at Stanford I enjoyed the creative pleasure of making two 16mm films. For my subject matter, I took ordinary people and their problems, an approach fitting Grierson's focus on society as it is. My initial film brought me into close contact with well-to-do elderly people living a luxurious old age in a high-priced Northern California nursing home. Filming at the home confirmed my earlier conclusions from having visited an old folks' home in New York that served lower income people: America's treatment of the general elderly population needs humane reevaluation. Yugoslavia further reinforced this opinion. Svetlana had mentioned that the toothless senior who carried my suitcase through the crowded tram would, in his later years, most probably receive care from his family. "It would be shameful if children could not manage to care for their aged parents," she said.

Rich or poor, in whatever land we grow old, we all face physical and sometimes mental breakdown. Care of the elderly, especially the poor elderly and the helpless elderly, is one revealer of both the individual's and the society's heart. Some of the world's peoples, lacking a governmental or social network to provide the personalized help needed in old age, and also lacking the financial means to pay for such services themselves, may look to the future with debilitating worry and fear.

I get such thoughts after meeting John Grierson. Besides intensifying my attraction to film, the great pioneer of the social realist film presses my social concern buttons. Despite bemoaning my situation in Zagreb, I thank any powers that may be for the opportunity to spend time with John Grierson.

Grierson's rich background and his lively cultivated mind belong to a treasure house from which he liberally allows me to draw. Obviously the old master relishes playing the father figure and mentor to the younger and less experienced. He welcomes my sincerity and seriousness; I value his nonjudgmental attitude to my inquisitiveness. During a meal or in his room while he rests, I pose many questions.

I make notes while we speak. This habit started when I was nine, and my love of writing launched my extracurricular career as a reporter/editor for school publications. Thinking about the films I made at Stanford, the second documenting a day in the life of a blind man, I ask Grierson: "How to discover if one has talent as a filmmaker?"

"That's easy," the grand old man of film replies. "Get some film and make a film called, 'I Remember.' Then there are no other filmmakers to follow."

Grierson heeds his own advice in reverse. He has just finished making "I Remember, I Remember," a biopic of his life in film.

Aspiring filmmakers can initiate their own training from an early age, he tells me. "I grew up in Scotland, a country without a tradition of art, but I had a mania for seeing. I used to shut my eyes at night and go over all I had seen on my way to and from school. I taught myself training in visual seeing though I didn't know why I was doing it. When first exposed to postimpressionist painting, that was no difficulty for me. There was no art tradition in my family or country, but I had trained myself in the art of seeing. If you have that kind of training, and you take to the cinema, wonderful."

"Is there a difference between what you look at and what you see? I mean, in the creative sense. Do you notice what others may miss?"

"Training in the art of seeing opens your eyes to artistic vision."

One question elicits an unexpected response. I inquire: "How did you get connected with film?" He taps the side of his head in disbelief and barks, "What a foolish question!"

If John Grierson is trying to make me feel foolish, he succeeds. Yet my foolish question leads to his pithy follow-up response: "It was there and I used it!"

When he was a young communicator in the 1920s, he simply took to the relatively new medium of film that "was there."

In plain and simple words, in the blunt style often projecting an "I know better than you" attitude, Grierson blurted out a good piece of general advice. In only seven words he transmitted a practical and powerful formula: "It was there and I used it!"

"The crisis of the world is there, here, staring us right in the face!" I exclaim. I am envisioning my America. Social unrest is rocking my country shore to shore in a tumultuous transition away from the conservative 1950s and early 1960s.

"So get busy and serve the world!" pronounces Grierson, nearly shouting.

"Sometimes we search and search," I begin, "and—"

"— and the answers are right before us!" growls Grierson, his eyes fiery and his bushy eyebrows flaring more wildly than usual. "It was there and I used it! Now *you* look at what is there and use it!"

"I'm doing the best I can!" I declare, raising my voice. "I'm doing the best that I can."

"Okay," says Grierson in a milder tone. "When the mind is cluttered, we don't see clearly. You will eventually, I know it."

His soothing change of manner helps my feeling of foolishness pass. If he is provoking me to probe myself deeper, I accept the challenge. Bracing myself for what at times is his theatrical wrath, I dare ask afresh about his first association with film. Once again the mellow teacher wishing to stimulate, Grierson answers: "I had a Rockefeller Grant at the University of Chicago. I noticed that the Hearst newspapers used short, active words to hit the reader with an idea. I thought, 'Why not do the same with film?'"

"What is your purpose with film?" I ask, back on the journalistic track.

"There is a film to be made wherever there are slums, malnutrition, exploitation, and cruelty." He answers wearily, as if he has expounded on this issue many times.

"It is there," I say, "and you use it."

"It's very simple," Grierson responds. "I wanted to put film at the disposition of the working class. Workers had no place on the screen except as comic characters. I wanted to give them their proper place in the public image."

He elaborates on his initial documentary, the trailblazing *Drifters*. At the time, Grierson held a civil service position as Films Officer for the Empire Marketing Board, a governmental organization promoting trade and a sense of unity within the various countries of the British Commonwealth. In addition to writing the scenario, directing, and editing the fifty-minute silent film, he wrote the publicity materials. Diverging from the British and Hollywood cinema of the time, Grierson took the film's subject and actions from real life. *Drifters* portrayed and conveyed the actual atmosphere of the previously unseen daily work of the North Sea herring fleet, the fishing ships and the crews. Instead of professional actors, Grierson hired workingmen. He shot the footage totally on location, out-of-doors.

"If two years before *Drifters* anyone had said I would make a film, I would have said he was crazy. I had to make *Drifters* because no one believed in my theories. The documentary film was conceived as a conscious political movement to present the working class on the screen. After I showed *Drifters* to the government, I asked: 'Have you ever seen a picture of the British working class?' The answer was 'No.'"

Grierson offers many points to consider.

"*Drifters* was a public sensation for two reasons," explains Grierson. "First, nobody had ever seen work presented as a heroic subject. Second, no one had ever seen the camera approach reality through the new way of cutting and montage. Film pieces were assembled to music."

The film premiered in London in 1929 on a double bill with the feature film *The Battleship Potemkin* by the Russian director Sergei Eisenstein, whose work influenced Grierson.

Grierson lyricizes the impact of the film image in time: "One image moving into the next is the important thing, equivalent to a boxing match where one force moves to the next. Image and continuity, image and counterpoint, movement and ideal. In *Drifters*, there is a ship with nets catching fish. Birds in the air, whale in the sea, conger eel below, and the wind comes up or dies down. At one moment you're busy with the net, and then someone looks up and you're involved in another world, and you pass from one to the other."

"Did you realize you had made a groundbreaking film?" I ask.

"It is impossible for a good artist to appreciate when he's made a good film," replies Grierson. "The greater the artist, the more he draws attention to a small part. He's not sure of the important part. I've never met a true artist who was sure of himself."

Grierson does not see himself as a film artist. "I think first and last of myself as a public servant," he tells me.

After *Drifters*, Grierson left directing to guide a group of young filmmakers. They formed the core artists who created the British Documentary Movement. The most famous documentary of that period was the acclaimed *Night Mail*, screened at Zagreb's Grierson retrospective. Produced by Grierson to promote the British Post office as a facilitator of modern communication, *Night Mail* follows the overnight mail train on its journey London to Scotland carrying only mail, no passengers. The film shows the postal services linking widely separated regions and people of different social strata. Grierson narrated the voiceover.

"This film suited the government because it needed to create a new relationship between the people and the old, lost British Empire."

The same principle applied to the film he produced for the Ceylon Tea Propaganda Board. *The Song of Ceylon* documents the cultural and religious life of the local people and the effects of industrialization and modern communications.

"The film portrays the tea-producing people instead of Ceylon as a place to be ruled," says Grierson. "The idea was to accept not only the modern world but also the proletarian nature of the modern world, and to fill the gap of the passing away of the old colonial empire."

At another moment: "The interesting point of the films I made is that all of them were presented for public authority with public authority. I have never made a private money picture."

Grierson's filmic productions, sponsored by government agencies, contained no built-in target figures for box office sales. Audience attendance figures had no effect on Grierson's creativity. This manner of working, similar to that of the Zagreb Film artists, gave him more freedom of creative expression.

On the other side of the ledger, Grierson had to fulfill the purpose for which the government agency or film sponsor paid the bill. This may be why Grierson put, as *Drifters'* last subtitle: "So to the ends of the earth goes the harvest of the sea." Even Grierson could not escape the economic considerations influencing most areas of human endeavor. His highly praised debut film on the herring industry was made for a sponsor wanting to sell herring abroad. The film's greatness comes from its introduction of artistic elements derived from Grierson's artistic eye.

In one of our talks, Grierson states: "As a matter of principle, I have never looked at a film after it was made. Don't look at yesterday, and don't read your own publicity. Look at something new tomorrow."

"What do you look for when you watch another person's film?"

"Communication from one unknown to another, from one country to another," he answers. "I might not look for a good story, but for a drama involving man and his fate, man and his struggle in society."

Social relevance buoys Grierson; he wants to explain to people what is happening all around them. The documentary film can dramatize public affairs with engagement and excitement, activating citizens to participate in government and social reform. I grasp the meaning of his oft-quoted statement that his films are the "creative treatment of actuality." Making society understandable to people through film is Grierson's mission.

"On another level," continues Grierson, "when I watch a film I look for visual beauty. My most constant requirement is visual beauty. I ask from a film exactly what I would ask from an artist or architect."

"Does this criterion hold for politically motivated films as well?"

"Exactly the same," responds Grierson.

"Are you saying that film artistry does not dilute didactic messages aimed to raise public awareness of issues?"

Grierson nods affirmatively, yet his reply is a non sequitur: "In the communist countries they claim to be socialists but, actively, they are not. They are content with their petty satisfactions," he asserts. "You can see it in Yugoslavia. There is a battle for the petty satisfactions in all socialist countries. The everlasting battle, even before socialism was invented, was between personal interest and public interest. The best statement of the dilemma is still in the *Dialogues of Plato*, in the debate about the execution of Socrates."

Referring to Socrates recalls my academic studies of the Greek philosopher and educator. Socrates holds up a mirror into which we can gaze even thousands of years later.

When Socrates was around forty, one of his friends posed a question to the Oracle of Delphi, the prophetic priestess in the Temple of Apollo in Athens. The ancient peoples of Greece and Europe believed that through the Oracle spoke none other than Apollo, the god of Sun and Light. Apollo personified the victory of the divine Light over darkness and evil. He represented "the immaterial and intelligible light of which the sun is but the physical reflection, and whence flows all truth."[16] The very structure of the Temple of Apollo itself gave profound counsel through the numerous wise maxims carved on its columns, among them: *Gnōthi seautón,* "Know thyself." There was also *Mēdén ágan,* "Nothing in excess." Another guiding motto was, "Let no one without clean hands come near."

Asked "Who is the wisest of all men," the Oracle of Delphi named Socrates. Puzzled by the oracular message telling him: "No one is wiser than you," Socrates set out to prove the truth or the untruth of the Oracle's declaration.[17]

Seeking notable Athenians reputed to be wise, among them statesmen, poets, and artisans, Socrates approached them as if he were ignorant but wanted to be taught. Pretending ignorance and humility belonged to his teaching method. Socrates presented himself not as a teacher but as a seeker of Truth.

Cross-examining the selected men, Socrates tested their claims to know what was truly worthwhile. "What is wisdom? What is virtue?

---

[16] *Larousse Encyclopedia of Mythology,* edited by Félix Guirand, English-language edition published by Chancellor Press, London, 1997 reprint of 1996 edition, p. 113; and *The Great Initiates* by Edouard Schuré, Harper & Row, New York, 1961, pp. 287–288.

[17] Dialogues of Plato, the record of Socrates's defense as written down by his student, Plato, in the *Apologia,* "the Apology," 21a.

What is justice?" he would ask, among other challenging questions. Through persistent questioning, he encouraged in others self-discovery of knowledge about the human condition. His queries proved especially tortuous and embarrassing for those in positions of authority, those whose priority was supposedly serving the common interests of the people and the society.

Socrates discovered that the so-called wise men could not give him suitable answers. His logical scrutiny exposed their confusions and contradictions. He found they professed knowledge without realizing their ignorance. Thus he concluded: The Oracle might be right; he had the wisdom others lacked. Rather than pretend he knew something he did not, he admitted his ignorance. The awareness of his own ignorance was apparently the wisdom to which Apollo referred.

Even as a "nonteacher," Socrates taught that everything in the world has a definite meaning. That meaning is not just the logical expression of its being, but denotes its intrinsic value as well. The meaning of anything is not what we take it to be. It exists objectively. Virtue or justice would still be virtue or justice even if there were no human beings to be virtuous or just. One had to be able to "see" the intrinsic meaning beyond the appearance of things. Such "knowledge" penetrates the mystery of life. Only by learning to "see" do we come to know ourselves.[18]

Socrates believed there was a best standard for human conduct and political rule; he did not claim to possess that standard. For him, the Supreme Truth was God and the immortal soul. He believed that all virtues converge into one, the "good," which is the knowledge of one's true self and purposes.[19] In very simple and clear language, he said: "The unexamined life is not worth living."[20]

Socrates's student Plato went on to say: "Individual souls are eternal, having existed before they came into bodies which are like prisons.

---

[18] With thanks for the explanations of Gordon L. Ziniewicz in "Plato's Socrates: The Apology: The Conscience of a Community." See: www.fred.net/tzaka/phil.

[19] *Columbia Encyclopedia*, Fifth Edition, Columbia University Press, 1993, p. 2554.

[20] Ibid, Dialogues of Plato, 38a.

Self-knowledge alone can make the soul free. This knowledge is not a new thing. It is a recall, a remembrance of what has been forgotten."[21]

Socrates regarded the public discussion of life's great questions a necessary part of valuable human existence. The sad truth is that anyone inspiring people to think they are not helpless slaves to the gods or to the political, social, and cultural establishment may be viewed as an annoyance, if not a danger, by those upholding the social fabric.

Sure enough, when Socrates was approximately seventy-one, in 399 CE, he was put on trial in Athens. The citizen jury heard a case against Socrates for religious heresy and corrupting the minds of the young. "Corruption" actually signified instilling the spirit of inquiry into the young men of Athens. Socrates was condemned to die by ingesting poison hemlock. Some considered his crime to be the crime of crimes: teaching people to think for themselves. Thinking for themselves, some of the young Athenian men with whom Socrates carried on philosophical discussions went on to question the Athenian government.

John Grierson is functioning for me as Socrates did for his students in ancient Athens. Perhaps Grierson thinks that my awareness of my own ignorance will fertilize the soil of my creative self-learning. He is helping me become more aware of my own higher ideals and those of society. Grierson's manner, at times intimidating and causing discomfort, shakes me awake to a wider and deeper way of seeing myself.

Although from a young age I have tended to live a kind of examined life, having started the rudimentary logbook at age nine, Yu-go-slave-ia is pushing me to look with increased intensity at my thoughts and my actions. As I slow down in Zagreb, I engage in a heightened self-scrutiny. I am speeding ahead from the unexamined to the examined life. The challenging Yugoslavian society is helping me know myself better.

---

[21] *The Basic Teachings of the Great Philosophers* by S. E. Frost, New York, New Home Library, 1942, pp. 174–175, as quoted in *Meditation and Spiritual Life*, by Swami Yatiswarananda, Sri Ramakrishna Ashrama, Bangalore, India, Third Edition, 1989, p. 41.

In the ongoing drama of life, as we seek to understand ourselves by exploration and experience, we may come to penetrate the veil of illusion covering the everyday process of living. We see through the dream, as did I, beginning in 1968, during my transformative stay in Yugoslavia, and as I have increasingly in the decades since. *(Photo Thomas Fogarty [1873–1938]; US Library of Congress)*

MOST LIKELY TO SUCCEED
Joel Blatt—Norma Eisner

When my high school classmates voted me—then still bearing the name given by my parents—"Most Likely to Succeed," they in fact elected me most likely to realize the American Dream. In those years, I was still caught in the imprisonment of materialistic goals as the school photographer, consciously or unconsciously, symbolically portrayed. *(Photo from* The Pioneer, *yearbook of the author's graduating class at Andrew Jackson High School, Queens, New York City. Courtesy Surya Green)*

When I entered the coveted gates of Stanford University, ranked high as a "dream school," I still believed that the American Dream could become the everyday reality of anyone willing to work hard in the democratic and prosperous American society with its free-enterprise system offering limitless possibilities for upward mobility. *(US Library of Congress)*

Before stepping into the American career world aided by the prestigious Stanford degree symbolizing social mobility, I got the call to work temporarily in a country ostensibly pursuing the Communist Dream—of creating a classless, cooperative, and sharing society. My destination: a distinguished animation film studio, Zagreb Film. This image is from a film cel drawn for me (and which I filmed as it was being drawn) by Zagreb Film artist Milan Blažeković (1940–), who was then directing the film *Gorilla's Dance* (1968) under the supervision of animation pioneer Dušan Vukotić (1927–1998).

For all the talk of worker equality and democracy I heard from Yugoslavs, and notwithstanding the valuable lessons I did learn on this front while in Yugoslavia, Tito's Third Way in many respects fell well short of its "Brotherhood and Unity" slogan. At Zagreb Film I, the guest worker from the West, personally experienced mainly lip service to this noble, unifying ideal. As a small but symbolic example, during a visit by Studio staff to Vienna in 1968, my co-workers assembled for a photo. I was not included. Am I wrong to think that "unity" connotes "all in the whole"—even an American, and yes, a "foreigner," temporarily in the company? By the way, standing tall among the colleagues and animators is, back row (left), flashing his trademark smile, Zagreb Film commercial director and my workplace supervisor, Želimir Matko (d. 1977). *(Photo courtesy Surya Green)*

Milovan Djilas (1911–1995), a top communist ideologist once regarded as the possible successor of Yugoslav leader Josip Broz Tito, missed more profoundly the truth of "Brotherhood and Unity." His criticism of Yugoslav policy and the rise of a "New Class" ruling elite landed him in jail for years. Here, in 1952, Djilas (left) is still in the good graces of Tito (right). *(ANP Foto)*

Josip Broz Tito (1892–1980) illustrates a Yugoslav version of the Horatio Alger rags-to-riches American success story. Born as a poor peasant, Broz followed the Communist Dream to attain the top position in the Yugoslav Partisan Resistance, was elected president of Yugoslavia five times, and was finally proclaimed president for life, leaving behind a legacy known as "Tito's Third Way."

"You Croatians, fight for freedom!" exhorts this poster of the Croatian Partisans of the People's Liberation Army of Yugoslavia (1941–1945). Yugoslavia did attain relative political and economic freedom as a nation but, forcibly seeking to achieve its promise of a better life for all, Titoism resorted to authoritarian oppression. *(Croatian History Museum)*

In authoritarian Yugoslavia, often I felt watched, if not by governmental authorities, then by Zagrebians, as if I had come from another world, which in fact I had. In turn, my observation of the Yugoslavs and their world helped me recognize the illusory nature and existential nonreality of my own American Dream society. *(Photos Surya Green)*

Presenting *This Wonderful World* on Scottish TV from 1957 to 1967, John Grierson (1898–1972) introduced audiences to outstanding international documentaries; in our interaction, he helped awaken my sleeping sense of social responsibility to help make a better world. *(Photo courtesy John Grierson Archive, University of Stirling, UK)*

From black nationalist leader Malcolm X (1925-1965), and the young boxing champ Cassius Clay (1942-), I might have absorbed some of the spiritual energy that kept them riveted on the inner search even while involved in societal tasks. Here, on March 20, 1964, the man who was just recently named (March 6, 1964) *Muhammad* (one worthy of praise) *Ali* (name of a cousin of the Prophet Muhammad) prepares to give his new autograph to Malcolm X (who received his own spiritual name, El-Hajj Malik El-Shabazz, later the same year). Both men very kindly gave me their autographs on the last day that, it turned out, Ali was still signing his name to the public as "Cassius Clay." *(Photo John Peodincuk/New York Daily News, via Getty Images)*

No photo exists of me with John Grierson, but I am reminded of his positive impact on my social conscience when I see myself here, in 1969, three months after leaving Yugoslavia, speaking (listening) to socially engaged American photographer-filmmaker-arts administrator Willard van Dyke (1906–1986). We were participants, Van Dyke the faculty chair, at the first seminar on cinema at the Salzburg Seminar in American Studies (Salzburg Global Seminar since 2007) in Austria. Back, left, is longtime *New York Times* film critic Bosley Crowther (1905–1981). *(Photo Henk Meulman, courtesy Surya Green)*

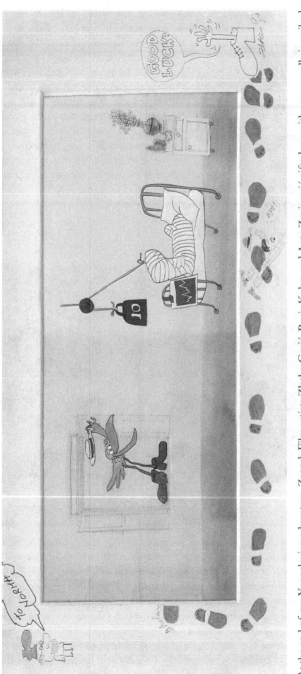

At the end of my Yugoslavian adventure, Zagreb Film artists Zlatko Grgić, Boris Kolar, and Ante Zaninović gifted me with a personally inscribed "goodbye" cel from the new Professor Balthazar cartoon series. With so much of life seeming symbolic to me, how to interpret why the animators gave me this particular image? *(Photo courtesy Sarya Green)*

A flower memorial, designed by Serbian architect-artist-philosopher and ex-Partisan Bogdan Bogdanović (1922–2010), marks the site in Croatia of the former Yugoslavia where once stood the infamous Jasenovac World War II concentration camp. The memorial's form makes me aware that, even from soil on which much human suffering has taken place, there can grow up a flower (albeit of stone, created from human artistic vision), symbolizing, to me, an immortal knowledge: the force of human goodness will always, ultimately, triumph over destructive forces unleashed in the world. *(Photo Petar Milošević)*

Holocaust memorials, like the one at Jasenovac and the Tree of Life at the Great/ Central Synagogue in Budapest, Hungary—erected in 1991 as a metal, weeping willow tree designed by internationally celebrated Hungarian artist Imre Varga (b. 1923)— honor those many human beings sacrificed at the violent hands of confused people who saw incorrectly the composition of the human family. The tree, each of its leaves engraved with the family names of Hungarian Jewish persons cut down because of their Jewish roots, transcends, in my view, this perishable world—its branches extending beyond the limitations of material nature, its leaves singing hymns that convey spiritual truths the everyday eye cannot see but that the inner self can feel, just like freedom. *(Photo Surya Green, 2015)*

13
Knowing Which Questions to Ask

Rather than philosophize with John Grierson about ancient Socrates, I choose the actual: "You say there is a battle for the petty satisfactions in all socialist countries and this is also evident in Yugoslavia. How exactly are Yugoslav socialists engaged in the everlasting battle between personal interest and public interest?" I ask him.

"Yugoslavia's filmmakers have been given the freedom to discuss the limitations and failures of public management," he responds, "and they seem to be concentrating on small pettifogging discomforts."

His answer has universal application even though he forms it in the framework of film: "A weakness in Yugoslav filmmakers is that they are unable to self-criticize," he states.

This last point is proved to Grierson's displeasure during a private screening of Zagreb Film's most recent documentaries. Afterward, at a specially arranged meeting with the filmmakers, Grierson delivers his critique. He can be a hard taskmaster, but he addresses the assembled Yugoslavian filmmakers quite gently: "I think the best thing we can do to help each other, if you will permit me, in relation to the films I have seen," he begins, "is for me to make some observations and talk about technique. I will be as courteous as possible, but I will not simply be courteous because that would be no service to anyone."

The translator leisurely converts Grierson's words into Serbo-Croatian, affording me plenty of time to jot down notes.

Grierson goes on: "I will merely say that when I see, in a communist country like Yugoslavia, so much attention paid to the life of the person and to the sufferings of the person, I think you are pursuing petit-bourgeois human purposes in a petit-bourgeois aesthetic."

Grierson's "petit-bourgeois," I sense, is not referring to a specific social class. His remark has broader reach, targeting people mainly absorbed in their own materialistic pursuits and concerns.

"I have the greatest feeling that, in the pictures I have seen, you are suffering from petit-bourgeois delusions. I expect you will now take to drugs and alcohol, and pursue the personal life even more intensely. I fear the worst from the petit-bourgeois freedoms in which you are now indulging."

He names a film and asks who directed it. "Is he here?" he inquires, immediately adding: "He didn't dare come here tonight." He evaluates the film, summing up: "The first thing about any documentary film is to know what questions to ask, to know what stones to turn over, so that you can see the light hidden behind the stones. One of the most important studies that any documentary filmmaker might make is to study the technique of the research reporter as developed, for example, by the magazines *Paris Match* or *Time*."

After offering his suggestions for Yugoslav directors and film critics, he announces: "The meeting is yours."

A questioner zeroes in on Grierson's social criticism. "Which films indicated so much of the petit-bourgeois atmosphere, this self-pitying, to you?"

Grierson dissects *Morning Chronicle*, the story of a woman working in a factory morning to night. The woman has no contact with anyone at work and no one has contact with her. At home, her relationship with her husband is equally silent. The two barely speak to each another.

"Someone told that woman not to smile," says Grierson. "Who instructed the director to make an unsmiling picture? Matko the producer? Instructed to make a woman's life look miserable? I don't know who is

Tito's minister of propaganda, but I am going to report this film. It is designed to give a bad picture of Yugoslavia in foreign countries. You have created a society under communism in which nobody smiles or can smile. This is sabotage of the worst order, and you ought to be reported."

The faces of the filmmakers darken. A few in the audience squirm in their chairs. A number make notes. Is Grierson coating his words with irony to make a point? Or joking? "Sabotage of the worst order . . . ought to be reported"? He will report the film to Tito's minister of propaganda?

Taking for granted the American ideal of free speech assured by my society, I adhere to the principle that a communicator in a democratic society has the right to criticize or expose authorities without fearing censorship, blackballing, or arrest. John Grierson's scolding of the Yugoslav filmmakers for the grim view of Yugoslav life reminds me they are struggling to present the truth they perceive. I also understand that, for a good portion of his professional career, Grierson served as a propagandist for government agencies.

From the perspective of film artistry, I concur with Grierson's next comment.

"When you are dealing with everyday life, there are compensations," he states. "The major thesis of any picture can be the boredom of life. For example, the boredom of the woman with the impersonal business of going to work, symbolized by the railway tracks. That was a nice touch, symbolizing the rut she was in. But it is the duty of the filmmaker to be true to the compensations. The compensations of going to work in a factory are that you meet other women. You probably have tea together. My main point is, when you are dealing with films that go to foreign countries, the image of your film must be true to life or it will only be damaging."

Matko stands and proclaims: "This documentary earned the director two Yugoslav film prizes."

Another man stands. He, too, wants to speak. Matko introduces him as "Professor Sremec." He is Rudolf Sremec, writer of Dušan Vukotić's Oscar-winning cartoon.

Sremec commences: "I had the opportunity to talk with many film critics at the Oberhausen film festival about this very film. Their feeling was that this film was not bad publicity for Yugoslav socialism. They understood, as a kind of strength, a society that can look at things inside that country as they really are."

The filmmakers nod their heads in agreement.

"Furthermore," Sremec continues, "this film gives a true indication of the conditions caused by our too rapid industrialization. A film like this could not have been made here ten years ago. The censors would have forbid it."

"Right!" a voice rings out.

"This is why we, the filmmakers here, like this film so much," concludes Sremec. "We consider it an indication of freedom of expression."

I comprehend the elation of the men able to produce and distribute *Morning Chronicle*. The Yugoslav filmmakers are testing boundaries in their controlled state.

A dialogue ensues between Grierson and Sremec. The professor explains that the dark and silent mentality of the woman in the film is appropriate to the character and nature of the Yugoslavian people coming from the countryside into the cities. Grierson counters that the film does not bring out the silent mentality as an inevitable part of Yugoslav life within a certain section in the population.

After a lively exchange, Grierson thanks the professor for his explanation. He sums up that the film means more to Yugoslavs than to the foreigner. Later, during the general discussion, referring to *Morning Chronicle*, Grierson concedes: "The film was interesting because of the questions the director asked, but he answered them like a technician, not an artist."

Sensitive to my own version of a gray, unsmiling Yu-go-*slave*-ian existence, I decide that *Morning Chronicle* successfully portrays the downbeat lifestyle the Yugoslavs patiently tolerate. I relate to *Morning Chronicle* in a subjective way that John Grierson cannot. He is unable to access the film's levels of meaning based on Yugoslav social and cultural interaction. He never tried to live as a Yugoslav. Did he ever have to endure social alienation or isolation? To me, the one-sided dark mood of the film helps it score its point. My own life in Zagreb helps me identify with the woman, feeling why she fails to smile.

Listening to the conversation between the East Europeans and the Westerner, I recognize anew my limited grasp of the Yugoslavian culture, mindset, and lifestyle. Remaining on the surface of Yugoslav life is not my goal. I wish to travel into the country's psyche as deeply as I can. It is natural to be among the Yugoslavs and to try, as much as possible, to live within their limitations. The only way to know a lifestyle is to live it. But can I penetrate the Yugoslav mentality without acquiring the language and understanding the country's history and culture before and after both world wars? Still, my life in Zagreb has allowed me to catch a repressed people's yearning for freedoms of all types.

During this precious upbeat week assisting John Grierson, I join the film master for many meals. At one of our first dinners, he orders as soon as the waiter hands him the menu. Then we wait, and wait, for the food to arrive. Impatiently he hails the waiter and inquires. "Just a few minutes," the man says apologetically. Grierson checks his watch. Clearly "just a few minutes" belongs to the imprecise Yugoslav manner of calculating time. He waves for the waiter again. He shows his displeasure. Somehow, Grierson's irritated attitude and his complaints about the tardy service do not capture me. I am delighted that the Yugoslav slow-motion time gives me "extra time" to explore with Grierson film, art, society, and Titoism. I keep returning our talk to these topics.

"Doesn't this slow service bother you?" he asks. "How can you sit there so calmly? Americans don't like to play the waiting game."

I laugh. "This patience is new to me too," I declare. "I'm simply glad to be here with you. Besides, I've learned that the Croatians operate on South European nonchalance."

The only time concerning me at this moment is the timelessness inherent in Grierson's remarks.

As the wait drags on, I say: "Compared to my busy life in America, I feel as if I'm in a rest home here. Am I so used to the speed and turmoil of my country that I cannot live without it?" When Grierson does not respond, I add: "I'm beginning to feel dulled. I'm not inspired, excited, or stimulated by anything in this place. Is it wrong to look outside yourself for inspiration and stimulation?"

Grierson replies in his sometimes indirect style, forcing me to ponder his statements. "The Yugoslavs are a happy people. There are no great disturbances."

"Maybe you'll have to make a disturbance to get us our food!"

He laughs and theatrically shakes his fist in the air, in the direction of the waiter, all in fun. Immediately he returns to the point he wants to make. "Let me illustrate by speaking of art. The Yugoslavs have no extremes in their art, neither the very good nor the very bad. This is bad for art. America has much disturbance; that is good."

"Good?" I question. "Two years ago, even Dr. King complained of living in a sick and violent nation."

"Out of disturbance can come harmony."

Grierson has the wise eye able to perceive the positive in the negative. Picking up his approach, I comment: "You are right. Disturbance can bring issues to light, enabling people to find solutions. Instead of despairing at my country's disunity and downhill spiral, I should rejoice at the positive power of change gestating within chaos."

"You learn fast," he says. "Sometimes extreme conditions are required to help people seek a harmonious balance. Consider the world of art. It's very difficult to be an artist today. The temptation for money is too great. Why should you be interested in art when your belly is full and you have a good-looking girl and a nice little house? Unless you are driven mad like the Americans into another kind of explosion."

"Are you talking just of the art world or society in general?"

"It's going so crazy over there that something must happen. The most exciting situation in the art world is happening in America."

"Because of the social upheavals? Because society's mental and emotional energies affect artists and their creativity? What happens when the artist attunes with the forces connected with disorder and destruction?

"It's good for art, good for America."

We agree that "art" is an expansive pallet incorporating various forms of creativity including film, literature, dance, music, and architecture. Life is art; art is life.

"The Americans can't go on being so superficial in the midst of so much energy and violence," he responds. "They're bound to become creative. That's what art is. You need to go through a period of disturbance first."

"What about that form of art which moves through and beyond the portrayal or dramatization of earthly challenges to a higher manifestation? As in forms of old religious art and the mystical writings of saints, sages, and prophets?" I ask.

The old master is tired and declares an end to our after-dinner talk. He concludes the evening's discussion by pronouncing: "Always retain a secrecy, a privacy. This is as true in life as in art." I listen attentively.

"The most important part of any art is that which is not stated, the undertone. Michelangelo always left a rough, uncompleted section in his sculptures. The undertone, the acceptance of the inarticulate communication, is the important thing. That is the style. Style is created not by what is written, but by what is not written."

In bed this night, I contemplate Grierson's advice regarding art and secrecy. The biggest retainer of secrecy, I decide, is everyday life itself, with all its inscrutable whys and wherefores. The secret of life, concealing the answer to the question of life's intention, is waiting to be unearthed by everyone seeking to know the eternal truths. A long road of discovery looms ahead.

The next day, Grierson asks to see my writings.

"Really?" I exclaim.

"Why not?"

From the writing samples I tucked into my suitcase before flying, I select several articles prepared for my Stanford journalism classes. That evening, in his room, I hand over the articles.

"Plenty of time this week," he says, flipping through the pages. "I'll read them."

The following morning Grierson announces grandly, "I have read every paper! Good work!" He pats me on the shoulder as if I am a colleague on one of his projects. "You're making people think. When people think, they tend to speak up more for their rights. Good work."

Grierson comments that my pen has led me onto the path of social service. His observation comforts me. It has bothered me that, for all my noble thoughts and ideals of equality, fairness, justice, and freedom, I was not one of the brave and motivated students or other high-minded citizens who risked their lives for the civil rights fight and, later on at Stanford, I did not put on my walking shoes to march for peace. I feel called to work for the betterment of society, yet I do not act on this call. I complain, but do not campaign. Grierson has confirmed that my pen is the tool of my service and has already brought me into the arena of social change.

He asks to hold onto my article, "Talk Radio in America," explaining: "Talk Radio has not hit England. Maybe I can do something with it."

He likes Talk Radio because it encourages citizens to discuss alternative opinions not usually represented in mainstream media, and can challenge the media to go public on certain topics. He is alert for ways to make the governance of society more transparent. He understands the power of effective mass communication to raise awareness, enrich the lives of people, and improve society. These are goals of the National Film Board of Canada he established. A government agency, the NFB produces and distributes films "to interpret Canada to Canadians and to other nations."[22]

"Coincidentally" enough, while at Stanford I wrote a paper on the National Film Board of Canada. Who better to vet the unpublished draft of "The Government as Filmmaker" than the inspirer-founder of the NFB himself?

---

[22] In the Massey Report to the Canadian Parliament in 1949, the NFB described its duties and functions as: "to explain and illuminate the common objectives of the people . . . to stimulate and strengthen the processes of representative government . . . to reinforce a sense of community . . . to emphasize not only the privileges but the responsibilities of a free society."

After reading the paper, Grierson commands: "You have to get this into print!"

He returns the paper with his editorial comments and suggestions written in black ballpoint. The paper is no exposé, but it does disclose that the National Film Board of Canada, a government agency under continuous government supervision, suffers from political interference. I describe three NFB films that ran into government opposition; they were either never released or were frozen for varying periods. My insider source was John Kemeny, editor-writer-director-producer at the National Film Board.

After Kemeny guest-lectured to our Stanford film class, I asked him for an interview. His talk sparked in me a theme for an upcoming film paper. Also, Kemeny came from Hungary. True, the area in the Hungarian part of the Austro-Hungarian Empire where my paternal grandparents were born experienced border changes in the twentieth century, finally winding up in Ukraine. At the time I met Kemeny, I located their birth villages in Hungary, where the Hungarian language was spoken when my grandparents were born. My grandmother replied, when asked, "I am Hungarian." And my father referred to his "Hungarian roots." My search to know the significance of life keeps bringing me unconsciously—and coincidentally?—into contact in some way with my Central European heritage.

Born in Budapest, John Kemeny began his career in film distribution and promotion in his native Hungary. One year after the Hungarian uprising in 1956, he emigrated to Canada. By 1958, he was employed as a film editor at the prestigious National Film Board. Occasionally he lectured at Stanford.

During our conversation, in a quiet, sunlit corner on the Stanford campus, Kemeny spoke frankly of the difficulties of making critical films for a government agency. He had to battle the Canadian government for release of the politically touchy film *Bethune, héros de notre temps* (Bethune, Hero of our Time). The hour-long biographical documentary, made in 1964 with Kemeny as co-writer-producer-editor and Donald Brittain as director, recounted the story of the visionary Canadian doctor. Norman Bethune was an early proponent of universal health care.

Born in Ontario in 1890, Norman Bethune dedicated his life to carrying out his humanitarian and democratic medical ideals. During World War I, he interrupted his medical studies to serve as a stretcher-bearer for the Canadian Army in France. In the late 1920s, as an established doctor, he specialized in thoracic surgery and introduced many innovations into the field.

During the economic depression of the 1930s, increasingly engaged with the socioeconomic aspects of disease, Bethune formed the Montreal Group for the Security of People's Health. The clinic, advocating that the main duty of medical doctors is to secure and sustain the health of all citizens, gave free medical treatment to people who had no funds for care.

Bethune's ideals are expressed in his words: "Medicine, as we are practicing it, is a luxury trade. We are selling bread at the price of jewels. . . . Let us take the profit, the private economic profit, out of medicine, and purify our profession of rapacious individualism. . . . Let us say to the people not 'How much have you got?' but 'How best can we serve you?'"[23]

Seeing the link between poverty and illness, Bethune realized that poor people could not be physically cured without having proper living conditions. Many doctors at the time considered his ideas of social welfare extreme. In the late 1930s, the Canadian government rejected Bethune's plan for a health system providing the same level of medical treatment for all people equally.

Bethune also became known for his services during the Spanish Civil War. In Spain, in 1936, he introduced a new method of blood transfusion and mobile blood banks, enabling the wounded to receive care immediately, in the field of action, drastically reducing fatalities. He spent the last two years of his life in China as a medical advisor, teacher, and surgeon. "Communist" was rubber-stamped onto his name.

---

[23] www.encyclopedia.thefreedictionary.com/Norman+Bethune#cite_note-15

In the 1960s, Norman Bethune was a risky figure to feature in a government-sponsored documentary. After the one-hour biopic aired on Canadian TV, the government instituted a distribution freeze. It was reported, Kemeny told me, that the government decided it was unsound policy to circulate a film stating so unequivocally that Canada had communists in her midst. "But I underplayed the political aspect and stressed Bethune's humanitarian work," he said.

Governments know very well the discrediting labels to paste onto those independent thinkers who question, and may seem to threaten, the Establishment. Persons who might possibly endanger the status quo of the ruling system may be ridiculed, resisted, and hushed. It took John Kemeny six months of haranguing to get the objections to his Norman Bethune film withdrawn. The freeze lifted, the film went on to become a success in Canada and the US.

Kemeny's newest worry, he told me, is government interference in the "Challenge for Change" series. CFC is a Film Board project using film as a weapon in the war on poverty and other challenging social conditions in Canada. Several of the CFC films outspokenly criticize the government's approach to problems of the native peoples of Canada, who are as deprived and isolated from mainstream Canadian society as their counterparts in the US. For more than one century, government policy required indigenous Canadians to lose their cultural identity and routinely subjected them to abuse.[24]

My paper mentions the film *Indian Dialogue*, in which Canadian native peoples discuss their concern for the loss of their traditional culture. They question those values of white people that presume that natives will change to the majority, white lifestyle. The article divulges that the then-Minister of Indian Affairs asked Kemeny to rephrase the

---

[24] In 2008, Canada instituted a truth and reconciliation commission to examine government policy, from the nineteenth century to the 1970s, that had required Canada's indigenous peoples to assimilate. Source: "Canada hears pain and Indian abuse" by Rob Gillies, Associated Press, Toronto, reprinted in the *Philadelphia Inquirer*, Philadelphia, June 2008.

CFC films to make a better case for the government. Kemeny refused. The Deputy Minister complained that the films "endangered the very basis of Canadian social structure." The Minister wanted to see, in the future, the unfinished versions of all films on native peoples and to have final editing rights. Kemeny told him this was "not proper."

Kemeny admitted to me, as I quote him in my article: "There is an unwritten policy of self-censorship at the Board, but we try to be objective about our work. Therefore, our Indian films will remain our edited versions."

While encouraging me to publish "The Government as Film-maker," John Grierson suspects that the same man who gave me the material about the suppressed films will try to stop the paper's publication.

"Kemeny's reaction will provide a test case for the relationship between the filmmaker and the government authority," declares Grierson. "He may feel that publicity can endanger some of the gains he's already made with his films attacking government policy toward native peoples."

14

Carrying Out Self-Examination

Although we are separated by a large gap in age as well as life experiences and accomplishments, John Grierson and I share a harmonious communion. Merely through his presence he transmits an invigorating influence. Age wrinkles his skin, and his body demands frequent rest, but the dynamic energy of his penetrating intellect belies he is entering his seventh decade of life. He exemplifies that one does not have to grow old in attitude. He also exhibits qualities, like stubbornness and impatience, associated with people who act as if they know better than others, as perhaps they do in certain areas.

During one of our dinners of the typical Yugoslav fare, Grierson amazes me by stating: "The most astounding revolution in my lifetime has been the revolution in food. There is a great variety of foods now, especially in America. There is a rich world of cooking. Horizons have been extended."

In pinpointing "the most astounding revolution" in his lifetime, Grierson disregards the revolutions in transport and communications and the many scientific firsts of the twentieth century. We are sitting in a socialist country and he does not refer to the Russian Revolution of 1917, which deposed the Tsarist autocracy and led to the creation of the communist USSR in 1922, radically changing the politics of Eastern

Europe and the world. He does refer to the student revolution of the past May in France.

"The revolution in France right now is against the feudal bureaucracy of the professors," he begins. "Professors, bureaucrats, and all other people who need their jobs are dangerous. They are the real parasites. When you get a world caught up with the bourgeois thing, it is a weak world because people cannot stand up to change. They cannot throw off their jobs."

I understand what he means, remembering that I could not refuse recording the TV commercial for the bug killer. In any system, one conforms and gets ostensibly rewarded, or dissents and risks getting beaten down. If workers fear losing their jobs, they may not dare ask for higher pay or better benefits. Most of those protesting and demonstrating for change in 1968 are the young, mainly students. They have no jobs they need to keep. Even when employed, young workers usually accept lower wages and do not speak up when they have grievances. They do as they are told. But what if masses of older people had no jobs, and circumstances prevented them from getting jobs? Would massive unemployment strengthen the unemployed mass to stand up to change?

Grierson returns the talk to food. He loves to cook. Looking at his plate, he comments wryly, "The revolution has not reached Yugoslavia."

Chuckling, I ply Grierson with tales of my Yugoslav diet. He listens attentively, sharing my insatiable interest in what people think and how they live. A narration of my food shopping excursions to the state-run grocery store greatly amuses him.

I describe my frustrating attempt to buy a one-day's supply of cheese. "The grocer sliced and kept on slicing. The man was very engrossed in the slicing. He never once glanced up. 'Stop,' I said. He went on. 'Stop, stop!' I repeated. He kept on slicing. I waved my hands near his face. I shouted 'Enough!' Finito!' He totally ignored me! I had to pound feverishly on the counter to halt his endless slicing!"

Grierson laughs heartily.

"Am I wrong to suspect a commercial motive for his deafness to my cries? Am I imagining he was out to get my money, pegging me as a rich American?"

Grierson's inquiry into where I live in Zagreb brings forth the account of my efforts to find a proper place. Grierson mentions *Housing Problems*, a documentary made in 1935 by young filmmakers he trained.

In *Housing Problems*, slum dwellers in their poor living quarters relate their housing troubles directly to the camera lens, a new method of filming.[25] Filming ordinary people in actual activities sought to represent unbiased realism. *Housing Problems* was one of the first documentaries to touch upon social conscience and citizenship.

Grierson extols the power of film to serve a larger objective beyond filmmaking. Film can focus attention on vital social issues, wake people up, set them thinking. Grierson voices the concern that society has grown too complex for citizens to understand; citizen participation in government has become perfunctory, apathetic, meaningless, and often nonexistent.

"What about all the engaged young people nowadays?" I ask him.

But Grierson is intent on conveying the thesis that film can involve citizens in their government with the same excitement generated by the popular press, simplifying and dramatizing public affairs.

Over the following days, encouraged by the importance Grierson attributes to questioning, I pose him many queries on film, work, and society. During one conversation, he shows he is no passive spirit content to let the questioning remain one-sided. He startles me and alters the atmosphere by asking: "Have you been married?"

I stay silent.

Grierson nods his head and comments: "I thought the answer is 'Yes.' Tell me," he coaxes in a gentle tone.

Our camaraderie deepens as Grierson transforms from the PhD sociologist-filmmaker into a psychologist. His investigative but kind

---

[25] Two decades later, this new method of filming would be called *cinéma vérité*, "cinema truth"—following real things happening in real time.

approach breaks through my reluctance to take up a sore subject. I am victim to the conditioning of the time associating a tinge of shame to the status "divorced." After knowing each other but a few months, I said "Yes" to Walter Green's proposal to elope. That "Yes" emerged as quickly as I later accepted my Stanford mentor's film job offer. Probably Yugoslavia "had to be," just as the marriage to Walter during my senior year at Barnard?

To be sure, Walter and I enjoyed a warm union of our equally inquisitive minds. After fireworks sparked between us in a Columbia University History of Theater course, we soared deliriously in love, at least as I understood "love" at age twenty-one. Had a force higher than human love led me into that college marriage? Though short-lived, it irrevocably changed my surname from *Eisner*, "made of iron," which brought up in me a strong but hard, cold, metallic feeling. The name "Green" bubbled in me the energy of spring and seeds bursting into life. Marrying Walter, I embraced my new last name as "more me." Sometimes I speculate how my Hungarian paternal grandfather came to carry a name of Germanic origin. Probably the name "Eisner" aided him. He needed to be as strong as iron when, as a teenager, he left his home country and culture to forge a life for himself as a stranger alone in a foreign land.

"Green suits you," John Grierson decides. He says my marriage name is "prophetic," a big clue to my life's purpose. Would Stern have concurred "no coincidence" at hearing the name change from Iron to Green? Rather than allowing me to catch my breath after tackling a topic I prefer to avoid, Grierson presses his advantage. Now he inquires: "What bloke are you running away from?"

Indeed, I had left a man behind at Stanford. Our friendship lacked future since his parents disapproved of me. Not only was I six years older than their adored son, I was divorced. When he told me their serious concerns, and expressed his own worry that I would "go gray" before him, I felt "old" and unfit. I began wrapping a colorful hair band around my head to try and look younger. Shortly after I arrived in Zagreb, minus hair bands, he slept with my best Stanford girlfriend, as she dutifully wrote to me with her usual candor. So, yes, Mr. Grierson, perhaps my departure for Yugoslavia was in part, though unconsciously, motivated by a wish to avoid heartbreak.

Grierson declares he cannot see me getting married for quite a while "unless you meet someone stupendous. A man doesn't have much to offer you except sex."

His ability to sense a past marriage and a current bloke does not surprise me. John Grierson's insight into human nature helped him become a trendsetter in the use of film for social purpose. The documentary film movement, he wrote in one of his many magazine articles, "was from the beginning an adventure in public observation."[26]

Our budding friendship intensifies as Grierson probes my psyche further: "What do you consider the most significant events of your life?" He wants to know less about my pleasures than the pains, challenges, and problems I have faced. I confide many personal details.

A skilled interviewer, Grierson poses a sequence of probing queries that reveal his understanding of human psychology. His blunt directness contrasts with his occasional indirectness. "What else are you running away from?" he asks.

Again I do not respond immediately. I take the time to think before answering, another fruit of my forced slowing down in Yugoslavia. My unsupportive Stanford boyfriend comes to mind. No, despite the predictable dead end of that relationship, I had not consciously sought an overseas job to distance myself from the people and the country I love. "Run away?" Never had I entertained such a scenario. On the contrary, Zagreb Film had run toward me, offering a unique educational opportunity. I left my American life behind only temporarily.

Grierson patiently waits for my answer. My words emerge slowly. "I . . . don't . . . think . . . I am . . . running away . . . from anything," I manage to articulate. "Not from the Stanford bloke, and not even from my esteemed if troubled country. Or . . . am I?"

---

[26] *Grierson on Documentary*, Edited and compiled by Forsyth Hardy, Faber and Faber, London, 1966, p. 18, from the Introduction, quoting an article of John Grierson's in the *Fortnightly Review*, August 1939.

"Are you?"

"Am I?"

Grierson smiles broadly. "I can wait for your answer," he says, nonchalantly glancing through a magazine. He ignores me, as if alone in his hotel room. Prickled by his sudden if feigned indifference, I can retreat, but I am ashamed to leave the room without giving any reply. I can regain Grierson's attention simply by avowing: "I maintain my conviction that I am not running away from anything in America," yet I cannot avoid noticing my rush of thoughts.

Images good and bad, sad and happy, race to me, hang on to me, pull at me. The face of the murdered Martin Luther King appears. So do the faces of the assassinated Kennedy brothers, and other images calling up my life in America. Sitting in Zagreb with the extraordinary John Grierson, I acknowledge to myself that my inborn American idealism and optimism have become casualties of the tumultuous disorder in my homeland.

"I am ready to confess," I announce. "I admit it, I am discouraged at what I view as my country's downhill spiraling."

The abrupt exit of Dr. King, I relate, caused me to question the murder of yet another leader trying to forge social change. My Stanford friends and I discussed the subsequent violence, rioting, burning, and looting; the loss of hope; the departure of young people to Canada and other countries.

"Late in this period the Zagreb Film contract arrived and I signed it."

Grierson nods victoriously. He has compelled me to admit something essential to myself. Circumstances had formed to extract me from America's unsettling atmosphere for a while, and they met with an unstated wish inside me.

"Taking a summer job in a foreign country simply offered me a summer break from the turmoil. It was not a 'running away,'" I insist.

Grierson listens attentively.

"Rather," I say, asking myself for the first time, "to where am I running, or traveling, and why?"

With Grierson I can speak freely, as through my pen to my log-book.

"In my childhood, I asked almost incessantly, 'Why? Why is this? Why is that?' My frequent 'Why?' so exasperated my father that he perfected an automatic reply: 'Y is a crooked letter.'"

"Knowledge increases one's capacity to see more," Grierson pronounces.

"I continued my why-asking, if not any longer to my father, then to school teachers and to well-informed and wise persons."

Grierson smiles, pleased with the intended compliment. "My tendency to question is a long-held trait."

"Good for communication work," he remarks. "Sometimes the questions are more important than the answers. Questions make you more aware of what you want to know."

"Behind all my questioning there burns a larger, plaguing question. As a child I wondered, 'Where? Where would I be if I were not here?'"

"And?"

"By 'where,' I did not mean a place in the world," I go on. "I kept asking myself: 'Where would I be if I were not alive?'"

Grierson tells me he has no answer to this question; each of us has to find out the existential answers for ourself.

Eventually Grierson inquires: "What do you want to do with your talents?"

"I am not sure," I admit. "I think my future intertwines with my writing. Since I was six years old, when I wrote my first poem, I wanted to be a writer. I have always been writing and asking, 'Why?'"

Grierson cautions me about timing. "You are twenty-nine," he states, as if comparing me with Methuselah. "By twenty-five, a woman should know her path in life. Men have until thirty."

His response jabs at my self-confidence. He can hit below the belt, this founding father of the documentary film. He challenges me to know myself better. Suddenly I feel less worthy, not up to my usual mark. Yet he does not make me feel old and unfit; he excites my sense of adventure about what lies ahead. For all my successes thus far—my achievements on the academic and extracurricular fronts, as well as on the job—I am lagging behind at knowing myself. Strangely, I do not ask Grierson to clarify the age guidelines he mentioned in his self-certain manner. Perhaps I am not ready to hear his explanation, yet our talks help me realize that to be of value as a communicator, I have to know myself better, more deeply. I understand that to recognize my path, I have to learn to identify and reduce my imperfections, while also learning to expand my humane qualities such as to be loving and caring.

John Grierson assists my arrival at more clarity. Like Stern, Grierson poses questions penetrating my mind and my heart. He, too, zooms in on the purpose of my stay in Yugoslavia by asking: "Why did you come here?"

I am unable to answer with the absolute certitude Grierson expects from a woman four years over his timetable for a female to know her life's path. I hedge his question: "Is not an experience in and of itself important?" Then comes up a question long occupying me: "Does everything happen for a purpose?"

Grierson does not give one of his characteristically self-assured replies; this is another answer I have to discover on my own.

"The Yugoslavs will be damn stupid if they don't exploit you," he sums up during one of our last conversations. "You can be valuable to them in many ways. At the same time," he adds, "a year at the Studio can be valuable to you too."

"Please elaborate."

"You can learn film production, meet all the international film people who pass through here, and make good contacts. However," he cautions, "Yugoslavia is a man's world. Women work very hard, but not at the top."

"In documentary filmmaking, the gender of the filmmaker does not matter," I say.

"In Yugoslavia, it is harder for a woman to get a creative chance," declares Grierson.

Again it is obvious that the country's socialistic ideal of equality has not transformed from theory into practice. The underdog position of women signals this lack. Despite Yugoslavia's proclaimed legal and representative gender equality, with unrestricted access to education and employment, men hold the scepter in the family, the workplace, and in the Party leadership.

"An old mentality is hard to change, but change is what Yugoslavia is about, isn't it?" I ask John Grierson on his last day in Zagreb.

A quizzical look is his answer, followed by his assertion: "If I were still working in film, I would hire you on the spot." We embrace in a warm farewell.

"Be wise where you invest your energies," he advises.

15
Glimpsing the Larger Perspective

lthough a female writer in male-dominated Zagreb Film, I am a welcome figure at the Studio; an American writer is a rare species here. When Matko asks my signature for the contract's extension, I recollect John Grierson's advice and agree to stay for another three months. Despite dragging myself through the after-work hours as if enduring a burden or serving a punishment, I continue to sense that the experience as a whole fits into a larger scheme for my life. Since my very young years, a gut feeling has been telling me that every experience is leading me somewhere quite specified. To date, this message remains based on feeling, not fact. For all his sagacity, Grierson could not shed any light on this question for me.

Always I have felt that life contains a profound inner meaning, but not yet have I discovered what that meaning could be. Not through religion, not through philosophy, not through work, and not even through the love of family and friends, have I uncovered why I was born. I learned about God in the synagogue but lacked attunement with the divine depths of Judaism. My family celebrated the Jewish holidays, but also the nonreligious aspects of Christmas and Easter. Perhaps, after the war, the family felt a pressure to assimilate somewhat into the predominantly Christian society. At any rate, my sister Bonnie and I hung up our empty stockings on Christmas Eve and the next morning excitedly retrieved them filled with small presents and sweets. We never had a Christmas tree, but we exchanged Christmas gifts; on Easter, we colored eggs and received from our parents chocolate bunnies and new Easter outfits.

So, for various reasons, I grew up knowing Judaism—and Christianity—only externally, and considered myself a secular person. Being raised in a Jewish family that practiced a nondogmatic and "hybrid" religion probably opened my mind to respect other religions. But I still have the question: Is there really, as some people attest, a perfect, omnipotent, omniscient incorporeal "Being" who is the originator and ruler of the manifested universe? If so, does such a Being influence human society as well as each person's individual life?

In Zagreb, I have time to ponder life's import and to contemplate my daily experiences. Always I search for meaning. Circumstances may provoke me to utter: "Coincidence?" Doggedly I ask myself: *Is there a Greater Power guiding me?* Frequently I remember my occasional sensation of blessed good luck. My intuition keeps hinting that there is more to life than my materialistic upbringing suggested.

At a very young age I started to wonder: *What is our purpose for being?* Not yet have I answered this crucial question. And, as John Grierson so mercilessly pointed out, I am already twenty-nine! The material shortcomings of Tito's Yu-go-*slave*-ia mirror my own shortcomings. My greatest lack, I realize, is not yet knowing the hidden truths of existence. Minus the answers to life's most important questions, how can I succeed in reaching my life's ultimate success, whatever it may be? My experiences are surely acting as my Oracle of Delphi, but am I catching all the messages transmitted?

I do perceive, thanks to Yu-go-*slave*-ia, that I am less free in my thinking than all along I have assumed. It has become clear that my American-bred conditioning holds me tightly in its grip. Even while dealing with the immediate challenges of Yugoslavian life, I project myself into the future. I mull over what doors the Zagreb Film job might open for me professionally. At other times I live in the past. This is not the past of the old Croatian capital possessing a rich cultural history tracing back one thousand years. My head dwells pretty much in my own past, caught up in thought patterns created over nearly three decades. Ambition, competition, and acquisitiveness exert a deeply rooted authority.

Social dictates bind me. I am noticing my slavery to social norms. For instance, I am programmed to believe that my value as a human being increases in accord with the quantity and quality of my official papers, such as my academic degrees and assorted awards, diplomas, and certificates. But the papers I earned in America denote pretty much nothing to most of the people around me in Yugoslavia. I start doubting the validity of this ingrained social standard.

Besides the enhancement conferred by official papers, I have been taught that my human value escalates according to what I wear, own, drive, and even eat. In Zagreb, it strikes me that judging a person by outer appearance is a habit I acquired while growing up. Society projects material guidelines that can indicate one's wealth and success. Clothing and shoes, bags and accessories, and other accouterments, especially those with brand names connected to high prices and social superiority, help define one's human identity.

My minidress clash with the cursing old woman tugs at me. The incident pesters me to rethink my tendency to follow the latest New York or California fashion trends. My wanting to abide by the principle, "When in Zagreb, do as the Zagrebians do," forces me to acknowledge that, at home, I allow myself to obey fashion commands telling me how to look and what to wear, what is "in" and what is "not with it."

During my Barnard years, however, I had become free from dress codes. In that period, many a conflict arose with my parents because they disliked my "unconventional" clothing. I defended my offbeat style by retorting, "Clothing is only an outer covering. It is who I am that matters." (Not that I knew then who that "I" truly was.) My reasoning fell on my parents' blocked ears. By the time I graduated from college, I found that to participate optimally in the work world I had to conform a bit to mainstream fashion. So my parents' thinking was not wholly incorrect; it was their combative approach to my developing ideas that proved faulty. Now, having lugged a suitcase of Fifth Avenue outfits to Zagreb, I know that fashion decrees influence me.

Emancipating myself from fashion directives will let me take, unwittingly, a tiny but conscious step along the road toward knowing my truest me. As I intuited in my college days, how I look cannot be equated with who I am. But "who am I?" remains a burning question.

I vent my thoughts to John Grierson in letters I send him after he leaves Zagreb, even as I wonder whether "the watchers" are also reading our correspondence. Grierson's responses help me feel less alone. He puts my experiential findings into a larger perspective. In one of his letters to me, he asks: "How is your Yugoslav odyssey going?"

"Ah, my dear doctor," I reply, "the life and working practices here are easy-going and lackadaisical if you are Yugoslavian. If you are American, you work hard. It is not official white slavery, for I am here voluntarily. Every week I get my thirty-two dollars worth of dinars. The Studio cannot complain. It is getting hard currency value out of me. And I am not complaining, simply observing. The entire world, including myself, may criticize America and Americans, but everyone is very happy to get our products and our know-how."

In one letter, Grierson again expresses disappointment with the present Yugoslav documentary films: "I saw little this time in Zagreb to make me believe they were devoting themselves very deeply to that art of theirs. Maybe I had a bad sample of films. Anyway, I am back with the notion that if that's the violin, it just doesn't play very well." He was referring to the Yugoslav documentary *Homage to Hands*, the story of a violinmaker.

I write him: "They seem curiously unambitious. The political system does not seem to inspire them. Even my chief at the Studio, one of the most Westernized Yugoslavs, lives every day with little organization and overall perspective. When he apologizes for something he has postponed, he invariably calls himself a 'lazy Yu-go-*slave*.' Although joking, there is an element of truth in what he says. I sometimes think they have to start the morning with their plum brandy just to get up enough courage to face the rest of the day."

John Grierson confirms my thoughts on the Yugoslavian system when he states, in his characteristic handwriting: "I think of your reactions to Zagreb as an important testament, for I have not before heard the Yugoslav relative conditions made so plain. I now seem to understand Djilas a little better."

Whatever understanding about Yugoslavia I give John Grierson, it is Grierson who enables me to perceive more deeply the benefits I reap in Zagreb. He expands my awareness of my own relative conditions. He stimulates me to discern that every experience, dark or light, has its compensations. He recognizes my creative passion. I am an anomaly to his age-based-path-knowing formula, yet he awards me his endorsement.

Certainly I am flattered that the respected British documentarist compares my critique of the Yugoslav lifestyle with the sharp political acumen of Milovan Djilas. It would be easy to take Grierson's praise at face value, congratulating myself for my sprouting ability as a social critic. I have no such illusions. I am at elementary school level in the knowledge of how society is run behind the scenes by the often-secretive workings of those in power.

The cable I receive from John Kemeny of the National Film Board of Canada verifies my naiveté regarding the manipulative ways of government. His words are ominously clear: "STOP SHOWING ARTICLE." A letter follows, mysteriously implying the negative repercussions the publication of my article could have.

A state of tension exists between creative artists in East European communist countries and their governments, but in Canada? I am reminded that, despite constitutional laws on the books, free speech in any society is never fully guaranteed if the speech is directed at a reigning government. A democratically elected government supposedly operates on behalf of the citizenry, but when threatened with the communication of an inconvenient truth or truths, a democratic government may use repressive actions to restrain critical speech, free press, and public disclosure.

John Kemeny's cable of censorship stuns me. His red-light reaction to my paper's publication confirms there is some self-risk involved with criticizing or exposing any government, even innocently. My article reveals insider knowledge of the Canadian government's attempts to suppress information that may reflect poorly on Canada's image. The little-known censorial aspect of the Canadian government's role as filmmaker is the basis of my article. Considering that the NFB produces hundreds of films a year, the extent of government interference is negligible. Nevertheless, after our interview Kemeny asked for the right of approval over my final text. Perhaps, having spoken so openly, he had nervous afterthoughts?

Agreeing he could suggest factual corrections or editorial improvements, I never imagined I was extending a right of censorship. Having given Kemeny my word, I have no moral option except to withdraw the text. How ironic. Kemeny complained about the censorship of his films, and then censored my article. Grierson's forecast proved correct.

Through this incident, minor yet major to me, I gain personal experience in the operational ways of government and politics. In the Yugoslavia of 1968, the populace knows very well the clamps on its personal liberties and freedoms. Lacking the freedom to criticize government policies publicly, Yugoslavs endure the freedom from punishment that comes by practicing silence. A democratic government, I had taken for granted, allows the communicator to serve the citizenry by explaining and exposing the abuse of power of any kind. Democracy is compromised when government or business influence the media from doing its communicating job to the utmost.

The censorship of my paper on the National Film Board of Canada makes me look askance at ever involving myself professionally with the machinations of government and politics. The borders of my personal core are fanning out. I sense that there are secrets more necessary to discover than the behind-the-scenes functioning of governments. There are revelations more significant than the methods democratically elected governments use to obstruct the communication of governmental unpleasantries. There are ponderings more crucial to share through my pen than those pertaining solely to societal events of the transient present.

16

Experiencing the Soviet Invasion
of Czechoslovakia from Afar

Marking time in my Zagrebian isolation, I think about the political conventions coming up in America. Both mainstream parties will select their presidential and vice-presidential candidates for the November national election, determining the further course of the Vietnam War. America is the place of action. The power of large numbers of people demanding social change rocks my country, setting the world's direction. And here I am cut off from modern civilization in a poor Balkan nation where the society's slowness lulls my daily gait.

Whether led to Zagreb by random chance or by a Higher Intention guiding my life's travel itinerary, I am living among the Yugoslav people in the general geographic area of my family heritage. Knowing of my Hungarian background, Matko delivers a marvelous surprise. Zagreb Film will send us, in company with the admired Dušan Vukotić, on a work assignment to the major film studio in Budapest, capital of the People's Republic of Hungary. I will gain entrance to the society where everyone speaks the mother tongue of my paternal grandparents.

Before I can step behind the Iron Curtain, tanks and troops from the Soviet army and four other Warsaw Pact nations invade the Czechoslovak Socialist Republic. Zagreb Film cancels our trip to Hungary, a Soviet-satellite state.

The invasion in the morning hours on the twenty-first of August shocks the Yugoslavs. Newspaper headlines thunder with Serbo-Croatian equivalents of "Czechoslovakia Occupied!" Life tumbles into disarray. Radios appear everywhere, blasting news of the latest developments far into the night. Bulletins, sounding like wartime maneuvers, interrupt regular programming. Zagreb Radio reports that nearby Budapest is "closed up." Neighboring Romania has mobilized.

Zagreb Radio lambasts the Soviets as "imperialists," "aggressors," and more of the same. The anxiety and fear behind the name-calling exacerbates the already tense atmosphere. Matko keeps me abreast of breaking events. British newspapers, arriving one day late, fill me in on background. "Nothing's as dead as yesterday's news" does not ring true for me in the Croatian capital. I snatch up every detail of the historic moment.

In Czechoslovakia, at the beginning of 1968, a new government came into power in response to a popular wish for reforms of the repressive Czech system. Alexander Dubček received the post of First Secretary of the Communist Party of Czechoslovakia. In March, World War II military hero Ludvik Svoboda became the country's president. His name, *Svoboda*, translates from the Czech language as "freedom."

The two leaders try to usher in democratic and humane reforms that will create, in the words of Dubček, "Socialism with a human face." A thawing of the country's frozen freedoms results in the "Prague Spring." Czechoslovakia reduces press censorship and tries to restore a democratic political life. For the first time since its liberation from Nazi occupation and its subsequent entrance into the Soviet orbit, Czechoslovakia proclaims the legitimacy of basic human rights and liberties. The government initiates a program of liberalizations while the people press for reforms at a faster pace.

Before Czechoslovakia's reform impulse can spread throughout the other satellite states, the Soviet Union invades. The USSR fears that the Czech "reformist heresy" will weaken the Communist Bloc in the Cold War struggle.

Tito, and Romania's party chief, Nicolae Ceauşescu, loudly oppose the Soviet invasion. Both denounce the Brezhnev Doctrine, the Soviet foreign policy declaring that the communist countries have the right to intervene in other communist countries whose actions threaten the international communist movement.

The invasion unleashes a veiled Yugoslav worry. Might the Soviets use military action against Yugoslavia, the rebel nation that rejected Stalin's grip twenty years earlier? People animatedly discuss 1956, when the Soviets crushed the Hungarian Revolution that sought to democratize the Hungarian communist system and end Soviet domination.

Zagreb suddenly clatters as a city of rifles. As if they have never stopped being fiery Partisans at heart, citizens flourish weaponry stashed in their homes since the wartime resistance against the Nazis. Trucks and sandbags, retrieved from storage, block the runways at Zagreb Airport. About fifty thousand stranded Czech tourists get shelter, food, and medical care in Yugoslavia while deciding whether to return home.

Zagrebians swallow glass after glass of *šljivovica* as they hotly debate the targets of a possible Soviet attack. Belgrade wins top place as prime candidate; Zagreb is the runner up. Yugoslavs assure me: "Unlike the Czechs, we will fight to the end!" "We will safeguard our independence at all costs!" "We have never been occupied by the Soviets and we will not start now!" "Of all the peoples conquered by the Nazis, our Partisans under Tito fought with the most armed resistance. We will do that to defeat the Soviets too!"

The Soviet invasion of Czechoslovakia brings me closer to the mindset of war than I ever before consciously experienced. A memory surfaces.

I am a toddler in a crib, in a room not fully dark, a small light burning. There comes an eerie sound, loud and continuing. All becomes dark. I am afraid. I call for my mommy.

The frightening sound, I learned years later from my parents, was the wailing of air raid sirens carrying out practice warning drills against enemy invasion. The pitch-blackness resulted from my mother lowering the window shades and turning off the light.

This crib incident occurred during World War II. In New York City, we were far from the killing fields of Europe, Asia, and Africa. Even so, the anxieties of war reached us across the ocean. The relatively minor crib incident apparently so affected me at such a young age that its lasting impression emerged as a vivid memory years later. One can only imagine the memories haunting children who have been directly involved in wars and other forms of violence.

Applying Grierson's principle that extreme conditions help people seek harmonious balance, the extreme human behavior of war represents a poor path toward societal advancement. Social equilibrium achieved through conflict, calamity, and killing is usually fleeting, while the suffering and trauma caused by violence remains for generations.

To the relief of all Yugoslavs in 1968, the Soviets did not invade Yugoslavia. Not then, not ever, did the USSR attempt a military intervention in Yugoslavia of the kind that reversed the Czechoslovakian reforms or put down the Hungarian Revolution.

Three weeks after the Soviet invasion of Czechoslovakia, I attend an international festival of student theater. In a building of the University of Zagreb, escaped Czech students perform a medieval miracle play using Christian mysticism to depict the passions and political struggles of the Prague Spring. In the aftermath of the Soviet invasion, the Christ figure crucified on stage symbolizes Czechoslovakia herself.

At the play's end, the audience erupts in energetic applause in a pulsating rhythm. People rise to their feet, visibly stirred. "Dubček! Svoboda! Dubček! Svoboda!" they chant. A powerful emotional outburst charges the hall. Some people weep openly.

A man's voice pierces through the din with song. Great fervor infuses his singing. The audience joins in. I recognize the "Internationale," the socialist anthem calling for workers to stand up and group together for their rights. If workers do not have rights, says the song, they have nothing. The audience sings for freedom to be enjoyed by all. Following the lead of the student actors on stage, audience members sing with their left hands raised in clenched fist salutes. Some people hold their clenched fists over their hearts.

The explosive theatrical event lifts everyone to an elevated space. I, too, imagine a society where all human beings will enjoy the freedom and justice and unity the students demand. Linked in spontaneous camaraderie by the mutual wish for political and intellectual freedom, the Yugoslav and the Czech students convey the message that all human beings deserve the same basic human rights. It is exactly as Milovan Djilas maintains: The people are not against the goal of socialism. They are against the use of totalitarian means to manifest socialism.

Personal discovery lets me know, better than any book or lecturer or film, how Tito's Third Way ideology translates into practice. Yet I do note how Titoism describes itself in its books. *Tito*, by the leader's official biographer, Vladimir Dedijer, quotes Tito speaking in 1952 with a delegation of the Socialist Party of India: "In Yugoslavia the man means everything. Our aim is to create, as early as possible and in an utmost humane way, a better life for our people, for all individuals and for the whole community."[27]

Dedijer, a Partisan fighter and close ally of Tito during the anti-Nazi struggle, sums up the Yugoslav attitude: "It is the attitude of a people striving in its own way to build a society in which there will be no exploitation of man by man," he says. That is an attitude "in which individuals will be freed of the fetters of the state [and] . . . fully enjoy all economic, social, and political freedoms."[28]

In socialist Yu-go-*slave*-ia, I neither witness nor experience the "better life" Dedijer mentioned. Nor did he. The sole member of the Communist Party of Yugoslavia to agree with Milovan Djilas about the emergence of

---

[27] *Tito*, by Vladimir Dedijer, Simon and Schuster, New York, 1952. Reprint, Arno Press, New York, 1972, p. 427.

[28] Ibid, p. 436

a "New Class," he was jailed. After a trial closed to both the press and the public, he received a suspended prison sentence. His branding as a dissident effectively blocked his further life in Yugoslavia.

In 1957, the journalist Elie Abel filed a story from Belgrade that began: "Recant or starve: that is the ultimatum served on Vladimir Dedijer by the Tito regime in Yugoslavia. Unlike his friend Milovan Djilas, now serving a three-year prison sentence, Vladimir Dedijer is a free man. He is free, but he may not work to support his wife and five children. He is free, but he may not travel out of the country. He is free, but he may not publish any of his writings, however nonpolitical, inside Yugoslavia. He is free, but his old friends are warned to shun his company."[29]

In 1959, Yugoslav authorities granted Dedijer a passport, and he and his family were allowed to leave the country.

After my months in Yu-go-*slave*-ia, although never locked literally behind iron prison bars like Dedijer and Djilas, or the cartoon character in *Elegy*, I experience "freedom" no longer as merely an intellectual abstraction. Freedom is a feeling. I can define the word "freedom" by consulting a dictionary, but how to describe in words what it means to be "free"? How to describe the *feeling* of freedom?

Perhaps the feeling of freedom might be compared to the lack of restrictions and attachments one may experience standing on a mountain. During a visit in my late teen years to the high-altitude ski area of Zermatt in Switzerland, over which the imposing Matterhorn mountain looms, first I gazed wondrously below at Earth's landscape in the far distance; then I scanned the whiteness of shimmering snow all around; and finally I looked up, at the mighty Matterhorn soaring toward an endless sky. The panorama of white and light expanded me to the outermost frontier of the universe and ascended me to gravity-free inner heights.

In Yu-go-*slave*-ia I feel, on the contrary, a lack of freedom. This lack constricts my thinking and being. The totalitarian system continually

---

[29] From the memorial resolution written by Dr. Henry Breitrose for Elie Abel, who taught journalism in the Department of Communication at Stanford University and was the Zagreb correspondent for the *New York Times*.

helps me see that I take my American freedoms and liberties for granted, just like my breathing. In Tito's society, I figuratively gasp from a shortness of breath.

Zagreb gives me an experiential taste of the futuristic society portrayed in the 1949 novel *Nineteen Eighty-Four*. George Orwell's classic satire portrays an imagined totalitarian regime in England. The character "Big Brother" symbolizes an authoritarian set-up in human form. Big Brother is Orwell's epithet for a dictator of centralized, absolute power. Faceless and invisible, everywhere present, Big Brother heads a government that closely monitors citizens.

In 1968, in Yu-go-*slave*-ia, the totalitarian Boss of the Yugoslav state has an identifiable face bearing the features of Josip Broz Tito. Portraits of Tito, smartly attired in military uniforms or double-breasted suits, hang in offices, banks, and shops. "The Leader" is ubiquitous. One day, the strong photo image unexpectedly takes on a living presence for me.

Walking in Zagreb, I come upon a mass of people crowding the sidewalk as if in wait for something. The road is devoid of traffic. Excitement enlivens the air, a perceptible change from the usual sleepiness. Once the highly charged Soviet-invasion scare passed, Zagreb's torpor reasserted itself. Today a dynamic energy ignites the gathered citizens I encounter. Emotional lightning fires the multitude when a shiny black limousine comes into view. Slowly the limousine drives down the street, motoring leisurely past the waiting people. All eyes rivet on the vehicle. As if on cue, the people wave the Yugoslav flags clasped in their hands. A man sitting in the car with a woman waves back.

"Tito! Tito!" shout the people, continuing to flutter the flags energetically. "Tito! Tito!" they roar. They seem genuinely ecstatic. The outpouring appears spontaneous.

"Tito! Tito!"

Perhaps those in the assemblage forget that Tito suppressed internal opposition by authorizing espionage and assassinations by the secret police. Possibly the politically motivated show trials, jailings, and executions of dissenters slip their collective memory. Disgruntlements about the past, or present dissatisfactions, as with the glaring scarcity of consumer goods, do not prevent those in the crowd from waving their flags with unbridled enthusiasm.

"Tito! Tito!"

Some people use their hands as flags, waving nonstop as if their lives depend on it. For all the flaws of the Yugoslav political experiment, Tito remains the esteemed Marshal of Yugoslavia, the Commander-in-Chief-superhuman hero of the Partisan forces who led the wartime resistance against the Axis forces. He is the larger-than-life President of Socialist Yugoslavia and President of the League of Communists of Yugoslavia. He is the mythic warrior who not only successfully led the country through a national liberation struggle and a socialist revolution, but who protected the Yugoslav identity by rejecting Stalin and Soviet-style socialism.

Josip Broz Tito is the masterly statesman who acts independently both of Moscow and Washington, managing to receive Western military and economic aid while refusing to become subservient. Maybe the flag wavers are, like Svetlana, still super proud that Tito, on an official visit to the US in 1963, was the last foreign head of state to see President John F. Kennedy alive.

"Tito has given our small but resolute country a unique image in the world community," Svetlana had declared. "He gives us an idea of who we want to be. Although he is called a dictator, most of us believe that our country, having so many national and ethnic groups living together, needs a strong leader like him. He is a dictator, but benevolent."

The people on the sidewalk burst with excitement, thrilled at glimpsing the benevolent dictator in person. Tito has arrived in town with his wife Jovanka to open the International Grand Fair, where Yugoslav products are exhibited for businesspeople East and West. The biannual event plays an important role in the economic life of Zagreb, Yugoslavia's second largest city and a chief economic center.

Standing on the sidewalk, I observe the people's flamboyant behavior. They wave and wave. I have to wonder: Is the Yugoslav ruler so beloved, or am I watching a government-staged event? Does not the citizens' exuberance also reflect the state's ideological power as symbolized by the charismatic Tito?

No political protest is allowed here. Only a few courageous citizens stand up publicly to the one-party line, and they pay a hefty price. Who on this street in Zagreb would dare hold aloft a placard expressing disapproval with government policies? Who in the crowd would publicly risk criticizing the government or its president? The flag-waving event underscores a basic human freedom unavailable to the Yugoslavs.

Whether natural or orchestrated, the spirited demonstration hailing Tito is impressive. Even I, the sole nonwaver in the crowd, can feel the dynamic magnetism of "The Leader."

17
Learning from Muhammad Ali and Malcolm X

My brief encounter with Tito from a distance, and with his cheering citizens nearby, once more accentuates the many enigmas of the Yugoslav society I cannot fathom. Concurrently, I sense there is much the Yugoslavs themselves do not understand about their own society. The phrase "make society understandable to people," the mission of John Grierson, rings in my ears.

Also still ringing is the impassioned fervor of the runaway Czech students crying out for their country's democracy and freedom. I mull over the emotional theatrical production that dramatized Czechoslovakia's political predicament. Singing the "Internationale," the Czech and Yugoslav students had joined forces in an East European version of "We Shall Overcome," the protest song of the American Civil Rights Movement. Overt racism in America is now unacceptable, but discrimination based on skin color continues. Having suffered my own experiences of prejudicial narrow-mindedness, I share Martin Luther King's dream of a nation where people will be judged by the content of their character. That dream symbolizes the dream of all minority peoples. Despite our skin tint, religion, gender, or any other distinguishing feature, we all dream of enjoying equal human rights and freedoms.

During one of my Zagrebian reflections, I recall a day that brought me closer to American black activism.

I am strolling on Fifth Avenue in Midtown Manhattan, admiring items for sale in the various clothing stores. Deciding to shut my window-shopping eyes for the day, impulsively I turn to walk along West 55th Street. I pass an art gallery packed with chattering people holding drinks. My curiosity piques. I stop to read a press release taped to the gallery window.

The Van Bovenkamp Gallerie is presenting, on this very date, the fifth of March, and at this very hour, a bronze sculpture titled "Ode to Cassius Clay." The gallery owner, the Dutch sculptor Hans van de Bovenkamp, created the artwork to portray "the supreme confidence which has always been an asset of the new champion."[30]

A week earlier, at age twenty-two, Cassius Clay stunned the sports world by defeating Sonny Liston, the reigning heavyweight-boxing champion. During the highly promoted TV buildup to the fight, I watched the boastful Clay proclaim his greatness. Endless times he repeated his self-promotional mantra: "I was born to be great. I am great and I will be greater—the greatest." His insults, rants, and snotty poems taunted his opponent. The chest-thumping attitude annoyed me.

I reread the press release. The hyperbole I dismiss as Clay's egoistic swaggering, the Van Bovenkamp Gallerie interprets as his "supreme confidence." Hmm, yes, certainly it can be said that Cassius Clay epitomizes the fullest state of certainty in one's own abilities. To my surprise, as abruptly as I turned onto West 55th Street, I find myself open to revise my opinion about the champ and his claim of greatness.

The door is ajar; no one checks for invitations; I enter. Once inside the gallery, I do not have to settle for merely viewing a sculpted depiction of the boxing champ. There, in all his self-assured glory, looms the flesh-and-blood Cassius Clay himself. I recognize him from

[30] Press release of Van Bovenkamp Gallerie, 18 West 55th Street, New York, March 5, 1964.

his TV appearances, but I do not see the media clown. Also absent is the irritating loudmouth braggart who broadcast, "When you're as great as I am, it's hard to be humble."

The champ stands in modest demeanor speaking in normal conversational tones with the people gathered around him. A friendly atmosphere prevails. Perhaps the positive thought of Clay's supreme self-confidence strengthens my own self-confidence. I walk over, extend my hand, and congratulate Cassius Clay on his world title. He returns a warm response. We exchange simple and polite pleasantries. Aware he hails from Kentucky, I ask how he likes my hometown. He mentions he will take a guided tour of the United Nations the next day with the man at his side. So focused am I on the champ that I do not even glance at the black man next to him until Clay introduces me to—Malcolm X!

I shudder. The controversial black nationalist is all too well known for his militant stance. He says aloud what black people say only among each other. The surname "X" he adopted after rejecting his family name of "Little" because it was "a slave name." The "X" refers to his lost tribal name derived from his African roots. He vilifies all whites for racial discrimination; all whites are devils. He accepts the "eye for an eye" principle.

Well, apparently not all white people represent the evil white oppressors. Malcolm smiles graciously at me. I peer critically at the tall, handsome, well-dressed man. Conversing with me in a charming manner, he gives me all his attention. Nonetheless, I cannot forget his reputation as a dangerous hater of white people. He is a disciple of Elijah Muhammad, a black supremacist leader. Followers regard Elijah Muhammad to be a modern-day prophet, as the double whammy of his prophetic name suggests. The son of former slaves, Elijah Muhammad is head of the Nation of Islam, a black American spiritual and political organization based loosely on orthodox Islam. Instead of Islam's principle of unity, Elijah Muhammad preaches separation of blacks from white society. He teaches that white society actively works to prevent black people from empowering themselves and achieving political, economic, and social success.

The longer I stand there, the larger beams Malcolm's smile, truly a winning smile. A gentle, good feeling passes between us. As much as I want to resist, I like him! This response, so baffling, overpowers my negative preconceptions. Malcolm's presence touches me more than his words.

Before leaving the reception, I ask Malcolm X and Cassius Clay to autograph the gallery's handout sheet. The boxing champion writes my name and signs his. He adds the message: "Good luck, 1964." I hand the paper to Malcolm X. We are side to side as he writes, in red ballpoint: "Bro Malcolm X." At this moment, Malcolm X does seem a Bro, and I a Sis. He makes a scribble in what appears to be Arabic writing.

"Peace, that means peace," he translates.

The following week, I read that Cassius Marcellus Clay has changed his name to Muhammad Ali-Haj. "Clay was my slave name," he explains.

Muhammad Ali will need all his self-confidence to overcome the public challenges of his new Islamic faith and his new identity. I admire his courage to change so publicly. My negative judgment of Clay in tatters, I reconsider, in a positive light, his flamboyant self-boastfulness. Clay-Ali cannot express himself through his cocky poetry or immodest declarations if he does not truly believe in himself. The absolute self-confidence that he personifies is his greatness itself.

Trust in his own greatness or, at least, in his potential for greatness, enabled Clay to rise above the discouraging circumstances into which he was born. Using all of his natural gifts, he transformed himself from a poverty-stricken boy who was an indifferent student into a top boxer. At the age of twelve, Clay devoted himself to mastering the principles of boxing. At eighteen, he won the Olympic gold medal for light heavyweight boxing at the Rome Summer Olympics. At twenty-two, he secured the boxing world's professional title. Ali's exceptional boxing skills, and his tremendous conviction in those skills, helped him reach the greatness he felt in himself from a young age. Without unquestioned self-assurance, he never could roar convincingly, and perpetually, with TV cameras rolling: "I am the greatest!"

In 1967, Ali refuses induction into the US Army based on his religious faith and his conscientious objections to the war. He declares he will not go to Vietnam to kill. His status as a Black Muslim minister, he contends, makes him draft exempt. Not even the powerful American nation can shake his confidence in his own right actions. Arrested in 1967 and found guilty for violating the United States Selective Service laws, Ali receives a five-year prison sentence, a ten thousand dollar fine, and loses all his boxing titles. His firm belief in his own powers helps Muhammad Ali hold tightly to his truth and his principles, going on to fight successfully no lesser opponent than the US government.[31]

Observing the career of Malcolm X, I note that he constantly transforms himself too. One week after meeting Malcolm X, I read he has left the Nation of Islam and formed his own Muslim organization. A few months later, he makes a pilgrimage to the heart of orthodox Islam in Saudi Arabia. He undergoes spiritually deepening experiences in the holy city of Mecca. He embraces orthodox Islam and takes again a new name: El-Hajj Malik El-Shabazz. In a huge turnaround, he says publicly that he no longer believes all white people are evil; he abandons racism and violence. Brother Malcolm asserts his willingness to cooperate with both blacks and progressive whites to secure social, civil, and political rights for black Americans. He announces his intention to bring to the United Nations the complaints of the black people against the United States.

Before Bro Malcolm can fulfill his humanitarian goals, three men angered at his break with the Nation of Islam pump sixteen bullets into his body.[32] Ironically, he is gunned down on the twenty-first of February, the first day of New York's National Brotherhood Week in 1965. Hearing of Malcolm X's violent passing, I sob as if he were indeed my bro.

Only years later would I realize that the energy I had felt in the presence of Malcolm X had been spiritual potency. This power had kept

---

[31] Muhammad Ali took his case all the way to the Supreme Court. In 1971, he won the appeal against his conviction.

[32] "Malcolm X killer is freed on parole," *Philadelphia Inquirer*, Philadelphia, April 28, 2010.

me in the present moment with the future El-Hajj Malik El-Shabazz, a place where my mind's past negative thoughts about Malcolm X had no force over my natural response to the intriguing man's winning smile. In the Now, I could feel the energy of brotherly love coming from him to me, just as I could feel my sisterly love traveling in his direction. Significant experiences often occur unexpectedly.

Meeting these two outspoken black activists altered my images of them. I ceased identifying Malcolm X as a white-hating, militant extremist. I stopped associating him with bigotry, hatred, and violence. My negative prejudgments withered. I came to respect Malcolm X as a courageous human rights activist. His life narrated the journey of a man never afraid to change, just like Cassius Clay–Muhammad Ali.

My opinion of Clay-Ali also dramatically reversed. He was not the egoistic clown manipulating the media for his own self-glory. I appreciated him as a principled human being and social activist. His freedom from doubt in his own right actions, especially as a black man living in a racially biased country, proved what Eleanor Roosevelt once said: "No one can make you feel inferior without your consent." Dismissing other people as inferior to ourselves may swell our self-confidence, but such confidence will be false.

During our brief exchange, I had felt Clay's very palpable energy radiating his secure trust in his own beautiful self. That powerful energy helped me spot the holes in my own self-belief. Did my original annoyance with the champ's flamboyantly self-confident behavior derive from my own insufficient self-confidence? Perhaps, unconsciously, I wanted to be as confident in my talents and abilities as the boxing champ demonstrated himself to be, and my former annoyance with him was really with myself?

In Zagreb, recalling Cassius Clay-Muhammad Ali and Malcolm X–El-Hajj Malik El-Shabazz, I acknowledge afresh the confines of my thought world. I had allowed media reportages to imprison me in narrow and intolerant thinking about the groundbreaking black leaders. In their actual presence, my eyes opened to larger dimensions of their being.

Thinking over my positive reevaluation of the two men, I ask my-self: *When we judge others, is a false superior attitude at play?* In response, I hear inner questions making me ponder: *Who are we to pass judgment on someone else's words or actions? Are we able to assess with godlike all-knowingness if someone else's character is good or bad? Does finding flaws in other people turn my vision away from seeing my own flaws? What is the state of my own character?*

Although aware of the Christ's noble instruction, "Judge not, that ye be not judged,"[33] I tend to fall victim to this human tendency. Not to judge myself too harshly, I picked up the habit of judging others as a child, growing up around people who routinely judged others.

Making negative judgments is common human behavior. We do it all the time. When I reject damaged produce at the outdoor market in Zagreb, I am making a negative judgment. Negative judgments are unavoidable in life. Our decisions to do this or to do that depend on negative as much as on positive judgments. Judgments can help us take actions and move forward.

Remembering my encounter with Muhammad Ali and El-Hajj Malik El-Shabazz makes me see how dangerous, faulty, and unfair it is to judge other people. My musings remind me that if we make judgments, our judgments can change, just as people can change. I resolve to stay open to change, and to be willing to release the past, including past judgments. This seems a requirement in the lengthy process of overcoming the habit of judging others.

Gaining delayed insight into the meeting with Muhammad Ali and El-Hajj Malik El-Shabazz, I grasp another big lesson: It is helpful to reflect on experiences closer to their occurrence. The sooner we detect the lessons offered, the sooner may we learn them. Or, as Stern said, "If you can really take the timely benefit."

Not yet, however, do I recognize that on arriving in Zagreb I had entered a classroom. Professor Yu-go-*slave*-ia is offering me initial teachings of an inner education I am not yet conscious I am seeking.

---

[33] Matthew 7:1–3

18
Seeing with New Eyes

fter months at Zagreb Film, I am fatigued from overwork. Loneliness engulfs me. My living conditions subject me to emotional stress. In this vulnerable state, I get sucked into the heart-wrenching soap opera of my landlady, her "no-good of an ex-husband," and his family.

Early one morning, the ringing of my landlady's telephone jolts me awake. I hear my landlady scream as if a stabbing knife is penetrating her. "*Umro? Umro?*" she shrieks. Without pausing either to put on slippers or bathrobe, or even to consult my *rečnik* for the translation of *umro*, I run into the hallway.

Ana, clad in a loose nightdress, her feet bare, hangs collapsed over the wooden stool near the phone. "Stef! Stef!" She throws herself into my arms. She sobs unabashedly. Additional words are unnecessary. The hand of Death has unlocked the emotional floodgates Ana sealed by denying her love for her ex. Anger and hate dissolve in hot tears of sorrow for "the wretch" who taught her the deepest meaning of grief and pain.

A knocking at the door interrupts us. "What is it?" loudly asks a man's voice in Serbo-Croatian. Hearing my landlady's heart-piercing cries through the walls, Ana's neighbors, in their sleeping clothes, have come to investigate. Ana conveys the shocking news in between her incessant sobbing. She calms herself enough to relate the tasks suddenly entrusted to her. She has to go to a hospital in the countryside to identify Stef's body. She has to inform her former mother-in-law. The old woman has no phone. Even if a telegram could reach her village in the rural Croatian outback, she is a simple peasant, unable to read. Ana asks: will I accompany her? The neighbor will drive us. His wife will stay home. I phone Matko and request the day off.

Very soon thereafter, I am sitting in the neighbor's car. During the long and tedious journey into the Croatian countryside, the only sound is Ana's weeping. We arrive at a complex of buildings, a sanatorium. The barrackslike structure looks deserted. Ana buries her face in her hands and utters pitiful groans. The neighbor leaves the car to go and inquire. I place my hand softly on Ana's back and stroke her gently. When the neighbor returns, she leans on him as we walk slowly toward a large cottage.

Inside the building, a uniformed woman hands Ana a paper. She signs it, taking only a perfunctory glance at its contents. Stef had been ill for twelve days but no one notified either his family or friends. A nurse leads us into a small room. Gray and austere, the room contains a simple cot, a chair, and a night table with a wind-up clock that has stopped. Cigarette butts form a heap on the floor. "He will sleep here no more," says Ana aloud to herself.

On the chair rests Stef's battered duffle bag. A doctor enters, speaks briefly with Ana, and displays the bag's contents, mostly undershorts, shirts, and trousers. As the doctor holds up each item, Ana mutters "*Dobro, dobro* [Good, good; okay, okay]" through her streaming tears. The doctor checkmarks each item on the list attached to his clipboard.

Picking up one of Stef's shirts, Ana presses it to her breast. The doctor hands her a wallet. Her hands shaking, she retrieves from it money and five photos of women. Two of the snapshots are of Ana at a younger age. The doctor indicates it is time to leave. Before we exit the room, Ana stuffs into the duffle bag a newspaper, a blue plastic pen cap, and a crumpled candy bar wrapper found in the night table. The neighbor and I coax her out of the last living space of her ex. We take her arms in ours.

In the courtyard, we encounter an open coffin. Ana emits a blood-curdling scream. Her sobs turn into deafening wails. Undoing our grip, she rushes to the coffin. I, too, am unnerved to see Stef's lifeless form covered by clear plastic sheeting. Through the plastic sheeting, Ana fervently plants kiss upon kiss on the dead man's lips. In death, Stef is hers completely. It costs us great effort to separate the hysterical Ana from the corpse. None of our words or embraces can pacify her. Two men lift the coffin into a truck.

At the next stop, a cemetery, two men carry Stef's body into a building and deposit it on a stone slab. Ana is inconsolable. The neighbor and I wrest her away, drawing her to the car. In silence, except for Ana's nonstop lamenting, we drive into an isolated rural area wet after fresh rain. The dirt road increasingly narrows. Overburdened, the mini auto struggles to travel the progressively muddy path until its wheels spin and spin, stuck in defeat. The neighbor turns off the engine. He will wait with the car and I will accompany Ana further. "Not far," she assures me.

Ana and I start walking on the muddy path. We choose the central section, avoiding the soft, pulpy side pockets. The mush thins into a brown soup encrusting our legs and soaking our shoes. A young boy tending cows gives directions to the village of Stef's mother. In the distance appears an old woman dressed all in black down to knee-high black rubber boots. She strides forward with a perfect gait while balancing a basket of cabbages on her head. Coming close, she points to our mud-soaked shoes and clicks, "Tsk tsk."

Ana sobs the words "Stef" and "*umro*." The cabbage woman utters several more "tsks" before breaking into full-throated grief. In the middle of nowhere, we meet someone who knows Stef and reacts to his death hyperemotionally. Would I respond with the same depth of heart to the death of Manny, my across-the-hall elderly neighbor on First Avenue?

Ana and I slog on. We wade through slushy grass fields, climb over fallen trees and rocks, cross streams helped by logs tossed above the rushing water to form foot bridges, and splash through rain-soaked pastureland. For nearly an hour, we hold our skirts above our thighs.

Eventually we come to a small grouping of houses. I hold my nose against the stench of feces. The bathroom in Ana's apartment falls well below my American standard, but it includes the basic sanitary facilities some Yugoslavs obviously lack.

The home of the as-yet unsuspecting mother is a one-room peasant hut. Flimsy curtains, not glass, stretch across the openings in the mud wall serving as her windows to the world. An elderly woman emerges from the hut. She tells that the mother is absent, lunching at a neighbor's house. The woman wears black, like the cabbage woman and the cursing old woman of the minidress incident. Fortunately, my minidress is now a packed up relic along with other American garments I find unsuitable for Yugoslav society. My clothing today, a dark knee-length skirt and plain, tailored blouse, can be no source of disgust. Besides, the old woman evinces little interest in me. Ana's presence absorbs her attention. Hearing the unhappy message, the woman plummets into hysterical sobs that drown out the clacking of the geese. Her frenzied emotion triggers an alarm. A young girl of no more than eighteen runs up. She wears heavily soiled, raggedy clothing. At "Stef" and "*umro*," she bursts into tears and dashes off. Collecting herself, the elderly woman motions us into the hut.

From the bright light of the sunny morning, we step into a dark interior. Chickens follow us; the old woman shoos them away. The floor is dry, hardened earth. I see no signs of electricity, gas, or running water. In contrast, Ana's apartment is a palace no matter how deficient I classify it.

The hut itself is clean and neat. The functional and very simple furnishings are handmade. There is a bed, straight-back chairs, a cupboard, and a table—all constructed out of wooden crates. On the hut's earthen walls hang Christian religious pictures secured by nails. Metal cans emptied and cleaned of their motor oil serve as receptacles for fresh vegetables. Putting aside conventional home decoration criteria, I appreciate again how lacks can nurture ingenuity.

Still, the clothes and towels hanging on nails are worn and dingy. Inviting me to sit, the elderly woman brushes away tears as she cushions the seat of my wooden crate-chair with a mucky towel calling up my fear of lice. Not wanting to insult the grieving woman who offers the cloth so kindly, I grit my teeth and sit. I do refuse, in the kind manner I imitate from the woman, a similarly begrimed towel for tidying up my muddied feet and legs. Flies buzz around the water bucket when the old woman dips in a cup to get water for her guests. "None for me," I motion.

The old woman and Ana cradle each other as they weep bitterly over Stef's death. Their sobbing is as nothing to the unnerving howls now charging the air. Outside approaches a small entourage of wailing people, among them the young girl, clustered around a small figure also wearing the cheerless black clothing. It is hard to believe that such a tiny frame can issue forth these intensely loud, anguished sounds of torment. The tears submerging the old mother's rugged, weather-beaten face cannot hide the good looks she gave her son. She and Ana embrace. The crying women engage in a short conversation. I mainly hear "Stef, Stef." Other words I do not understand. The talk completed, the two women part cordially. Ana says we have to go back before dark.

As we hike to the neighbor's waiting car, Ana maintains a contemplative silence. Perhaps she has no tears left. We stick to the same obstacle course through the pathless fields and over streams. In my own silence, I reflect on the simplicity of lifestyle witnessed, simpler even than the materially deprived existence of Zagreb. I just saw with my own eyes what I had read about in the Zagreb Film catalog for the documentary film *Putujuči Kino* (Mobile Cinema): Yugoslavia consists of many rural expanses where people live with neither basic amenities, health services, newspapers, radio, TV, nor shops. Mobile cinemas on wheels bring remote communities film screenings "to open for them a window into the world."[34]

---

[34] *Putujuči Kino* (Mobile Cinema), documentary film written and directed by Ranko Munitič, 1964.

The living conditions of Stef's mother make poor Americans look rich. America's poor living on low welfare payments stay in places with more comforts than the humble abode of Stef's mother. The needy families on my social investigator caseload lived in decrepit and ill-kempt buildings, but they had strong shelter from the elements, and so too they had electricity, hot water, toilets, fridges, and TVs.

Although I classify the Croatian villagers as "very poor" by Western economic definitions, I noted that around them hung no atmosphere of poorness or deprivation. Moreover, I saw them relate to each other as more than good neighbors. I sensed a close bond. Comradeship seemed to provide a fulfilling source of contentment and well-being, a wealth in itself. A palpable inner strength and dignity gave these people an air of richness.

My perception is growing that feeling safe and contented in a society depends less on our goods and more on our relationships. Am I romanticizing the situation of the poor Croatian villagers based on a snap judgment?

Night has fallen when we return to the city from the depths of peasant life. Ana's apartment now ranks as grandiose. I intend to spend longer than usual in the bathroom to scrub myself squeaky clean. The gas heater finally produces hot water and I step into the tub. Showering away the caked mud and smells of the raw nature, I am thankful for my accommodations in Ana's home rather than pining for my all-equipped Manhattan apartment.

The tub's slow drainage system empties the accumulated water. I clean the tub and run a bath. Lolling luxuriously in the warm water, I close my eyes and imagine myself at home, soaking in my own bathtub, the inconveniences of Yugoslavia behind me. When it is time for the draining, I yank the bathtub plug. The bathroom becomes an instant Venice! Immersed in my musings, I did not remember the hole in the bottom of the bathtub. I remembered it after showering, but the relaxing bath made me forget the need to open the bathtub plug barely a hair's breath for a slow drainage.

Nevertheless, my grateful attitude remains even as I step onto the flooded bathroom floor. My gratitude stays, too, during the fifteen minutes I need to soak up the water using tiny towels, no mop available. My hands ache from continually wringing the water into the metal clothes-washing tub. Before I retire for the night, Ana tells me that at five in the morning she will see "the wastrel brought to his last rendezvous."

I arrive at Zagreb Film at two the next afternoon. Matko dictates letters to Western film companies until six. Delaying my return to Ana's sorrowful atmosphere, I eat dinner in a restaurant at Trg Republike and walk aimlessly around. When I come upon a cinema screening the 1962 American film *To Kill a Mockingbird* in the original English, I buy a ticket and escape my reality for two hours. Close to eleven, quietly I slip into Ana's apartment. She is still up, waiting for me, insisting on my company. Unable to refuse, I work at the kitchen table on a Studio assignment until nearly two in the morning. With Ana sobbing at my side, I write subtitles for a feature film.

A few mornings later, the doorbell rings. Ana is in her bedroom and I open the door. There stands the dead Stef's elderly mother with a man who looks like a younger version of Stef. The mother's black ensemble appears new. Her face is clean and forms a neutral backdrop to her eyes still red from crying. Before I can utter a word, she and the young man storm past me into the apartment. Loudly they call for Ana.

This time the two women do not exchange comforting hugs. The old woman glares angrily at Ana. She and the young man address Ana belligerently. The mother claims my room for the young man who is, indeed, Stef's brother. She and her son demand Stef's clothes and his belongings. Ana vehemently refuses. The old mother gets enraged; she and her son curse and scream. Ana screams back that they can have the clothes but the room is hers! There is not one calm moment in which to discuss the distribution, perhaps even the sharing, of Stef's things and the room. The ex-wife is no longer a member of the close and caring countryside family.

The uproar continues. I expect that any minute the next-door neighbors will knock on the door. Then Ana runs into her bedroom and emerges carrying a plastic bag of clothing and other items. She flings the bag out the front door.

"Go, go, and don't bother me again!" Ana yells in Serbo-Croatian, pushing the two from the apartment.

"We'll be back!" threatens the mother. In a hybrid language evidently concocted for my understanding, the son growls: "*Američanka* out!"

Stef's death, the discharge of Ana's suppressed love for him, and the release of his possessions give a new boost to Ana's self-confidence. Six years after divorcing "the devil," she is finally free from the forced coresidency that the housing shortage compelled.

The night of the shouting match with her ex-in-laws, Ana wakes up screaming. She sees Stef's face on the wall and is frightened, as she tells me the next morning. Night upon night, the same occurs. My sleep disturbed, I awake exhausted and groggy.

Ana keeps a candle burning next to a photo of Stef. The snapshots of Stef's girlfriends she has thrown on the kitchen table, where they become stained by falling bits of food and breadcrumbs. Nearly whenever I am in the kitchen, Ana enters and obsesses on Stef and his harem. I try to understand the main thoughts occupying her mind and attempt to comfort her. The pages of my *rečnik* turn over many times; I absorb many new Serbo-Croatian words. It fascinates me to learn the meaning of *ljubomora*. A combination of *ljubav*, "love," and *mora*, "nightmare," the word translates into English as "jealousy"—quite accurately, "love's nightmare."

During this taxing period, Matko presses me to sign a contract extending my stay for another six months. Like a capitalist employer, he offers inducements: "The Studio will find you a proper place to live. The Studio will do all it can to help you. The Studio will arrange Serbo-Croatian audiovisual lessons." Regarding the latter, he cannot say anything definite. He has to discuss the proposal at the workers' council.

By now I am well aware that Yugoslav timing saunters from one immeasurable minute to the next. My patience will again be tested during my wait for the Studio's decision concerning the language lessons. Knowing the self-management procedure of endless meetings

and consultations resulting in slow-paced decision-making, I assume
there will come no resolution until the day of the contract's expiration,
if then. The Studio overloads me more than an American employer
would, but without giving the material rewards and perks customary in
the American workplace.

"I have to think this over," I tell Matko.

19

Becoming Wise in the Workplace

Coming from American society, in which employers consider it normal to get as much worker productivity as possible, preferably for the lowest costs, I am accustomed to working hard. Perhaps my willingness to pour my talents and energy into the Yugoslav job signals to the Studio that there is nothing amiss in not offering more than the originally stipulated salary.

Matko pushes me to spend longer hours for the benefit of Zagreb Film. Yet when I labor late into the evening, he is at his desk too. Despite joking, "I am a lazy Yu-go-*slave*," he tirelessly drives the chariot that the frisky horse of Zagreb Film flies all over the world. It is Želimir Matko who is largely responsible for bringing the Studio's respected name and films to international buyers, schools, and film festivals.

Even with their lackadaisical style, the Yugoslavs drive me excessively, well beyond the borders of their socialism's supposed caring for the worker. The accounts ledger of our employer-employee relationship is distortedly out of balance. The Studio's benefits from my daily grind equate lopsidedly with my meager dinar payments and the zero interest in my welfare. Accepting the imbalance, I demonstrate my unawareness that Lady Justice has tied her blindfold around my eyes. I do not grasp the extent to which I allow myself to be exploited by employers—whether they work for their own or their shareholders' profit or for the benefit of the state.

John Grierson tries to warn me. He writes: "Tell Matko for me that he must exploit you in the best capitalist manner, because you are a very, very clever American girl and he badly needs one such."

I wonder if the facetious suggestion is intended to remind me I did not go to Yugoslavia to chain myself into exploitative conditions. Grierson's message I do not have to convey; Matko surely received Grierson's witty exhortation directly.

In Yu-go-*slave*-ia, as at home, I give my utmost. Apropos any activity, in my subconscious runs an insistent question my Uncle Sam taught me to ask at a very young age: *What do I gain? What can I become, or be, or have, through the completion of this task/work/activity?*

My Uncle Sam is, of course, the personification of the United States government, the nation, and the American people. Not fat or jolly like Santa Claus, Uncle Sam is a serious-looking elderly gentleman with white hair and neatly trimmed goatee who is eye-catching in his outfit reminiscent of the American flag. He wears a white shirt, red bowtie, blue jacket, red-and-white-striped trousers, and a white top hat decorated by white stars on a blue band.

It was my Uncle Sam who initiated me at a very young age into the American belief system. Uncle's teachings reached me through my parents and other family members, the school system, the media, and my life in New York City. My Uncle Sam strengthened my faith that anyone can achieve the American Dream of happiness based on worldly success; any goal or dream can be realized through one's conscious choice, determination, competition, and hard work. I was a happy Am-er-*I-can*, motivated by the standard American mantra: "I can!" Uncle Sam's instructions provided an invaluable source of guidance, encouragement, and support.

As well, early on, I was indoctrinated into the Horatio Alger line of positive thought permeating American society. In nineteenth-century

America, the prolific American writer Horatio Alger (1832–1899) inspired young people with his easy-to-read rags to riches pocketbook novels of capitalistic achievement and financial success. Alger's adventure stories narrate how poor boys (emphasis on boys) can attain success through hard work, honesty, and courage. Over one hundred American Dream success novels, bearing titles such as *Do and Dare; or A Brave Boy's Fight for Fortune* (1884); *The Western Boy or, The Road to Success* (1878); and *From Farm to Fortune; or Nat Nason's Strange Experience* (1905), have sold over two hundred and fifty million copies worldwide.[35]

When my parents reduced the volumes on their bookshelves, they gave me their copy of the Alger novel entitled *Frank's Campaign; or The Farm and the Camp*. The story, set at the beginning of the Civil War, focuses on fifteen-year-old Frank Frost. After his father enlists in the Union army, Frank postpones his education to take care of the family farm. In the book's preface, Alger wrote: "*Frank's Campaign* is the record of a boy's experiences, by which the cares and responsibilities of manhood are voluntarily assumed, and nobly and successfully borne. He supplies his father's place while the latter is absent in his country's service, and is enabled, by a fortunate circumstance, to pay off a mortgage resting on the home farm.

"Nothing is claimed for the young hero which may not be achieved by an energetic and manly boy of the same age. It is hoped that the record of Frank's struggles and final success may stimulate the boys who may read it to manly endeavor, and to a faithful and conscientious discharge of whatever duties may devolve upon them."[36]

Horatio Alger gave the hope and encouragement that any boy (girls not mentioned), through hard work and honesty, and actions based on trying to do what is right, can fulfill his material goals. Positivism energizes America even when the society goes through periods of confusion regarding what is "right" and what is "wrong" behavior.

---

[35] www.horatioalger.com

[36] From *Frank's Campaign; or The Farm and the Camp*. Copyright page of book missing. No publisher information available.

I grew up respecting such Americanisms as: "There is no substitute for hard work." Those supportive words issued from the influential American inventor-businessman Thomas Alva Edison (1847–1931). A classic example of American ingenuity and material attainment, Edison patented over one thousand discoveries, including the phonograph, telegraph, and the incandescent light bulb. He was one of the first inventors to apply the principles of mass production to the invention process.

Apparently Edison needed one thousand tries to invent the light bulb. When a reporter asked how it felt to fail one thousand times, Edison answered: "I didn't fail one thousand times. The light bulb was an invention with one thousand steps."[37]

Besides teaching me to adore hard work, my Uncle Sam trained me to worship Lord Money, the universal deity of the global secular religion. If the oatmeal in my childhood years probably lacked chemical additives, it contained the hypnotic message my Uncle Sam mixed into it through my mother's true-believer hand: "Eat and be strong, my dear American child, so you can work hard and earn lots of money. Success depends on the personal accumulation of wealth and more wealth, things and more things, status and recognition."

Ever since I can remember, I have embraced the American value system exalting success based on competition. Competition emphasizes winning. When we do not compete well we are often underestimated and discounted. Despite years of honing my competitive skills, I do not relish the galloping heart, the butterflies in my stomach, and the toilet runs that the act of competing may activate in me.

While I do not like the nerve-wracking aspects of competition, I do appreciate recreational competitive sports based on teamwork. Dribbling the ball during our high school volleyball games, I felt differently about competition than when listening to my heart thump and my stomach jump as I awaited my next word in a spelling bee. Reaching upward

---

[37] Reported in "An Example of Detailed Perseverance" published in *Awakening*, Monthly Bulletin of Women's Council, Sri Aurobindo Society, Puducherry, India, June 2010, p. 13.

to slam back a volley across the net for our team charged me with pleasure, not a fearful anxiety as might shake me during a written classroom exam. During sports competitions I was not a lone individual trying to better myself over other individuals. I was part of a group cooperating for a shared goal. Sometimes a small delicious sensation arose in me, the thrill of cooperation and unity. Competing in team sports helped me learn to accept the highs of a win and the lows of a loss without emotional seesawing. I could go on, emotionally undefeated, even when we lost a match. Teamwork in sports symbolizes teamwork in society, but already in high school I felt that my country glorified the principle of competition to excess.

In Zagreb, my competitive behavior is useless. Interestingly, this particular Yugoslav lack, of competition, I am enjoying. Mulling this over, I get the insight that competing is not my natural instinct; competition is a learned behavior. My society demands, if not dictates, that I must compete and perfect my competitive skills.

A clarity afforded by my more peaceful mind, one result of the general slowing down, lets me realize: *Hey! It is not the American society per se that has been forcing me to compete.* No, more insidiously, the need to compete, so I perceive in another "Aha" moment, derives from my fear of being a "loser," especially in comparison to the successful and happy professionals and celebrities portrayed in magazine articles and TV reportages. While encouraging me to devote my life to Success, my society engendered in me an emotional insecurity and fear of failure. Fear of failure in the "Most Likely to Succeed"?

The question is why, while in this country of Titoist dictatorship, do I feel that my own country, the Land of the Free, is also a dictatorship? If I am not literally a slave to the American system, I am surely a victim.

As a thunderbolt flash comes the understanding: *There is no one to compete with in life except myself.* Therefore, I have to become a better person not by competing against others to raise myself up in society; I have only to compete with the less-than-perfect person I myself was yesterday in order to make myself less imperfect today and tomorrow. This lights-on perception is a breakthrough. I can drop the competitive habit that causes me upset. Whoa, not so easy. The attitude of competition is firmly anchored in my psyche. Throwing off the competitive habit will require effort and time.

Crucially, I recognize that my motivation to compete and excel in the eyes of others also originates from my insecurities. Winning, or being near the top of the competitive pyramid, helps me dispel doubts and lack of confidence in my own abilities. No wonder the encounter with Cassius Clay-Muhammad Ali and Malcolm X-El-Hajj Malik El-Shabazz surfaced during my stay here in Zagreb.

Yugoslavia is building my self-confidence. Now I am able to sit alone and silently in the Studio canteen not feeling compelled to establish myself as a first-rate person through spoken words. I am experiencing, albeit still minimally, the power of being indifferent to what others think or say about me, whether positive or negative.

It is exactly as Stern declared: one's core needs to be strong. Only then can we function at top form and fulfill our purpose in life. But what is my purpose? At the very least, I have to redraw my definition of "success."

My success in Yugoslav society is nonexistent. A foreigner falls outside the Yugoslav norms of accomplishment. Besides, when one does not speak the language or understand the culture, success in any society can dangle out of grasp. Here, more often than at home, I remember my immigrant grandparents. Unlike their adjustments as strangers committed to a long-term stay in a strange land, I am in strange Yugoslavia but temporarily. I have no need to compete for success as defined by the Yugoslavian Dream, whatever that dream may be. I feel no pressure to prove my worth as a human being except by bringing my Studio assignments to the best conclusion I can. In general, my being a "winner" in Yugoslavian society depends on my ability to meet and overcome the daily challenges. For such winning, chiefly my inner qualities count.

Whatever success means to Yugoslavs, they are pursuing it in their own distinctive style. Yugoslavia is heading toward a future that is perhaps the envisioned egalitarian paradise, and perhaps not. Whatever the destination sought, its citizens are not leaping breathlessly to the cooperative form of society. At Zagreb Film, where workers take all the indeterminable Yugoslav minutes they want to complete a task, the slowness of being tackles and shackles my running feet.

Yugoslavia shows me an extremely reversed image of my speedy American tempo. The Studio's easygoing atmosphere compels me to stop dashing in the fast lane. On the Titoist road of life, there simply is no fast lane; there is no high-pressured, competitive rat race. Releasing my habitual ways enables me to view those habits as if they are somehow separate from me.

My speed reduced to a turtle's, I have time to observe my life while I live it. I have more opportunity to explore my inner attitudes. Now I understand I am looking for a life and a society of balance. My unconscious search has improbably led me to a Yugoslavia endeavoring to make a better life for its people by means of a unique social experiment. Perhaps a "better life" in a "better world" will integrate the best of the capitalist and the socialist systems while improving on each?

Regarding my own "better life," it is evident I have to disable the conditioning that has fettered me to a self-centered mindset lacking deep content and contentment. To become a better person, where to go or stay? During moments of isolated quiet in my rented room, I chew over the query: *To sign, or not to sign? Remain in Zagreb or leave?* I imagine various scenarios. Repeatedly I ask myself: *If I said "Yes!" so spontaneously to the job offer, why the struggle to figure out whether to accept the new contract?* The "guidance" I sense from time to time refuses to send forth assistance.

My family and friends, receiving my letters, know absolutely my next step. Unanimously they proclaim: "Come home! Come home!" While contemplating the "better life," I now muse: *Just where is "home"?* Stef's death intensifies my nagging urge to know the answers to life's existential questions.

Before deciding whether to sign or not sign, I tell Matko: "I am drained." I request two weeks off. Matko agrees, but there is a stipulation: "Your vacation will be American style."

"American style?"

"The Studio has no legal obligation to give you a paid vacation. It's the same in America, where no law guarantees workers paid vacation time."

"I think I can manage without the two weeks' lost salary. Sixty-four dollars, isn't it?" I remark sarcastically. The biting tone ushers from my mounting dissatisfaction with the Studio's treatment of me. "Don't all Yugoslav workers get paid vacations?"

"Yes, but you are now a Yu-go-*slave*, have you forgotten?" Matko responds, winking. "Before leaving on your vacation, you will have to sign another three-month contract."

"Why? I haven't yet decided to stay or not! That's the whole point of the pause!"

"A break in the time span will complicate the work permit." He avoids my quizzical glance.

"I see," I say, and I really do see. "Then put in the contract a two-weeks' notice clause."

Matko, startled at my uncustomary hard tone, nods his agreement. "If you will stay on," he adds, "I'll teach you the film business. Later on you could get a job in distribution and travel widely."

"I'd rather make my own films than sell the films of others."

"Well, after you've assisted me some more months, I could let you be an assistant to a film director."

"Really?"

"On a volunteer basis."

"Oh."

The unpaid time off and the signing of the new contract arranged, I desire a breather not solely from Zagreb. I need to leave Yu-go-*slave*-ia itself. Otherwise I might have visited Belgrade again. A few weekends after meeting the government bureaucrat at the Esplanade Intercontinental

Hotel, I traveled to Yugoslavia's capital city. The man's promise to show me around evaporated when I read his apologetic note left in my hotel. He had been called out of town. This disappointment aside, the visit progressed spectacularly. Musicians serenaded me with traditional folk music below my hotel balcony. Touristy though it was, and schmaltzy too, I loved it. At dinner in the hotel, a friendly Serbian couple came over to speak to me. Midstream in our talk, they invited me to sightsee Belgrade with them the next day.

The city captivated me, as the government man had assured. He was wrong, though, about the paucity of shopping. I saw stores carrying shoes and clothes even I would buy. But the subtle topped the weekend. On the train back to Zagreb, I vividly remembered my entrance into the mysterious atmosphere of a Serbian Orthodox Church, the powerful congregational singing, and the surprise of my lips spontaneously kissing the icon of Jesus.

As much as Belgrade had intrigued me, after the emotionally charged episode with my Croatian landlady and her dead ex, I resolve to get away from the entire country Titoism built. Where to go? I sort through the business cards collected over the summer. Inexplicably, Stern's card is missing. Searching everywhere, I cannot find it. Examining the cards received in Pula from film people based in London, Paris, Rome, and The Hague, I bypass the exciting Big Three of European cities. Unaccountably, The Hague draws me.

"If you want to stay longer in Europe," Otto Milo had told me, "come to Holland." I phone Otto, a respected Dutch film columnist and cartoonist. He repeats his invitation. I ask him to book me a reasonably priced hotel for a two-week exploratory stay.

Parting from Ana is not easy. She cries, embraces me, and points to the front door. She has affixed an additional lock as protection against her aggressive ex-brother-in-law's promised return. I feel compassion and sorrow for her predicament. Nevertheless, I cannot continue living in the troubled situation. I am sure Ana has the strength to get through her crisis. The housing shortage guarantees she will install a new boarder for the room under threat, though perhaps not at an inflated foreigner's price. Hopefully her next boarder will be a Serbo-Croatian speaker with a good listening ear. I move out and deposit my luggage at Zagreb Film. Before boarding the train to the Netherlands, I send a letter detailing the contract dilemma to John Grierson.

20
Crossing Borders

At the train station in The Hague, Otto Milo welcomes me. He exhibits the graciousness of style I connect with European refinement, a character trait he shares with Svetlana. In Pula, by the swimming pool or at the open-air film screenings, Otto strolled in casual beach-resort costumes. In the chilly, late Dutch autumn, he dresses in a dark blue pinstriped three-piece suit set off by matching shirt and tie. A smartly tailored dark blue woolen coat, draped capelike over his shoulders, tops his outfit. A blue and black colored woolen scarf nicely complements his pitch-black hair, black mustache, and black-rimmed glasses. Milo is an attractive man, ten or fifteen years my senior. We ignite no romantic spark for each other. I feel that he just genuinely wants to help me, no strings attached, à la Svetlana.

Picking up my suitcase, Otto escorts me to a nearby hotel. The reception desk of the small and traditional Dutch hotel is located on the lofty peak of a very steep and narrow staircase. We climb and climb. I tease Otto: "Do you Dutch build such mountainous stairways to compensate for your very flat landscape?"

"No, no," replies Otto, seriously explaining: "We build narrow and steep to conserve space in our tiny and densely populated country."

The hotel room contains all modern amenities and is spotless. Otto is pleased the room satisfies me. Over dinner, he asks about my finances. "Still racking up the big pile of dinars?"

"They're burning a hole in my pocket with nothing to spend them on," I joke.

"You know, we Dutch are proud of our thriftiness," responds Otto. "Others call us frugal. You better hold on to your reserves. You need a nest egg should you decide to establish yourself here."

Why not stay at his house for my two-weeks' break, he suggests. "Especially since you forfeited a big pay check for your Dutch holiday!" A warning follows: "My place lacks a woman's touch."

What home of a professional Dutchman can be worse than my minimal living conditions in Zagreb? I accept Otto's offer, as I had Svetlana's, sight unseen.

The next evening, Otto fetches me from the hotel. A taxi brings us to his home in a suburb of The Hague. Immediately I grasp his aptly descriptive "bachelor's quarters." Scattered news publications and assorted papers cover the living room floor. Instead of getting upset, as I might have before adjusting to Matko's office, I burst into laughter. "Well," I state, "maybe you'll let me contribute a woman's touch."

Otto leads me into the kitchen. The kitchen has no refrigerator and only a two-burner hotplate. To my astonishment, there is not one pot for making food. "I do have a kettle," Otto informs me. "Voilà!" he exclaims, putting the kettle into action to boil water for tea. "The limit of my cooking skills," he declares matter-of-factly.

Although wrapped in my warm American winter coat sent to me by my parents, sitting in the living room I turn literally blue from the cold, northern European November. A tiny oil stove carries the burden of heating the fairly spacious house.

Otto's accommodations do not reflect the Dutch reputation for cleanliness and order, but I am thankful for his generosity. Soon I comprehend why the household and the heating fail to get his attention.

An astute film critic and cartoonist enriched with a witty drawing pen, Otto labors more than full-time for a daily newspaper in The

Hague. He leaves home at nine in the morning and arrives back to sleep at one in the night. All his meals he eats in restaurants.

Like a kind uncle hosting a niece visiting from abroad, Otto nestles me under his insider's wing. He includes me in his schedule and helps me arrange mine. By day, I explore The Hague's numerous touristic attractions and museums. Certainly I window shop, almost literally straining my eyes to peer into each attractive store, as had the Studio workers during our short excursion to Austria. A few stores I enter. Obviously my "acceptation of less" still has to overthrow my consumerist habits. At the American Express office, I am delighted to receive a telegram from John Grierson. He cables: "Send me another note when you have had a holiday and time to think it over. Have a good time in Holland. Grierson."

Otto listens to my adventures during our restaurant dinners. After the dinners, we socialize at one of his favorite cafés or at *Nieuwspoort* (Gateway to News), the international press center near the parliament building. Journalists, other media people, and politicians mingle over drinks with the understanding that conversations do not leave the building. Otto introduces me to his media network. Smartly clad in formal three-piece suits, Otto distinguishes himself sartorially from his journalistic colleagues who mainly wear sporty outfits. In their cozy cafés and meeting spots, I observe them enjoying substantial nourishment from their famous national beverages, Dutch beer and *jenever,* juniper berry-flavored gin. Often they drink the two together, taking the beer as a chaser.

Otto and his colleagues encourage me to "try life in Holland"; they say I can obtain writing assignments in English, one of the country's working languages. Otto proposes I lodge in his bachelor house. The same generous spirit of helpfulness that I associate with Svetlana flows through him. *It is people, not systems, that make or break this world,* I think.

Clarity dawns on my Yugoslavian situation. My decision emerges: *Leave Yu-go-slave-ia!* More accurately, rather than "make" a decision exercising my power of logic, I "see" the decision. It reveals itself. Finally I spot "the decision" confined in unfolding circumstances and events.

Someone else might have recognized the decision much earlier. For me, the timing seems perfect.

I have become aware that "coincidences," circumstances, events, experiences, and also relationships incorporate signs and messages offering guidance. Additionally, I am growing alert to internal cues. When I am about to take or continue a particular action, sometimes I feel uneasy. Any such unpleasantness I interpret as an indication to cease the action in question. Similarly, a good feeling, and/or perhaps a thought conveying, "Yes," convinces me to see that thought or action through to its end, no matter the difficulties or sufferings involved.

To dismiss the mounting communication from both without and within, I sense, will not serve my ultimate good. On the contrary, I have to give the signals increased attention. An inner urging advises: *Stay longer in good old Europe.* How can I ignore the message? The stay in Zagreb has extended to nearly three times the initially stipulated two summer months. The possibility of working in the Netherlands energizes me.

"I'll be back!" I assure Otto as we part on the train platform. Over my shoulder hangs his Super 8 film camera, on loan until my anticipated return. In Zagreb, I will start my "I Remember" film.

The train slows to a crawl on reaching Yugoslavia. Quickly, however, a Yugoslav conductor appears to demand an extra fee for this "Special Express." A measured confidence strengthens me as the train chugs into Zagreb. The scene is familiar and I know how to proceed. In a state of triumph, I ignore the imploring taxi drivers and catch the tram to Zagreb Film.

The chubby-faced blonde woman at reception greets me warmly. Matko is not his cheery self when I walk into his office. Before I left for the Netherlands, he professed deep regret for my housing problems. He guaranteed that the Studio would find me a suitable living place. "We want you so very much to stay on," he had asserted. Now he admits, guiltily: "No one has arranged any lodgings."

It is a sunny November day, but I see mainly the dark cloud of inertia hanging over Zagrebian life. "This is just the way they do things," I mumble under my breath, out of Matko's hearing.

"Would you like coffee?" he asks. At least this bit of hospitality is an improvement over my July arrival.

"I'd like to use your phone."

Instead of spending endless Yugoslav minutes in his office waiting for a next imprecise step to be taken, I phone Svetlana.

"The Studio has not arranged a living place."

"Again? Come here."

Soon I am closing her elevator gate behind me with a little thud. On her landing, her door swings open as if she has been listening for my return.

"My dear!" she exclaims. "Don't you know by now they will never change?"

"Can you blame me for concluding that the Studio's management board attaches no importance to my well-being?" I respond.

Svetlana unpacks the gift bag from Holland and, seeing the contents, sets water to boiling. We talk over cups of Dutch Indonesian tea and Dutch *stroopwafels*, two-layered thin waffle cookies filled with caramel syrup.

"Does the brotherhood slogan not equally apply to the sisterhood, including the foreign sisters?" I ask. "Is it wrong to question why the Studio, especially with its council representing the workers' interests, has not assisted my housing need?"

"So is it," replies Svetlana. "Best to have no illusions. How else can I accept my own life here?"

"Is inaction an ingrained part of the Yugoslav character?" I wonder out loud. "Oh, sorry," I add. "You are Yugoslavian. I didn't mean—"

"And proud to be," she retorts, cutting me off. "I know our strengths and our weaknesses. It takes all kinds of people to make up a society." Abruptly she stops, weighing her next words. "It is true," she finally says. "The Studio has remained complacent to your human needs. But," and she pauses before stating, "you have given a very American reaction. You see in a very American way."

I am puzzled. "Meaning?"

Svetlana puckers up her lips as if debating whether to go on. Then she continues: "Don't you think you look at your situation only from your point of view? Everything revolves around your needs. Your American-formed thinking is like a child's: 'I need a living place, I need companionship, I need help, I need, I-I-I. . . .' Persistently you wait for understanding and actions to originate from others, even though you recognize human shortcomings. When your colleagues do not open their hearts and their homes to you, you are disappointed and you suffer."

Her words sting.

"It is very true. Your co-workers show no empathy to you as a foreigner undergoing culture shock in a strange land. They do not try to see your situation through your eyes. Yet you, too, fail to try to put yourself in the shoes and the feelings of the people around you. Even though you stress learning from experience, pardon me for saying so, you relate to 'empathy' primarily as an intellectual understanding. It is very obvious you were raised as a self-centered capitalist. Do you try to imagine the walk of life in your colleagues' shoes?"

Her words cut into my very image of myself. I do not have to ponder her critique. She is correct. I do fail to try to put myself in the shoes and the feelings of the people around me. Just as the hearts of my colleagues do not activate their hands to reach out to me, I do not empathize with the circumstances of their hard lives. I bear my own shortcomings, but not theirs. The lesson of "reach out to others," personified by both Svetlana and the Turtleneck Man, has not penetrated me.

Perhaps my Studio colleagues were too shy, or ashamed, to welcome me into their modest homes? Instead of bemoaning my fate of isolation, couldn't I have stretched my hand in cross-cultural friendship? Couldn't I have gone to my Studio co-workers one at a time and invited them for coffee together with my *rečnik* and me? My colleagues and I might have gotten to know each other not as Yugoslavs and an American, or socialists and a capitalist, but on a deeper level as human beings sharing the same human condition.

I had written to John Grierson: "They have their own troubles at staying alive and go about it very seriously." My statement was correct, my empathy lacking. I did not wonder: *How may I be able to help them in some way?* One asks that question only when self-interest does not form one's main motivation. Svetlana's observations are accurate. I concentrate on my own needs as my central reference point. I wait for my colleagues to come to me. Svetlana's brutally frank appraisal hurts.

"Don't feel bad," purrs Svetlana. "We cannot condone their actions and you say you are here to learn, right?" I nod and grin, as if her arrow-sharp words have not pierced my heart.

"Now tell me about the Dutch!" she commands.

Glad to change the subject, I narrate my two weeks' respite in the Lowlands. Svetlana vicariously enjoys my Dutch adventures. Again she expresses delight with the presents I have brought, especially the selection of exotic kitchen spices. "Indian curry powder! I've never had it, never used it!" For the next days, the pungent blend of exotic spices infuses practically each dish Svetlana prepares. One especially tasty curry lunch she improvises from a recipe in a German magazine.

I decide not to accept Svetlana's invitation to stay. Her boyfriend's summer beach resort job is over and he visits frequently. "I'll be fine on my own," I declare. I have absorbed her lecture. My colleagues' indifference to my well-being highlights my own deficiencies in loving. Despite my professed ideals of caring about others, I function within a very self-centered existence. I lack true compassion for those not my blood family or friends. Under the surface of my relations lurks a trace of the materialistic "what's in it for me?" calculation. I feel so ashamed.

21

Embracing the Positive within the Negative

While hunting for a new room, unaided by the Studio, I live out of my suitcase at Svetlana's. Every day I arrive at Zagreb Film displeased that the Studio management acts oblivious to my needs. Several animators show concern for my predicament, especially Boris Kolar. Nobody has any suggestions. Matko avoids me. He leaves papers on my desk in an uncustomary hurry to get away, saying he is involved in nerve-wracking budget meetings.

During these days, I run into Ana on the street. Astonished to see me in Zagreb, promptly she begins to cry and pulls me into her embrace. The apartment is being painted, she reports, and she is so lonely there now. "Look at the bags under my eyes," she insists. She pulls open her coat to reveal her loss of weight. Continually she weeps, terming me her *kinder*, her child. "Will you come and have dinner?" she asks.

Svetlana and I visit rooms for rent. After a short search, I accept an accommodation mainly because of its proximity to Zagreb Film. The landlady asks for a hefty deposit and I have no choice but to pay an outrageously inflated foreigner's price.

Clean but bare, the room contains the standard bed, small table, one chair, and a minisize electric room heater quite inadequate for the oncoming winter. As usual, there is no fridge. The landlady tells me, through Svetlana's translation, "The hot water heater has exploded and will take one week to fix." I refrain myself from asking, "Is that one week by Yugoslav time?" The landlady will provide hot water in a bucket until the heater is repaired. She and I will take turns cooking on her two-burner hotplate.

"I'll manage," I assure Svetlana. "It's only temporary."

"Everything is temporary," Svetlana responds.

"I'm getting the idea."

As we leave, Svetlana inquires how this room differs from the "horrid place" Comrade Matko took me to see on my arrival day in Zagreb. Her question makes me pause, and smile. She winks and says: "Come on. We have cause to celebrate. Let's go for a drink."

My resignation is no surprise to Matko. We determine my last workday and I agree to round out all my assignments. Released from a project brought successfully to its conclusion, I feel my mood dramatically lighten. A perky bounce enlivens my step. I wish away my days in Zagreb. Life is so short and I am still trying to hasten my passage through time. *Slow down!* urges the constant reminder.

The task of relegating Zagreb to the past preoccupies me. I contemplate the end of my lonely confinement. As a child, I recall, often I left the company of my parents and my sister Bonnie while they sat in the living room watching TV. In the quiet of my bedroom, I treasured my aloneness to read, write, and draw. As an adult, speeding in the fast-forward American society, I forgot my childhood friendship with Aloneness. Slowed in Zagreb, and alone by circumstances, I now remember my former appreciation of solitude and silence. *A pity you did not remember at your old American pace,* I chide myself.

Finally I accept, and even relish, my Zagrebian isolation. I can now feel comfortable even when alone. I have won another victory in the battle to conquer my weaknesses and improve myself. My readiness to leave Yu-go-*slave*-ia has reached its climax. Visions of colorful Dutch tulips, turning windmills, and wooden shoes dance in my head. My suitcase is already half packed.

In this crossover state, during the countdown of weeks remaining in my prison sentence as a paid female slave in a totalitarian society, finally and fully convinced that *the time to leave Zagreb is now!*—at this very peak of my certainty, when I am confident, calm, and peacefully sure about my decision, I am turned topsy-turvy by an unforeseen event.

Walking on Trg Republike, I meet a colleague from the Studio. His companion is a man whose beaming smile is so large and dazzling that my heart jumpstarts and assumes a quicker beat. His sparkling eyes captivate me. Some pockmarks, not at all unsightly, give his skin an uneven texture. A dark blue coat accentuates his sandy-toned hair.

"Mario," he says, extending his hand.

"Mario? Is that a Yugoslav name?" I estimate he is a few years older than I am. "Sounds Italian."

"Czech, émigré, here years, with mother," he answers. He is an engineer. "You, Zagreb, how?" he asks. His English fits into the punctured pattern of communication forming most of my conversations in this society. On my side, my tiny grasp of Serbo-Croatian grammar limits me to expressing myself mainly in sentence fragments consisting of nouns or basic verbs accompanied by hand and eye movements. The language barriers notwithstanding, there is an unspoken yet tangible communion between this Czech man and me. Our first date quickly follows.

Mario comes to fetch me in a brightly polished car. "This car," he says proudly, helping me into the front seat, "I buy recently, brand new." Buying a car brand new, I understand, marks a great achievement in Yugoslav society. People may wait on a list for up to three years before receiving a car. Is ownership of a new car a Yugoslav status signal? He parks near the restaurant. Walking away from the car, Mario pats the fender in a "thank you" gesture.

At the restaurant we order dinner, clink glasses, and break bread together. The bread melts in my mouth, less coarse than usual, and the house wine romps extra merrily through my system. The caloric intake is skimpy compared to a nourishing exuberance I absorb in this man's presence. He, too, yields to the unexpected state of happiness in which we wondrously find ourselves, not only thanks to the wine.

When Mario and I can bear to end the glorious evening, we leave the restaurant. Immediately our hands rush to each other as two attracting poles of a magnet. Hands entwined, we stroll to his car, slowly, to prolong the inevitable parting. The energy of love has reentered my corner of the universe, lifting me to its breathtaking heights. Curious how life "just happens." My grim existence in Zagreb, colored dull in varying shades of gray, suddenly revels in rainbow hues. Especially in the worst of circumstances, there is no resuscitator like love. My spirits fall below sea level at the parking place.

"My car!" Mario shrieks.

The spot is empty.

I, too, stare in disbelief. We had been floating on sunshine in a heaven of love's enchantment; the shock of the car's disappearance plummets us back to Earth and gloomy Zagreb.

My new friend's distress is not easy to console. The car represents years of his hard work and savings. As well, the theft of the car will sadden his mother. That assumption disturbs him more than the theft itself.

After the unfortunate end of our dinner date, thoughts about the missing car and its rightful owner engross me. The theft of Mario's car forces me to consider a side of the Yugoslav citizenry Svetlana earlier mentioned. Some citizens have devised their own selfish version of socialism's message of cooperation and sharing en route to a better life for all. Does the car snatcher embody those Yugoslavs who do not feel connected to their brother and sister comrades in one interdependent communal oneness? Stealing is one of the oldest occupations, but does not a citizen in a visionary society have the patience to wait for the promised better times?

All Yugoslavs have grown up chanting *"Bratstvo i jedinstvo"* (Brotherhood and Unity). Not everyone takes the oft-repeated slogan to heart. Yugoslavians are no different from other people whose country has officially embraced a high-minded catchphrase. How often is there a discrepancy between what we mouth and how we act?

"In God We Trust," the modern slogan of my own birth country, was adopted by law in 1956. How many Americans have this trust? Actually, the motto fits with the governing materialistic values. "In God We Trust" appears on all US coins and paper currency.

"*Bratstvo i jedinstvo*" rallied the Communist Party of Yugoslavia as it came to power during World War II. The slogan energized the Partisans against the enemy Axis occupiers who used "divide and conquer" to provoke discord among Yugoslavia's diverse ethnic groups. "*Bratstvo i jedinstvo*" evolved into a guiding principle of the socialist revolution and national interethnic policy.

Of course, values of communality cannot be imposed by legislation in the same way that a society can develop a punishment system to discourage the negative social act of stealing. Stealing reflects, at the very least, the condition that some people are not satisfied with what they have or what they are. This dissatisfaction can be discouraged, or punished, by human law. Car theft in a socialist country striving for brotherhood and unity supplies additional evidence that human nature is the same everywhere. Weaknesses and strengths are embedded in us no matter the ideology or form of government propelling our country.

Nonstealing, not taking what does not belong to us, not even a box of paper clips from our employer's office stocks, constitutes a tenet of ethical conduct. We practice ethical conduct voluntarily. Nonstealing is merely a guideline. When implemented, nonstealing helps us better regulate ourselves as individuals and as societies.

All of us are, after all, entangled to a lesser or greater extent in the universal cycle of human desire, discontent, and frustration. Guidelines suggested by moral, ethical, and spiritual trailblazers can benefit us. As Stern asserted, "A society that professes one thing and does another is not moral."

My musing on the car theft intensifies my yearning to see Mario. The next evening we eat a snack together in a café. Then we visit a nightspot on Trg Republike. In a large, two-storied dance palace made romantically atmospheric by soft lighting, couples dance to the recorded hits of the British pop singer Engelbert Humperdinck. A crowded bar serves beer and Dalmatian wines. Although some young Yugoslavs might be disgruntled in their gray world, in the dance palace they create a merry private reality.

During this second appointment, Mario announces his plan to buy another car. To save on costs, he will search for a low-priced model needing repairs he can make himself. Will I accompany him to the used car lot? "Certainly," I say, exhilarated at the invitation. This Czech man lacks the sophistication of a Westerner, and his English is minimal, but his character shines through as kind and unencumbered. His genuine smile and his deep-going eyes conceal no deception. Unlike the ER doctor and the Turtleneck Man, he conveys the attitude that he does not regard me as an object, a plaything, or a means to acquire mucho mucho dollars.

A tram brings us to the used car lot in a distant section of Zagreb. Located entirely out-of-doors, the car lot positions a new aspect of Zagrebian life under my magnifying glass. It is a swarming beehive of activity, a marketplace and a social center. Around each vehicle, all East European models predominated by the Yugoslav Fiat, gather perhaps twenty-five chattering people, mostly men. With an interest in detail, they passionately examine and discuss the cars they scrutinize. The cars are definitely more eye-catching than the foreign woman in their midst. I receive very few of the usual gawks accorded my non-Yugoslav look.

In the Yugoslav society of scarcities, the people hunger for many things. The used car lot depicts the situation graphically. Mario and I press in closer. I lift Otto's camera from its case.

I am ready to press the start button when I hear the Croatian equivalent of: "Stop filming!" The authoritarian tone batters my ear. An icy male voice barks an order one needs to obey, or else. My finger instantly drops from the button as if a tendon has snapped. Uncomfortably near me is a middle-aged man wearing, yes, a belted trench coat. He could have stepped out of a Cold War spy thriller. I would laugh at his stereotypical garb if the moment were not so deadly serious.

In what absurdity am I now ensnared? As a tourist innocently films during a vacation, I am merely filming in a public area, but I forgot that the place is Yu-go-*slave*-ia.

My fearful reaction to the trench-coated man hurls me back to the day I extended my work visa. Matko wrote down the address of a government office and sent me there alone. "You can manage very well on your own," he said. "You are an American."

Gray and cheerless, the designated building meets my preconception of a government office in a communist bureaucracy. Entering the door, I sense impending danger. Almost literally, I gasp for air. My nose is stuffed, and breathing through my mouth helps only partially. Svetlana's "free air" phrase attains a literal meaning. A nervous tremor rattles me.

After a long wait on a hard wooden bench that numbs my bottom, I am directed into a small room. Essentially bare, it contains only a desk, piles of papers, and Tito's portrait. The official who processes my visa application asks questions in a monotone. He registers my answers while never glancing at me. His cold and impersonal style makes me feel as if I am a nobody, a nothing, only the number written on my visa form. I could be standing before him naked and he would not notice. A thought flashes of the Hungarian relatives I never knew because they perished in the concentration camps. Did they have to face a seated Nazi official who decided who would live and who would enter the gas chamber? I tremble. I do not feel safe, just as my mother said she would not feel safe in a communist country.

Encountering the trench-coated man in the used car lot, I am shivering. Not bothering to show any ID, the man demands I put away the camera. "Or," he threatens, "I take film, camera."

The force of habit dares me to question Mr. Trenchcoat: "*Zašto?* [Why?]" As can be expected, no conversation in any language is possible. One does not question or argue with law enforcement officers in a police state or, probably, anywhere.

"Come," declares Mario, grabbing my hand urgently, leading us quickly from the lot. Once I am breathing normally again, I ask him: "What objection can there be to filming people in a used car lot?"

"Power, control," Mario sums up succinctly. "You foreigner, American. I, Czech. Secret police, always watch."

In Zagreb, living inside a goldfish bowl populated by gray fish, I have undergone the loss of my anonymous and unmonitored privacy. I am not so alone here as I initially thought. The car lot experience puts me on more constant alert. In a surveillance society my comings and goings may be secretly observed. I have no constitutionally protected right either to move freely or to photograph in public. Our day's outing abruptly curtailed, Mario suggests we visit his home.

His front door opens into the living room section of a small, one-room apartment.

"Cozy," I say, noting the traditional naïve paintings of village scenes and villagers decorating the walls. The primitive art creates an atmosphere of childlike innocence, emanating freshness, delight, and optimism.

"Czech countryside," says Mario. He is pleased I appreciate the paintings and the Czech ceramics and carved wooden folk art assembled on a low table. I admire a hand-stitched cloth of colorful flowers and birds covering an overstuffed chair. The room projects a cherished existence, far away but not forgotten.

Mario lives in the tiny flat with his mother. They have only one room but it is solely theirs. His bed occupies one side. She sleeps in an alcove at the other end. Many Yugoslavs are forced by the housing shortage to live in small apartments with family members, friends, and even strangers, sharing toilet and cooking privileges. Space may be divided into private sections by sheets.

Mario says they are lucky to have their own place. Even so, they have applied for a larger apartment. The rents in Yugoslavia are very low as part of state-run housing, but there is a sign-up list for apartments. "Wait time years, perhaps decades," he estimates. Unless, he adds, one is part of the elite of Party and government officials. I wonder if Mario and his mother have learned to endure waits, delays, and the general inertia without fuming.

Shortly after our arrival, there appears a diminutive figure dressed all in black. Mario goes to her and they embrace.

"*Američanka*," is the lone word I catch as Mario introduces me to his mother. He speaks to her in the Czech language. "*Máma*" smiles shyly. I get the idea she has been expecting me.

"Simple village woman, no schooling," Mario states as his mother motions us into the kitchen. All the while she points to the worn wooden floor. It is not to the water staining she directs my sight. The floor is disfigured by a hole large enough to fall into and that must be carefully avoided. Mario tells me that a friend will help him make the repair.

Relieved that I am aware of the kitchen danger lying in wait, Mario's mother removes bowls from a cabinet and resumes stirring soup on the stove. She is really petite. Her very wrinkled face makes her look too old to have a son in his early thirties.

"Not knowing," responds Mario when I ask Máma's age. Her small village kept no records.

Máma wears a flowing, ankle-length skirt and long-sleeved blouse. The traditional head kerchief is tied under her hair. Her interaction with Mario shows that she rivets her life on caring for her one and only child. Her son shines as the light of her world. Now I am included in the mix as she ladles a thick vegetable soup out of the large metal pot and cuts chunks of bread. Watching us enjoy her delicious soup, she nods, satisfied. She springs to replenish our bowls. Softly she pats Mario's back.

Observing their relationship inspires memories of my Hungarian grandmother. She, too, doted on her son, my father, her life's reward. She also excelled at cooking and baking and making traditional dishes, always getting special praise for her stuffed cabbage and other culinary reminders of her homeland. Sometimes, at home, she wore a kerchief, making her face appear broader, more Slavic.

The soup is an appetizing prelude to a mouth-watering meal of Mario's Balkan favorites that Máma prepared as she happily sliced, chopped, and mixed. After dinner, Máma refuses my help to clean up and waves Mario and me into the living room. He draws my attention to particular pieces in their collection of Czech folk art. Máma carries in a tray of her homemade cookies dusted with nut shavings. "So good!" I exclaim after my first bite. She grins, lays the tray before me, and gestures, "Eat!"

Instead of sitting, she turns on the phonograph. Out pour the buoyant strains of Czechoslovakian folk music, violins predominating. Rather than merely listening, Máma begins dancing around the room. She holds her arms on high, as if offering herself heavenward. Her arms move gracefully, like branches of a young willow tree caressed by a gentle wind. Máma takes on the air of a very young girl so light she could float away. In the soft lighting, her wrinkles vanish and she transforms into an ageless being. She becomes an angelic presence whose shining face exudes pure joy. Occasionally she beams at me. I am impressed by her freedom to dance unselfconsciously before me, as if I am her intimate acquaintance. The longer she dances, the less my reaction interests her.

Máma's outstretched hands call us into a small circle suitable to the cramped area. Mario pushes the chairs aside to widen the dancing space. He lifts me from the chair and around and around we three whirl until we twirl down, our arms wrapped around each other's shoulders. We sway as one with the music. A glorious energy transports me to somewhere in the Czech countryside. Gradually I am elevated beyond Earth. I enter a light-filled expanse. My body pulsates with indescribable acceptance and belonging. Eyes closed, I almost forget where I am. The music stops, no one moves.

Slowly we unclasp and the spell breaks. The circle dissolves. Mother and son exchange knowing glances. Mario sets a tender kiss on her forehead. She glows. She bubbles around him. He bubbles back. I sense that his education and his engineering job are less the source of her pride than his respect for her and their devoted bond.

Nothing can top this moment. Wishing to freeze it in time, I suggest we end the evening. But the spell is not broken. Máma brings me into a firm hug. Her physical strength awes me. On the way to my lodging, Mario and I hold tightly to each other's hand. Meaningful squeezes tell me more than any verbal declarations.

My subsequent visits let me further witness Mario and his mother showering love on each other in a continuous give-and-take. Into this agreeable domain they gather me. In the presence of their warmth and solicitude, my feeling for Mario goes deeper than a thump-thump-thumping of my heart and excited tingling of my flesh. My Zagrebian loneliness fades into memory, underscoring that life is always changing.

Having risen in love, I view all through love-activated eyes. My heart connects me not merely with these affectionate people but with everyone. The recognizable blessedness and gratitude pulse through me. Love's rays of light burn up the clouds in my Yugoslav sky. I am so glad to be alive! Mario reminds my heart that to feel close love and tenderness for another is to beat in a rhythmic joy surpassing words.

Máma demonstrates the same lesson. She does not try to expel me as an intruder. She does not consider me a thief stealing her son's love and leaving her less. She does not compete against me for her son's attention. She neither fears me nor wishes to eradicate me from her son's life. Her attitude signals that I am more than worthy for her precious son. The kinship between the two of them has simply expanded into a larger familial network. Their earnest acceptance is a soothing balm for the hurts I sustained in the relationship with my Stanford beau.

Frequenting Mario's cozy Czech home in Zagreb brings to mind the birthplaces of my paternal grandparents. Both Schmuelhersh Eisner and Dvorah Braun were born in small villages in the Kingdom of Hungary when it was a partner in the Austro-Hungarian Empire. After they left Europe, border changes following the Empire's defeat in World War I placed their two Hungarian villages, on the River Uzh, officially inside Czechoslovakia for some time. The Holocaustic actions of Herr Hitler robbed me of my East European relatives, so it is probably healing to imbibe the close feeling of family with these goodhearted Czech people. I did not mention my Jewish roots to Mario, and he did not ask, but I cannot imagine that he and his mother hold any anti-Semitic beliefs. They represent for me all those Czechs and other East Europeans, plus Germans as well, who condemned, and perhaps even actively opposed, Hitler's demoniac policies.

In the cozy realm nurtured by Mario and his mother, centered around a love based on giving rather than on taking, I feel part of a remarkable togetherness. Even while we have little grasp of each other's language and culture, how to account for the moments of heart-oneness with Mario and Máma? More than once I remember the three of us dancing intertwined in joy. Is linguistic and cultural understanding not needed to experience unity with people? Some experiences obviously cannot be explained or understood by the mind. I conclude: *Yes, human beings do have the capacity to relate to each other deeply without jealousy, selfishness, and possessiveness.*

Máma is always cheerful. Never do I spot darkness shadowing her face. The society's flattening energy does not ground her high spirits. She radiates an internal environment of balance and strength. Máma seems to maintain her equilibrium unperturbed by outer influences, whether of down-or-upbeat quality. She exemplifies that outer repression need not suppress one's inner happiness. Is she expressing that the sunny person can hack through the difficulties of life better than the sorrowful person? Her example presents in yet another form the recurring message I get in Zagreb: *Learn to create your own inner harmony and peace. Then you may live anywhere.*

One evening, after we have savored yet another tasty dinner of Balkan specialties, Mario announces that his mother is planning our wedding. "Since met," he adds. As if on cue Máma, giggling shyly, delivers a box into my hands. I unwrap brand new stainless steel kitchen utensils. Máma points to Mario and me. She is blushing. I am embarrassed. Awkwardly, I hand the package to Mario. Seeing my flustered reaction, Máma discreetly retreats to the kitchen.

Mario and I sit in the living room. The phonograph is spinning out Czech folk music. I say I understand. Máma assumes that a romance automatically leads to a formal union. Again I note the vast differences between Yugoslav norms and values and those I know from New York and California.

With all delicacy, I tell Mario that marriage is not in my thoughts. He shows no surprise. In our initial meeting, I had cited my upcoming departure for Holland. We both regret his mother's disappointment.

A special learning period has reached natural closure. Love's ability to lift me to sublime emotion and heightened awareness reminds me there is a greater significance to my life, and I have not yet found it. Although transported to a blissful state, love has not deluded me. I do not wear rose-tinted glasses. Yu-go-*slave*-ia remains a gray, harsh, and secretive society. The seed of my me cannot come to further germination here, not even with a supportive Mario at my side. This very real romance is also a mirage. Mario and I share a communion transcending words, but language forms a barrier. My elementary Serbo-Croatian does not allow us to converse at any depth. Mario, for his part, speaks rudimentary English. It is his proficiency at voicing the language of love through everyday behavior that captivated me.

Mario, the Czech-Yugoslav, and generous Svetlana, and hardworking Matko, represent all that is positive in the Yugoslav society with its simple, natural, and authentic lifestyle. The Yugoslavs are a good people, I decide.

Yet I feel perplexed, sad, disappointed, and a little bit angry. *Why, after resolving to leave this puzzling land, have I met caring and loving Mario who causes me to treasure, rather than wish away, my final weeks in Zagreb? Why has my lonely stay in the Croatian capital transformed into a happy idyll? I had made peace with my isolation and loneliness. Why has that peace been disturbed?* Now I have new heartache caused by the imminent parting from Mario.

I accept my willingness to take risks and assign myself the responsibility for having plunged myself into the Yugoslavian adventure. Perhaps Mario is the answer to a prayer I did not make. Perhaps he is a gift of the Universe, a reward for my Zagrebian sufferings and pain. I recognize again: *Within the negative is the positive, if only we can see it.*

The very end of the Zagreb Film job mirrors my emotional conflict since meeting Mario. Finishing up the final tasks for Matko, he tells me he enjoyed our working together. Matko hands me a "To Whom It May Concern" reference letter. On the familiar Studio letterhead, in typewritten words, he "highly, and warmly" recommends me to any film production house. "All her work was done to our complete satisfaction, very conscientiously," reads the second paragraph, "with a very detailed penetration into the meaning and eventual message of each individual film. We have been greatly impressed by her abilities during her stay with us."

An unexpected sadness, born of the knowledge that Zagreb Film will now be in my past, besets me. This feeling intensifies on the day of my leave-taking from the Studio. One by one, the artists come to say goodbye. Their hugs and kisses and best wishes for my future throw me into an emotional ocean of both joy and sorrow.

They present me a parting gift. It is a book, in Serbo-Croatian and English, about the artistic creations of Andrija Buvina, a thirteenth-century Croatian sculptor and painter. One of the animators, Milan Blažeković, leafs through the book's photos with me. He admires the wooden doors Buvina sculpted in his masterly Romanesque style for the Cathedral of St. Duje in Split on the Dalmatian coast. "Go Split," he advises. I should see for myself the magnificent carvings that depict fourteen scenes from the life of Christ.

The animators also give me a personalized memento. It is a framed animation cell from *Izumitelj Cipela* (The Inventor of Shoes), the first cartoon in the new Professor Balthazar film series for children. The three directors of the film, Zlatko Grgić, Ante Zaninović, and Boris Kolar drew on the cel's mounting frame for me. At the top left is a smiling Professor Balthazar. My name emerges from the eccentric inventor's mouth. On his head, the professor sports a green shoe placed upside down. I gulp, remembering the upside down images during the film screening with Stern. Indeed, looking at life from a different angle in Yu-go-*slave*-ia changed my perspective, helping alter the quality of my life.

Is there any symbolism intended by the drawing of upside down shoes, and in the color green? Is there being suggested that Miss Green walk in another's shoes? Their animated films vividly evidence that the Zagreb filmmakers weave subtle messages into their images.

Footsteps drawn around the cel mounting each say "Boris." The footsteps lead over a supine Ante Zaninović, who is waving his hat and saying "Bye!" Out of the last shoe a hand waves "Good Luck" above the signature of Zlatko Grgić.

I am touched but tortured. *Why did this show of affection, and Mario, happen so late in the game?* I agonize to myself: *Reward or Punishment?* I am still debating the question on my departure day.

Unlike the sweltering July morning of my arrival, Sun is not shining in late November. A chill mist hovers over Zagreb. I am bundled up in my winter clothes. The collar of Mario's dark coat is upraised for the nippy day. Mario drives me to the train station in his recovered stolen car. Miraculously, the car reappeared before he purchased another one secondhand. He gives me a basket containing a chicken Máma baked for my journey to The Hague.

Love's sweetness fills every pore of my being. But my revitalized heart now hurts with the same intensity of ache as it felt ecstasy in Mario's arms. *Don't go!* my heart exhorts me. My mind rattles, confused, not sure whether to tell me to leave or to stay. Independently, as if energized by a power not their own, my legs climb the train steps.

In the open doorway, I stare through wet eyes at Mario standing on the platform. Mario's eyes water too. My hand makes a small waving sign; he waves back in slow motion.

Mario's friendly face is clouded behind a total solar eclipse. It is the remembrance of his usually sunny face, lit up by his gleaming smile, and his sandy hair combed neatly, a few strands attractively grazing his forehead, that embeds itself in my memory.

The conductor's whistle sounds the "all ready to go" signal. My heart moans. My eyes release more sad tears. At the train window, I wave and wave. Mario waves and waves. I watch as the watched becomes a receding speck in the mist.

Despite the pain of separation, I feel a sense of rightness. Once again, Yu-go-*slave*-ia allows me no choice. I have to leave and the timing remains *now*.

"*Doviđenja* [goodbye]," I whisper with a sigh, not knowing I am also saying goodbye to a part of myself left behind in Tito's Yu-go-*slave*-ia.

22
Going-from-*Slave*-ia

The twenty-eight-hour train ride to the Netherlands offers ample time for contemplation. I gaze out the window while actually looking inside myself. The journey glides into a traveling version of my reflective solitary evenings before I met Mario. Excluding the gift weeks enjoyed with him and his mother, in Zagreb I suffered a shortage of breath.

Inhaling every day in a country lacking "free air" confined me to a dark space that was the entire Yugoslav society of the drab, the grim, the lacking, the secretive, the fearful, and the unfree. Yet when my simple lodgings transformed into silent sanctuaries for contemplation, I started glimpsing the light of my own self-understanding. Self-confrontation obviously belonged to the deeper intent of the stay in Yu-go-*slave*-ia.

On the external level, as an American in the unfree Titoist society, often I felt watched. If the plainclothes secret policemen were not always observing me, the citizens were. The scrutiny was mutual. Our language, patterns of dressing, thinking, and behaving so differed. Only now, safe in the train, the Balkan society receding into my past, do I feel free from that unfree land. Yet Yu-go-*slave*-ia helped me peek behind the veil hiding what in my own *slave*-ia needs changing en route to my better life.

What creates the "better life" and the "better world"? I muse as the train chugs on. *And does the better world include everyone, no matter how different we are from each other?*

I review my life in America. Our education focuses on our own self-interest. There were reasons enough that John F. Kennedy spoke his memorable words: "My fellow Americans, ask not what your country can do for you, ask what you can do for your country." I have to confess that I give this oft-quoted statement mainly lip service. What do I do for my country except indirectly, as a responsible citizen obeying society's laws, voting, paying taxes, and contributing to the growth of the economy as a consumer?

My sojourn in Yu-go-*slave*-ia expanded my understanding of who I am as a citizen in society. In the mirror held up by John Grierson, I recognized myself as a person aspiring to express myself through my own creativity while helping the world become a better place. Grierson noted that my pen has already brought me on the road of public service. I know I still have to connect to a cause or issue meaningful to me. To succeed at knowing what is more meaningful for my life, apparently I have to lose the less meaningful. How to do this? And what is "the meaningful"? In various ways, I sense there is a greater freedom I have not yet discovered.

Yu-go-*slave*-ia helped me realize my lacks of freedom not only as a citizen in present-day society. Life in Zagreb taught me that freedoms of speech, assembly, and movement are not just human-made laws written into a national constitution. I experienced in nonfree Zagrabian society that freedom is also an inner need. Like breathing, "freedom" is essential to our human existence. But, just as we breathe on automatic pilot, we may be unaware of the inner state of freedom. Yu-go-*slave*-ia made tangible my inner need for unobstructed breathing in a state of true freedom, though I still have no idea what this "true freedom" might be. Will I get help from "the guidance" that has ostensibly led me to Zagreb?

In Yu-go-*slave*-ia, I became more conscious of the unconscious search engaging me. The sensation of feeling blessed gave me sustenance. The blessed feeling helped me endure the baffling Yugoslav situation, not tiring and not giving up, as if I were advancing to a beloved place or person awaiting me down the road.

A sixth sense conveys that my spontaneous "Yes!" led me to Yugoslavia with purpose, assuring me that there really is a Higher Purpose. My rationality encourages me to dismiss such notions. It seems unthinkable that a "conscious Power," greater than my own will, wants, and wishes, influences my steps. Yet my affinity with a Greater Power apparently exists. From where else do I get the feeling that "coincidences" are not so coincidental? Is there a "cosmic cause" governing "coincidence?" From where derives my thought that our daily life contains signs and messages offering guidance for our ultimate good?

On the train, moving toward the Netherlands at the predictable Yugoslav slowness, I ponder "time." It takes no time and no great insight to confirm that I regard time "in a very American way," as Svetlana might formulate my tendency. Americans are raised with time as part of the consumerist mindset. We consider time as a possession and a form of finance. I tend to "spend" my time, *my* time, in activities positioned around me. My time is *mine*. Time is my fortune, my "money." I am a rich person able to spend my days as I decide, as I deem to allocate my time resources.

The blaring light of post-Zagrebian reflection exposes that I am not very generous in giving freely of my free time simply to help out others for free. Sharing my wealth of time by doing good for others voluntarily and selflessly, I can act like a tightwad. When I give my time to civic activities, do I donate just to donate, asking nothing back? I volunteer for good purpose organizations, but their names do dress up and give prestige to my CV; I give financially to registered charities, and they deliver tax credits or ego boosting. Several times I fundraised for the Actors' Fund when I was a professional actress and singer. The Fund's retirement home in New Jersey for elderly members of Actors' Equity could possibly be a living place for me one day. Would I have helped fundraise had I not had a somewhat vested interest in the project and, as well, had not received in exchange for my volunteering free tickets to Broadway plays? Clearly my level of compassion and service to others needs a serious ascent. My heart needs stretching to embrace "us," and my mind needs to grow beyond the thought, *What will I get out of this?*

Glimpsing unpleasant truths about our own selfishness surely can hurt. Only remembering I am quick to help my family and friends lessens the pain. Perhaps, eventually, I will identify all people as my family and friends? Taking a positive view, in the Grierson manner, I discern that the loss of my so-called American good life in Zagreb has revived my childhood aspiration to live a do-good life.

I make an accounting of my American good life. It was not loneliness that had motivated me to pack my New York appointment book with a succession of leisure-time activities. Sense-gratification, arts appreciation, and the social need to stay updated on the cultural scene had sent me scurrying from the latest well-reviewed film to theatrical must-see to concert to exhibition to lecture. The constant round of activities had distracted me from taking the time to know myself better. My busy Manhattan existence had not fanned to flame my childhood spark to help bring forth a better world hand in hand. Using my leisure mainly for my personal benefit had diverted me from active participation in the problems and needs of my society. In sum, my dashing American feel-good free time cost me much more than the hours, energy, and money I invested to get back material reward, knowledge, and pleasure.

Yugoslavia obliged me to think outside my usual boxes. I got intimations that to be truly successful, I have to stop revolving myself solely around myself and what is important merely to me. I got hints that every thought, word, and action has a repercussion and an influence affecting a larger circle than the narrow one formed by self-centeredness.

The train speeds up after entering Austria. A long sigh rushes from my lips. I catch a whiff of my breath, smelling musty, reminiscent of the rental room visited with Matko. The room needed fresh air, but the window was closed. Following my musty exhale, spontaneously I inhale deeply. I jerk in my seat, giddy, as if jolted with a hit of pure oxygen. Svetlana is right. The air of the Free West is liberating.

In Zagreb, a feeling of suffocation and unease became habitual. The uneasiness also resulted from the piercing self-scrutiny demanded of me by Professor Yu-go-*slave*-ia, a most exacting headmaster. Challenges in Zagreb compelled me to face my dark inner places.

It takes honesty to admit one's deficiencies. To change requires courage, as the transformed lives of Cassius Clay and Malcolm Little exemplify. I am really glad I did not try to flee the Yu-go-*slave*-ian social experiment in which I had, after all, confined myself voluntarily and which I shared with a whole nation of citizens who, by contrast, had little choice in the matter. I am thankful I did not run away from my personal attempt at self-management in a workplace where "Brotherhood and Unity" apparently did not include the *Američanka*. I am grateful that difficulties did not send me scurrying home to my alleged good life left behind. Yu-go-*slave*-ia confirmed my ability to endure despite serious obstacles.

To be fair, I have to acknowledge that my American training in competition helped me survive Yu-go-*slave*-ia. My competitive society taught me: "I am not a quitter." Retreating from difficulties does not belong to my American mindset. In addition, New Yorkers do not usually give up. In America, even while immersed in the culture of "feeling good" and instant gratification, I learned to persevere in the face of troublesome situations.

Yu-go-*slave*-ia did not allow me to fly away from the battle of life. I had to face up to the various problems. I had to experience my experiences; for instance, my own existential loneliness. Outer, societally caused loneliness forced me to confront my inner aloneness. I learned it was more productive to become intimate with the inner state of aloneness than try to escape from the feeling of loneliness. The power of aloneness brought me into deeper touch with my inner needs, feelings, impulses, and also my inner resources. I had to deal with "feeling bad." Ironically, the worse I felt, the more I realized that mere "feeling good" is a vapid goal to pursue. I understood that one pays a hefty inner price for following the trend of disguising or suppressing unpleasantness and living in a feel-good bubble.

Zagreb pushed me into self-critique more probing than ever previously I had carried out. Negative qualities, attitudes, and habits came up for review and I examined them. How to gain release? Not yet did I know how to transmute the negative into the positive.

Staying the course in Zagreb, I passed a test I had no idea I was taking. That was a secret testing of my inner strength, an exam for which my life to date had provided a continuous preparation. Severe as it was, the test in Zagreb did not conjure up the usual feelings of overall nervousness and other unpleasant sensations I sometimes felt before taking an exam at Barnard. In Zagreb, there was no physical teacher assessing improvements in my powers of patience, flexibility, perseverance, awareness, acceptance and self-correction. No professor took up a red pencil to mark *A,* maybe *A+,* or *A-,* and hopefully no form of *B,* on my invisible exam paper. (By the way, Professor Rauch gave me an "*A,* Excellent" for my book report on *The New Class.*)

In short, there were no others in my Zagrebian classroom. There were no other persons with whom to compare myself and my performance; there was only me.

Professor Yu-go-*slave*-ia belonged to that school of education fitting with my preferred learning method, whereby here-and-now experience is the best teacher—a school in which we also try to learn from the past, thus having no reason to reinvent the wheel, and we try not to repeat mistakes. Professor Yu-go-*slave*-ia inspired me to realize: *I have no need to better others, as in beating or defeating, but only to "better" as in helping myself and others live a better life.* To do that, of course, I need to better myself, improve my character. I am beginning to trust that what I truly am, my real self unhampered and untampered by societal identity and my own unresolved issues from the past, will one day manifest itself.

My inability to speak Serbo-Croatian in the Studio canteen also bore unexpected fruit. After lunching in silence among chattering people became my new normalcy, the need to prove myself verbally lessened. No longer did I feel obliged to present myself to others in any special manner. If the inability to communicate with the Studio workers and the animators prevented the closer contact I desired, the forced muteness intensified my powers of observation. My weak Serbo-Croatian encouraged me to watch more and talk less.

Another discovery: I complained that the Yugoslavs did not help me, yet the behavior I wanted from them, I did not practice myself. What had I done to indicate I cared about their lives? My hypocrisy is simply my ignorance, or my unawareness. Svetlana's frank assessment of my deficient empathy was another reminder of the dangers attached to judging and misjudging others. It is easier to see flaws in others than in ourselves.

Growth in my concern for others led to another totally unanticipated consequence: I overcame my fear of communism or, rather, socialism. Caring bridges with loving, or learning to love. In aiming to stretch my boundaries of caring and loving, I embraced a simple and obvious truth: all people are human beings. Communists and socialists are human beings like anyone else. Whether we are capitalists or socialists or Americans or Germans or women or men or white or black or whatever, all of us are essentially the same in our human condition. Recognizing we are all human beings motivated by the same basic drives, needs, instincts, and inner nature furthers us to accept people for what they are from within. We all desire to live happy, peaceful, and fulfilling lives.

Savoring the train journey for the insight it showers, at one point I muse: *Is my view of Yugoslavia too somber?* Had I not made an adverse prejudgment, just as I had about Cassius Clay and Malcolm X? There is no denying that I imported into Yugoslavia a negative bias. My college studies, public opinion, media reports, and *The New Class* led me very naturally to regard unfavorably a dictatorship watched over by a secret police. Not surprisingly, even before my arrival I saw Yugoslavia through the gray clouds formed by my own negative prejudgment.

Before going to Zagreb, I was quite the stranger to the everyday functioning of Titoist politics and economics, the customs of the multiethnic Balkan culture, and the Serbo-Croatian language. From my very first day in Yu-go-*slave*-ia, the window of Yugoslav socialism was half-blocked and shaded. I got a sunless view of Yugoslav society. While open to see positive aspects of the Titoist system, more often

I spotted the negatives. My superficial understanding of the country's political and economic system, and my judgmental preconceptions, undoubtedly led me to misconceptions, misperceptions, and misinterpretations. Did not all of this fuel my dark outlook of the Yugoslavian experiment? I question myself: *Did my anticommunist conditioning, and my lonely outsider life as a quasi-Yu-go-slave, influence me to paint Yugoslavian society in tones grayer than appeared to the native Yu-go-slave?*

Probably my bleak perspective in Zagreb also owed its dark tint to disgruntled locals. My American optimism made me an alien to the grim mentality embodied by the unsmiling woman in *Morning Chronicle*, but had my disappointments with America's defects unconsciously drawn me to Yugoslavs equally unhappy with their government's national policies, the "like attracts like" principle at work? Svetlana and the Turtleneck Man, not to mention Drago, fit into the category of "malcontents." Alas, I let the gloomy local atmosphere overwhelm my normally optimistic American spirit. Negativity breeds negativity. A mind weighed down by negativity is a heavy burden to bear. Better to let positivity breed positivity, as I experienced in the presence of Mario and his mother.

The surge of insight continues. The outer circumstances of my life in the Titoist society formed not the only restrictions on my freedom. I felt captive in my body and mind. In America, Land of the Free, I always considered myself a free person. This illusion shattered in Yu-go-*slave*-ia. I noted that everywhere I am, I take orders from my various attitudes, desires, and habits. My conditioning imprisons me. It has become uncomfortably evident that the chains binding me to my own *slave*-ia are attached to my habitual ways of thinking and behaving. My past thoughts and emotional experiences color my reactions to events in the present. They motivate my actions. My initial responses to Bros Cassius Clay and Malcolm X and *Herr* Stern are merely three examples. Only I have the power to go beyond my own limitations. To grow further, I have to reduce my inner obstacles and expand my borders.

Bidding farewell to the lacks, deprivations, and inconveniences making up my daily life in Zagreb is no hardship. I am relieved to put behind me Tito's experiment in brotherhood (and sisterhood) and unity.

At the same time, I thank the Yugoslav society for compelling me to live in ways more natural and less complicated, if less comfortable, although more fruitfully reflective, than ever before I knew. The daily tests shifted my chief focus from externals to my own inner nature. Yu-go-*slave*-ia confirmed my hunch that a better life is based on more than material attainment. I am living to learn, while learning to live.

Traveling toward the land of the Dutch, I resolve to accept, without complaint, what I have or do not have at any moment. I will try to accept what I am, or am not, at any stage of my life, even while I will continually strive to improve myself. I resolve to become a better person than I was yesterday.

The challenge to better my own self, to attain to my nobler qualities, is the competition engaging me now. Like many people forming resolutions, I know I am taking on a gigantic task that will cost me quite some immeasurable minutes to implement fully—when I can recall my resolution.

In Zagreb, able to see my American life from afar, I perceived that my first two decades had schooled me in the unequaled greatness of American society. The third decade, the social, protesting Sixties, opened my eyes to America's imperfections. Viewing America from a distance in Zagreb, I acquired a renewed admiration for my birth country. I saw I had neither understood nor appreciated the true riches of my homeland. Despite its defects and immaturities as a nation, "Melting Pot America" offers a lifestyle of citizen freedom I did not cherish until I lived in a nation of reduced freedoms.

Having undergone the Yugoslavian restraints, I am really grateful to my European grandparents for my inheritance of American citizenship, freedoms, and the opportunity to attain the American Dream. I greatly respect their courage, which enabled them as teenagers to cross the vast Atlantic Ocean heading into an unspecified future totally on their own. Had they stayed in their birth countries, all eventually imprisoned inside the satellite system of the USSR, a harsh existence determined by oppressive Soviet Communism and anti-Semitism would have been their fate.

My train reaches the border of West Germany and halts. Uniformed men, speaking German and packing guns in holsters, walk through the carriage. They are checking travel documents. My papers are in order, yet a wave of insecurity upsets my composure. My life is momentarily in these persons' control. Handing my passport to the German officer, a tremor nonpluses me. Am I reacting nervously to crossing another border into the unknown, or am I suffering symptoms of my allergy to things Germanic? If the latter, this hypersensitivity confirms again that I need to rid myself of my German antipathy. *No, no, no, I cannot be a reverse Siegfried!* Herr Stern has had a multilayered inspirational effect.

Both Stern and John Grierson pointed out that Zagreb Film exploited me. Was it not I who allowed the exploitation? Going to Yugoslavia was never about money, and willingly I had accepted low wages and poor terms in exchange for the unique adventure. After all, it truly seemed that the Studio lacked the possibilities to pay more. Of course, the Studio could have compensated me in nonfinancial ways, such as arranging suitable lodgings and taking an interest in my general welfare.

For the questionable treatment dealt me at Zagreb Film, I have no one to blame except myself. I let Yu-go-*slave*-ia use me as a commodity. Even while thinking I was a free American in unfree Yugoslavia, I accepted dictatorship in the Yugoslav workplace. I had done the same in my own country, every time I accepted lower pay than a man for the same job. Problem is, exploitation can be hard to detect. "Invisible exploitation," just like "invisible prejudice," often hides behind friendly veneers.

In socialist Zagreb, some people misused me to an extreme. Besides mistreatment in the workplace, I came across landlords asking unreasonably high rents for little more than bare boxes with a door and a (generally closed) window or two. Did greed or need or old conditioning motivate these people? My housing problems reinforced my conclusion that political attempts to bring more fairness and justice among people will fail unless supported by the individuals' own uplifted attitudes and behavior.

On the subject of uplifted attitudes—namely, my own—I am glad to acknowledge that my forced involvement in Zagreb's housing problems also taught me a subtle lesson in the giving, sharing, and distribution of personal resources. Circumstances literally forced me to donate to the well-being of Ana and Stef, to step into their troubled lives as an unwitting benefactor. Would I have helped the couple had I not received a rental room in exchange? Would I have given them their needed funds voluntarily, giving simply to give? Again comes the unavoidable conclusion: My heart needs to expand to love inclusively, unconditionally, selflessly. My "things to do" list keeps getting longer and more challenging.

Musing further on my housing problems, I decide that my present desire to help better the world is fed more by my intellect and social conscience than by my loving heart. I am at the developmental stage where I am always open to aid those close to me; unfamiliar persons usually remain outside the direct line of my generosity. My slowness in extending a hand of assistance to strangers reveals the extent of my training in self-centeredness. I am very much wrapped up in my own "I."

The basic caring and sharing principles of socialism, which the Yugoslav society failed to demonstrate to me, dear Mario and his dear mother represented, as had dear Svetlana before them. I recognize that Mario's unconditional and nonexploitive love differed markedly from love I had known previously. Mario exemplified the principle of loving just to love. I sensed no calculations of: "What can I get from this woman? How can she benefit me?" If there is a totally accepting and nurturing love, I felt it flow from Mario. No insecurity or fear pressed me to wear a girlish hairband in his or his mother's company.

Mario appeared on my path as a godsend, but not when I most needed an upward surge, not when I would have most welcomed assistance in counteracting my Zagrebian gloom. His restorative love arrived after I had dropped my lonely frame of mind. By the time we met, I was cheerful, excitedly day-dreaming about my new start in Holland. Perhaps Mario was indeed a reward for my endurance of Yu-go-*slave*-ia? Or had my changed, upbeat approach merely attracted positive-minded Mario to my side, like attracting like?

The train halts at the Dutch border for passport control, and my grandparents again come to mind. Desiring a better life, they had journeyed to America. Following the pattern of early twentieth century mass emigration, after entering the Promised Land they learned English and looked for work. Good at sewing, my Hungarian grandmother found a job making buttonholes in men's vests and suits. My Hungarian grandfather, apprenticed to a jeweler, established himself as an artisan skilled at repairing lockets and watches. My Latvian grandfather sold women's garments and became a prosperous shop owner. My Warsaw-born grandmother settled in New York City at six months of age and grew up to be a hardworking mother and wife who assisted her husband, my grandfather, in the store. After he passed away, she maintained the business.

I, possessing the Constitutional freedoms inherited as a second generation American, including the unquestioned freedom to dream my own dream, have returned to the continent of my grandparents' birth. Not that I seek to make my fortune in Europe. Living in materially deprived Yugoslavia confirmed my thought that material fulfillment is only one measure of happiness, just as is emotional fulfillment. Now I know I am searching a fulfillment that speaks to my existential origins.

The high school student voted most likely to succeed is succeeding—in learning the lessons pointing out the direction of her life's true success. To what Promised Land am I heading? Or being led?

23

Rounding Out Yugo-Nostalgically

Despite my initial impression, my Zagreb Film art house movie did not reach the end of its reel with my waving "*Doviđenja,* goodbye" to Mario at the same train station where my Yu-go-slave-ian odyssey began. The conclusion occurred three months later.

In February 1969, I traveled from my rented room in The Hague to Salzburg, Austria. There I attended a three-week seminar on cinema at the Salzburg Seminar, an American nonprofit organization bringing together Europeans and Americans to exchange ideas for global change. Among many scintillating conversations, I enjoyed talks with faculty chairman Willard Van Dyke, director of the film department at New York's Museum of Modern Art. The well-known American photographer and documentary film pioneer was, like John Grierson, a film elder of social conscience. He, too, had dedicated his professional life to the use of film for social purpose.

Seminar concluded, Van Dyke visited several European cities scouting films for the museum. After meeting Želimir Matko in Yugoslavia, he wrote me a letter. On stationery of Zagreb's Esplanade Intercontinental Hotel, Van Dyke penned: "Matko asked me if I knew you and I said I did. He asked me about your ability as a writer, and I answered truthfully that I liked your film reviews and I thought your piece on the Salzburg Seminar was excellent. He expressed concern that he had not really had time to properly explore your capacities and that they had been a little bit cruel in that they paid you a Yugoslav salary and threw you into the problems of living on it. He excused himself by saying you had indicated your desire to really understand how Yugoslavs live. I asked him if you knew Serbo-Croat and since he said you did not, I suggested he had been less than fair."

Matko had evidently done some soul searching. Perhaps he would make improved financial and personal arrangements for the next American helping Zagreb Film. Van Dyke's letter stamped "The End" on my Yugoslavian story, or so I thought.

The completion received its double rounding out when I heard that my Studio colleague who wanted "go Amerika" for the "mucho mucho dollar" had won the Yugoslav National Lottery! "Coincidence?" Or had Mr. Turtleneck's overpowering wish for big money drawn the top lottery prize to his ticket? I became conscious of the power of wishing, especially as I still harbored many wishes myself. The phrase "You get what you wish for" had not yet divulged its profound meaning, and dangers, to me.

The double completion resolved into a triple ending with the news that the Turtleneck Man, after celebrating his win by throwing a huge party, contradicted Yugoslav slowness by running through the prize money mucho mucho quickly. My sympathy for him increased. Was it better to have won and lost all, than never to have won? The update came via Svetlana.

Svetlana and I corresponded until our letter writing petered out in the early 1970s. During the Yugoslav Wars in the 1990s, I wondered about her safety in Zagreb. My Yugoslavia file did not produce her address. Having forgotten her not-so-easy-to-remember Croatian last name, I could not trace her.

Apropos names, "Svetlana" is not her name. I wanted to protect the identity of "Svetlana" because I added imaginatively, but factually, to some of our conversations recorded in this book. I think "Svetlana" might have said the words I attribute to her vast knowledge. In case she might not have agreed with all quotes, I have changed her name. If we would come again into contact, and if she would permit, immediately I would write her real name.

Whatever artistic liberties I have taken in portraying "Svetlana," I have faithfully depicted her kind generosity. Even if the Studio undoubtedly pressed "Svetlana" initially into the role of my helper, her example of heartfelt giving to a stranger has remained with me. Our extensive discussions and her loving actions, treating me as a friend, stimulated me to try and see the truly good residing in people. To see the truly good requires, of course, penetrating beyond the surface of things and stopping to judge others.

Perhaps Svetlana's statement, "It would be shameful if children could not manage to care for their aged parents," also seeded itself in me. By the time my mother entered her nineties, I spent longer periods in the US caring for her 24/7. My sister Bonnie and I, in close teamwork, were privileged to help our mother reach the end of her nearly ninety-nine years' long life in her own home, in her own bed, with us at her side. Part of this book was therefore written in Wynnewood, Pennsylvania, usually late at night after the finish of the day's care-giving.

But I did not mention to my mother, quite a judgmental person, Yugoslavia's help in pinpointing my tendency to judge people from their outer appearance and/or behavior and/or what I know of their past. Remembering fondly my jersey minidress loved by my American friends but abhorred in Zagreb, even by progressive "Svetlana," I observe that "looking outward" and placing excessive attention on externals is a general conditioning that captures us very early.

My snap judgment about well-dressed and well-coifed "Svetlana" worked out positively. Similar instant judgments distanced me from people, such as the travelers at the Zagreb train station. Their appearance told me we had nothing in common, not even our mutual identity as human beings. In the same way, the peasant woman in Zagreb evaluated me. My minidress and fishnet stockings represented immorality to her and so she cursed and spit at me. My clothing, in fact, reflected how numbers of young women were then dressing in America.

The social revolution of the 1960s had already brought dynamic changes in attitudes. Among them, young women broke out of the mainstream convention expecting daughters to dress like their mothers in below-the knee skirts and twin cardigan sweater sets accessorized by pearl necklaces. No longer had daughters to follow precisely in mom's footsteps leading to marriage, childbearing, and full-time housewifery as prescribed by the patriarchal society. Many of us rebelled against the limitations set by "a man's world." In the 1960s, the miniskirt was for some people a symbol of female liberation.

Unknowingly, I was part of a growing women's rights movement using diverse means to free females from second-class citizenship. If I suffered a lack of self-confidence in certain areas of my being, I did not lack confidence in my feminine power. This feminine power, though, could bring me into touchy encounters with men who misinterpreted my free-spirited open-mindedness as an invitation for sexual engagement. I did not wear a miniskirt to lure men into the bedroom, but to assert my independence from male dominance.

Nonetheless, wearing my minidress in the Zagreb of 1968 was an error in judgment. The cursing and spitting incident obviously arose from the failure of my sound judgment to decide what is or what is not appropriate in social situations; it was also a lapse of my good judgment to know how to avoid embarrassment and/or distress. Dressing immodestly was, furthermore, a poor value judgment. That poor value judgment revealed something about my poor values at the time, when I was more affected by outer rather than inner influences.

Whether I made a good or bad judgment to honor my word to John Kemeny is still a matter to ponder. In my view, I had never given him final editorial approval over my paper examining governmental interference with films of the National Film Board of Canada. Thanks to that experience, I directly absorbed the painful lesson that free expression is not always free, not even in apparently free and democratic nations. It was no revelation that totalitarian Yugoslavia, with its one-party rule, used surveillance and censorship to control people. But in Zagreb I reeled from shock when John Kemeny blocked the publication of my Stanford article, as John Grierson had correctly forecast.

By the way, I did not take Kemeny's demand as the last word on the subject. I made some editorial improvements Grierson recommended and resent the paper. Kemeny wrote back that John Grierson had discussed the article with him. He would send me his opinion after reading the revision. Grierson's intervention ultimately had no effect. Kemeny stuck to his original position. I vowed never again to jeopardize my press freedom.

John Kemeny left the NFB three years later, having produced, written, or edited eighty films. He went to Hollywood and free-lanced as an independent commercial film producer. Returning to Canada, he also worked for TV. His films won a host of prizes or nominations in Canada and internationally, including at the Berlin, Venice, Cannes, and Hollywood Oscar film award events. When he passed away at the end of 2012, the *Toronto Star* wrote his obit under the headline: "John Kemeny, forgotten giant of Canadian film, dies at 87."[38]

Kemeny lived long enough to see Canadian society acknowledge the example of selflessness demonstrated in the life and work of Dr. Norman Bethune. Although generally unknown while alive, after his death Norman Bethune received deserved recognition. Kemeny's 1964 documentary was followed in 1977 and in 1990 by two biographical films starring Donald Sutherland, the noted Canadian actor, as Bethune.[39] Books, films, theater plays, and TV series about him, statues erected in his honor, and hospitals, schools, streets, and awards named after him, recognize Norman Bethune's manifold contributions to the medical field. Six decades after his death at age forty-nine in 1939, Dr. Bethune was inducted into the Canadian Medical Hall of Fame. In 2004, Canadian TV viewers voted him the twenty-sixth

---

[38] www.thestar.com/entertainment/movies/2012/11/27/john_kemeny_forgotten_giant_of_canadian_film_dies_at_87.html

[39] *Bethune* (1977) and *Bethune: The Making of a Hero* (1990)

greatest Canadian. Bethune Memorial House, a National Historic Site operated by the Canadian government in Ontario, commemorates the life and achievements of Norman Bethune.

John Grierson remains a name linked with Canada as well. The groundbreaking Scots film pioneer and founder of the National Film Board of Canada took his last breath in 1972. That same year, in London, the Grierson Trust was established to commemorate Grierson. The trust organizes the annual British Documentary Awards, presenting "The Griersons," which recognize outstanding films in nine categories.

Želimir Matko left this life in 1977. Willard Van Dyke, who sent me the letter containing Matko's reflections on our work together, passed on in 1986.

Scanning my remembrances of Matko, I notice that these pages depict him as a hard taskmaster extracting as much labor as possible from his highly skilled but lowly paid American guest worker. Though quite true, this description is partial. A very pleasant atmosphere existed between us in the Studio. I sincerely believe that Matko overworked me not merely for the prosperity of Zagreb Film or the nation's film industry. More essential to him, I think, was the ultimate success of his country's experimental socialistic system. Incidentally, the Piretoks bug spray film, for which I recorded the English voiceover, won First Prize for television commercials at the Chicago International Film Festival.

Mario? Ah, dear Mario. After leaving Zagreb, I sent him and his mother a thank you letter. He replied, and I quote him: "Dear! Thank you for your very lovely leter. May muther was raly surprcsed haveng it and now she is proud of your satisfided. (Because of coking) Please wrote me and I'll never forgat you al best to you for next voyage. Good by, Mario."

Holding Mario's note today, a flow of mental snapshots and pleasant thoughts flash by. His words affirm his ability to love unselfishly. He did not write of his own wants regarding us. His wishes were for me. I should have "al best" for "next voyage." I sense no sorrow or pining for what was not. Rather, streaming to me is the upbeat energy that buoyed me in Mario's presence, the pure joy of loving just to love.

It does seem that Mario appeared on my path, as it looped through the Yu-go-*slave*-ian maze, in answer to a prayer I had not made, praying not yet then on my agenda. But, as with any prayer asked either consciously or unconsciously, I received an answer. As is usual in the prayer process, the answer came in its own timing and manner of expression having nothing to do with my hopes, wishes, or expectations.

Knowing Mario better late than never, and the brevity of our friendship, highlighted the truth that neither suffering nor pleasure are permanent states but come and go. The underlying depth of this message eluded me at the time. Now I understand more completely that life is not absolute in the sense of being perfect in quality or nature. Life has its ups and downs. We can interpret circumstances only with the awareness we have at any moment.

Mario and I did not seek further contact. The language hurdles would have made correspondence torturous at best. As with "Svetlana," I would cherish seeing again this unforgettable person—whose name really was Mario. His love free from self-interest incredibly enriched my heart's memory bank. Keeping true to his love offered, without asking anything in return, and accepting unconditionally what I voluntarily gave or did not give, Mario did not try to bind me. Like Yu-go-*slave*-ia, he nurtured my progress on the road to freedom. Years after our contact I understood that the human longing to love and be loved arises from our inborn urge to feel whole, full, and complete within a larger Whole that is full and complete.

I would love to re-meet anyone from the then Zagreb Film, including the Turtleneck Man, and certainly also Ana. Ana is the real name, as is Stef. Curiously relevant to the unhappy living situation of Ana and Stef years back, the present-day economy in many reaches of the world is forcing belligerent couples in numerous countries to continue living together because they are unable to afford a divorce or separate residences. A judge in Spain set a precedent in 2013 when she ordered a divorcing couple to divide their apartment down the middle to create two independent abodes.[40]

Certainly I would be pleased to meet any offspring of my European relatives who may have survived World War II. In 1977, based on information my father belatedly supplied from the papers of my paternal grandmother, Dora Braun Eisner, I wrote to the International Tracing Service. I inquired of ITS, the Germany-based Holocaust documentation center, about my grandmother's brother, Alexander Braun, born in 1897 in Sopron, Hungary.

Photocopies of wartime records evidenced that the Nazis arrested Alexander Braun in France in 1943. "Reason given for incarceration: *Jude* [Jew]." Alexander Braun survived the internment camp Drancy outside Paris, the infamous concentration camp of Auschwitz in Poland, and the extremely cruel Mittelbau-Dora, a work subcamp of Buchenwald concentration camp in Germany [41] Perhaps the name of his last camp helped Alexander recall his sister Dvorah, who emigrated to America when he was only five years old and whom he never saw again. In 1977, I learned that Alexander Braun had died in Paris in 1971.

Concerning my maternal family history, I have to add that my cousin Robert Silberberg, the genealogist among us grandchildren, says there is controversy about the 1871 birthplace of our grandmother. It was most likely Warsaw, as the family's oral history attests and was listed in the 1880 Census of the United States. It might also be New York City, as written on the 1920 census form. Bob thinks Warsaw may be accurate.

About Otto Milo, real name, he and I kept contact until I left The Hague in the early 1970s. Thanks to Otto and his gracious loan of

---

[40] "Judge in Spain Partitions Home of Feuding Couple," by Dan Bilefsky and Silvia Taulés, *New York Times*, September 13, 2013.

[41] The International Tracing Service (ITS), in German *Internationaler Suchdienst*, in French *Service International de Recherches*, located in Bad Arolsen, Germany, is an internationally governed center for documentation, information, and research on Nazi persecution, forced labor, and the Holocaust in Nazi Germany and territories it occupied.

the Super 8 film camera, I have moving images of Zagreb 1968. Otto passed away years back.

Even after his official retirement, my film professor Henry Breitrose continued living in his solar-paneled house in Stanford, California. As professor emeritus, Henry taught a variety of film courses. He stayed involved in a plethora of activities. Besides editing books and writing novels, Henry held honorary and elected positions in the professional film world. He lectured and presented papers internationally. For years he was Vice-President for Publications and Research of CILECT, the International Association of Film and Television Schools. Henry departed for the "film world beyond" in the autumn of 2014.

Another distinguished academician, my six-years'-younger Stanford beau, is an active dean emeritus of the US university where he has made invaluable contributions to the school's communications program. Is it not ironic that he, who so feared my going gray before him, himself went totally gray and then lost most of that, while I still sport a full head of predominantly brown (natural, not dyed) hair? Perhaps his fear of gray hair played a role in the falling out of his own gray hair? A photo on his university's website shows a professor who is nearly bald. My relationship with him, flawed by his fear of my older age and by my lack of self-confidence in the face of his parents' disapproval, vividly points to the truth that we will suffer less when we accept more the processes of life.

My trust in life's processes strengthened in Yugoslavia. There I first asked myself seriously: *Am I just living my life haphazardly, or is there a rhyme and reason behind "coincidence" and apparent guidance?* Now I share the certainty of Stern's declaration: "There is no such thing as coincidence."

The meeting with Stern upraised my mind. In the beginning, I had collided with his distinctive German accent. As we spoke, I stumbled less and less over his pronunciation as the content of his words captured me. Is this why I thought his English improved as our conversation went on? Afterward I realized that *Herr* Stern and I had traveled on the wings of his accent past the Nazi killing fields and even past present-day Germany. Rather than remain fixed to a specific area on Earth, our talk had soared into a universal arena. We conversed in a place of attunement indifferent to our individual personalities and identification with a particular country or religion. "He is German" eventually expanded to: "He is a human being. We are all human beings."

In an inner landscape, Stern and I came together in a unity transcending outer differences, a unity both similar and dissimilar to the oneness I experienced with Mario and his mother. Engaging with Stern, I was able to leave my prejudicial attitude behind in the past, at least temporarily. Even while old thought patterns, negative judgments, and biased thinking tried to command my reactions, my heart stayed ajar to the present, as the encounter with Cassius Clay and Malcolm X had earlier demonstrated.

Curiously, about seven years after leaving Yugoslavia, when I was established in Amsterdam as a freelance writer on transformational and spiritual themes, one of the largest markets for my writings outside the Netherlands arose in Germany. Several German magazines regularly translated and published my articles. A German editor and I became friends. A German publisher brought out, in German translation, the first edition of my first book.[42] Perhaps my positive associations with Germany and Germans, and my understanding that we cannot and must not condemn later generations for their ancestors' evil deeds, also influenced my parents. During one of their trips to Europe, they included a visit to Cologne in their sightseeing program.

The natural unfolding of my life itself helped me fulfill my wish to dissolve my old German antipathy. Not that I gained liberation from prejudicial and small-minded thinking helped only by "coincidence" or the guidance. It took self-effort and growing awareness to transmute my predisposition.

Today increasing numbers of us, linked by technology, are overcoming prejudices and inborn attitudes of racial superiority or inferiority.

---

[42] *Der Ruf der Sonne: Eine spirituelle Reise: Ausgangsort Indien (The Call of the Sun: A Spiritual Journey: Starting Point India)*, by Surya Green, Verlag Hermann Bauer, Freiburg im Breisgau, Germany, 1993.

Nowadays, more easily than previously was the case, people enter into friendships and alliances, if not love-partnerships and procreation, with people of other nations, cultures, races, and religions. The mixing of peoples, helped by the World Wide Web and the widespread migrations of political, economic, and ecological refugees, is brewing a global population of less biased and more open-minded human beings. Thanks initially to Yu-go-*slave*-ia, I am one of them.

In so many areas, my Yugoslavian experience was essentially a training program that helped me in my process of determining who and what I truly am. Yugoslavia, helping me radiate further out from my core, functioned as an unexpected venue for my self-knowing and self-improvement. My experiences in Yugoslav society enabled me to take initial strides toward mindful living. The Yugoslav lifestyle induced in me changes that most likely I would never have thought of, much less have implemented, had I remained in America at that time.

Certainly the relatively Spartan Yugoslav society fulfilled my unconscious wish to get away for a while from conspicuously consumptive America, not that I lived easily with the fulfillment of this wish. Especially at the beginning of my stay in Zagreb, most missing my large fridge with freezer and comfy bathtub at home, I disliked the stark lack of material comforts and refinements. Yearning for my possessions helped me discern that not all the objects occupying my Manhattan apartment were necessities.

Circumstances in Zagreb compelled me to exercise a new simplicity. I had no choice. Yu-go-*slave*-ia essentially removed my freedom of choice (except the choice to leave Yugoslavia itself). Even while curtailing some of the freedoms I took for granted, the lifestyle helped loosen me from American excess. The lack of consumer items, advertising, and marketing promotions lessened my urge to shop and to buy. In a natural and spontaneous manner, I lost the compulsion of "wanna have; must have, want more; don't have enough, have too little." As well, Zagreb Film's improvisational work ways showed me the creative fruits of doing more with less and letting necessity be the mother of invention.

Life in Zagreb gave me only the choice: flee or adapt. On the very basic level of food, scarcity required me to adjust my food attitudes and reevaluate my food priorities. Forced to break my habit of indulging in whatever I wanted to eat, whenever I wanted to, Zagreb compelled me to take on reduced food consumption, eating from need and not purely for pleasure or greed. Food graduated into being a health advisor, commencing at the breakfasts shared with "Svetlana." I ate less and appreciated more. No longer did I consider food primarily for my sensory enjoyment. Although taste still counted, I gave thought to what I ate and how. What I put into my mouth should preferably help maintain my health, strength, and energy.

My new thinking about food naturally extended to American frozen TV dinners, packaged meals, fast foods, and take out. I pondered whether the manufacturers of prepared foods and their advertising agencies had brainwashed me to think that cooking my own food was a chore, and that "convenience foods" would free me from "kitchen drudgery." I could not escape the thought that maybe it had just been my own laziness, rather than the "inadequate time" in my busy New York schedule, that persuaded me often enough to bring in dinner from a shop instead of cooking for myself. Had I turned into a slave of my own laziness rationalized as "lack of time"? Or was my supposed lack of time simply my lack of awareness?

Zagreb, requiring me to cook from scratch, empowered me to reclaim the preparation of my own food. Composing and cooking a meal using fresh ingredients lifted me with a feeling of triumph, as if I had defeated an internal, down-pulling energy within myself. In addition, I noted the taste and energy benefits of eating food brought fresh from the market. So had my grandmothers shopped and cooked. Never had I seen tinned or boxed food in their kitchens.

While in Yugoslavia, I had no inkling I had arrived at a crossroads of my "I" focus. I was oblivious to the unusual education in self-awareness presented me. Forcing a control over my senses and my mind, Yugoslavia helped me decelerate, develop patience, and reflect with more insight. I was starting to value what I have rather than mourn my lacks. I was moving away from my American inclination to want more to an extreme.

Compelled by Yugoslavian scarcity to detach abruptly from my learned tendency to buy on whim and in excess of my actual needs, I had to confront my conditioned attitudes. I admit that de-hooking from my indentured lifestyle of abundant and careless consumption was no voluntary act of ascetic renunciation. Yu-go-*slave*-ia pressured me to surrender material excess. I had no choice but to comply. Forced to quit superfluity cold turkey, I did not experience the tremors and sweats that may come when kicking off addiction to a physical substance, but I did go through a period of mental suffering filled with debilitating complaint, desire, and regret.

In the end, the release from thing-orientation proved freeing. Yugoslavia validated my childhood intuition that the accumulation of money and matter is not the foremost goal of my existence. Yugoslavia confirmed that running breathlessly in a competitive race just to accumulate mucho mucho money or acquire name and fame is not the most purposeful use of my life. I began to think seriously about my success and happiness in nonmaterial terms.

After some mental tweaking, I found myself functioning quite well unburdened by the acquisition of a wide array of things and foods. Even while the phrase "content with less" was then intellectually unknown to me, I was beginning to feel the experiential meaning of those words. When basic necessities such as food and shelter are met, and comforts and luxuries are unavailable at any price, we realize how little we really need for our fulfillment. We grasp that our contentment does not derive from our consumption and possession and enjoyment. We experience that we do not discover the "more" in life by using the latest electronics or attending the top entertainment event. In Zagreb, within myself at a depth I had not yet penetrated, there simmered the germinal thought I would hear expressed years later as: "True abundance is really sufficiency."[43]

---

[43] With thanks for thoughts expressed in *The Art of Cooperation*, by Benjamin Creme, Share International Foundation, Amsterdam, London, Los Angeles, 2002, pp. 31–34.

Regarding consumption, never had I been a consumer slave. In America, I had not mindlessly followed the orders of the consumer society to buy this, own that, replace the old, get the new, buy buy buy. I had not fallen captive to manipulative advertisements creating false needs and desires to stimulate the consumption of products. Never had I let consumer items prey on my insecurities and fool me into thinking that they could be a measure of my worth. But at times I bought needlessly, without thinking, carelessly. Zagreb put a screeching halt to my unaware consuming.

To resist shopping and buying is to resist a way of life. Now I know that as we grow in understanding and wisdom, we do not need all that is pushed on us from outside. Wisdom reduces our outer needs. We gravitate to essentials, a graduation that is liberating.

If not enslaved to consumption, I was surely enslaved to the work system that exploits women by favouring men. After my stint as a guest worker in Yu-go-*slave*-ia, where I was treated "a little bit cruel," as Matko later admitted, laboring extended hours for low pay while my human needs were ignored, I started to think about exploitation as a general phenomenon. It amazed me to realize how habituated I was to exploitation. No one likes being exploited, yet we all accept exploitation of one sort or another, including the exploitation of Earth seen as a lifeless thing to be utilized for commercial gain.

I resolved not to accept exploitative circumstances from any employer again. I had never been a slave to wages although, unconsciously, I acted as a slave to the work process. Getting more satisfaction from a job well done than from a paycheck, I served every employer as a devoted follower of the American work ethic. Matko spotted this quality in me and used it to the Studio's advantage.

I can now thank my lucky stars—or, rather, my life's guidance—that my Stanford film mentor had not proposed my summering at a film studio in Japan. The phenomenon of *karōshi*, "death from overwork," became noticeable in Japan in the late 1960s, around the time I was in Yugoslavia. Pressures to keep up with co-workers, to outcompete competitors, and to increase market share at the expense of competitors resulted in unreasonable shifts for Japanese workers as part of a six-or-seven-day workweek. The practice of long days at a frenzied pace has led to a terminal malady termed "occupational sudden death," caused by stress-related heart attacks and strokes.[44] Varying degrees of *karōshi* exist in all societies, even when the phenomenon is not named, systematically studied, and statistically documented.

In Yugoslavia, and later on in the Netherlands, I not only avoided *karōshi* but also eluded burnout, by now the number one disease in the Dutch workplace. To raise awareness of burnout, affecting one in eight Dutch workers, in 2014 the Dutch government instituted a "Check your Work Stress Week." Both employees and employers participate in activities organized on themes of burnout symptoms, treatment, and prevention.[45]

A good number of people enjoy little or no pleasure in their work: "It's just a job." Many individuals endure jobs they do not like solely to survive. Even while management continues to pull in perks and bonuses, workers may have to suffer longer days at lower wages with shorter rests. The workers slave away, fueled by the fear of losing income. This is no unfounded fear when employees may be fired from one day to the next. The practice of immediate dismissal exists in many countries, together with hiring practices that make it difficult, if not impossible, for older dismissed workers to find equivalent employment and payment. I remember John Grierson's words: "People who *need* their jobs are dangerous. They are the real parasites. When you get a world caught up with the bourgeois thing, it is a weak world because people cannot stand up to change. They cannot throw off their jobs."

---

[44] "Death from Overwork," by Boye Lafayette de Mente, *Asia Pacific Management Forum* online magazine, May 2002: www.apmforum.com/columns/boye51.htm

[45] "Check your Work Stress Week" is an initiative of the Dutch Ministry of Social Affairs and Employment (SZW). The awareness campaign is part of Dutch government policy whereby employers take account of workers' specific circumstances in the different phases of life, including work life. The aim is to keep workers healthy, motivated, engaged, and thereby productive so they can go on working longer than the former employment cutoff age of sixty-five.

Economic downturn, causing the re-examination of work and its influence on self, others, and the planet, is bringing more people to the discovery: "We work to live; we do not live to work." Just like the counterculture hippies of the Sixties, more people today prefer work that neither harms nor exploits, and allows the qualities of cooperation, caring, and sharing to function visibly in society. Simply by having such "We-thoughts" helps the world by adding positive energy into the collective consciousness.

I thank Yugoslavia for functioning preemptively for me. Yugoslavia helped free me from the outer-oriented success standard of amassing ever more prestigious job titles and ever more income so as to afford more material possibilities and possessions and social status. Living in a society that offered little on which to spend, except basics, confirmed my thought that quality of life has nothing to do with money and all that money can buy. The key to my true success, I discovered, resides in my ability to stay open to see, learn, and grow from my experiences while endeavoring to give something meaningful to society.

24

Summing Up in the Now and Looking Ahead

In Yugoslavia, in the 1990s, nationalism won over communism. The federal Yugoslav nation fell apart. One by one, in their own timing, each of the six socialist republics successively declared themselves independent nations and opted for the free market economy and the privatization of formerly "social property." In these independent successor countries, now numbering seven, there has emerged a psychological and cultural phenomenon termed "(Yugo)nostalgia," "Yugonostalgia," or "Yugo-nostalgia."

Yugo-nostalgia refers to a nostalgic emotional attachment to idealized desirable features of the former Yugoslavia. "Experience the spirit of the old good times!" was the slogan rallying visitors to a 2013 exhibition in Belgrade that focused on the everyday life of Yugoslavians from roughly 1950 to 1990. The exhibition's brochure defined Yugo-nostalgia as "nostalgia for something that was unique and authentic, which is now missing from the cultural realities of the former Yugoslav republics."[46]

---

[46] "Between (Yugo)Nostalgia and Utopia" by Biljana Purić, published in the online bimonthly *New Eastern Europe*, July 18, 2013.
www.neweasterneurope.eu/interviews/803-between-yugo-nostalgia-and-utopia

"Yugo-nostalgics" who are old enough to have lived in the former Yugoslavia perhaps expected an easy good life under democratic capitalism. Now citizens of a successor nation, they remember a Yugoslavia in which socialist ideals may not have met reality, but people were at least assured of their basic needs. There was economic security and, for some, at least, a sense of socialist unity. Every citizen possessed the wealth of guaranteed employment, financial security, and medical care. Education was free, and even the poorest but qualified peasant child could undertake a university degree, all expenses covered. Virtually everyone had work, paid vacations, and could leave the office by two or three in the afternoon. The society essentially lacked violent personal crime (which makes the mass violence and the brutal sexual atrocities committed during the Yugoslav Wars all the more shocking). No unconscionable economic disparity separated the populace, although communist party members received perks unavailable to non-Party citizens and there were differences between the richer and poorer republics.

Yugo-nostalgics—of whom, admittedly, there may be more in Serbia (which mightily lost the 1990s war) than Croatia (which achieved its independence)—including those born after the Tito era, yearn for the simple, natural, slower-paced, and socially protected Titoist lifestyle. They confirm the observation Milovan Djilas made decades earlier that most of the people living within the Yugoslav system were not opposed to socialism, but to how it was being achieved. The remarks of Djilas apply to any political system. He eschewed the emergence of a political bureaucracy that keeps itself in power as a ruling elite possessing special privileges and economic preference, an advantaged minority apart from the people.

Longing for the old Yugoslavia, however, infers criticism of the successor nations. The epithet "Yugo-nostalgic" therefore also has a negative connotation, implying that Yugo-nostalgics are anachronistic, unrealistic, and unpatriotic enemies of the neoliberal capitalistic Balkan countries. Comparing the daily lifestyle in the twenty-first century Balkan nations with everyday existence during Tito's Third Way, some Yugo-nostalgics find that capitalistic democracy does not necessarily offer the "better life" citizens thought they were missing in socialist times. People have obtained freedom of speech at the expense of steady employment and personal security. Some Yugo-nostalgics regard contemporary capitalism as slavery. They have gained material comforts at the price of their freedom of free time. Some feel chained to an ongoing competitive struggle filled with debilitating insecurities, anxieties, stresses, and fears absent in the former Yugoslavia. Probably these people do not remember the fears and tensions inherent to knowing that any kind of opposition to one-party rule, even just critical vocal expression, could land one in jail

As a Yugo-nostalgic scientist now living and working under the free market system told me: "I am an ex-Yugoslav who lived in the Golden Age. In Yugoslavia, I was free from my work at two in the afternoon to visit friends and family and take it easy. I miss the brotherhood and unity that gave a feeling of 'us.' Today it is 'them and us.' Now I go from pajamas to work clothes to pajamas. I am under a lot of stress and have only the weekend to rest and recuperate before starting the pajama to work clothes to pajama workday routine all over again. I am not happy living like this."

Yugo-nostalgics gaze fondly back to a more fulfilling way of life. Invoking a depoliticized memory, they hanker for the Titoist past remembered as a utopian socialist society.

They forget or overlook that Yugoslavia was a totalitarian state. People were monitored and controlled, and the one-party government dealt severely with citizens who pointed out discrepancies between Party ideology and actual Yugoslav conditions. Yugo-nostalgics sentimentally focus on the positive qualities of both the Titoist system and the late Josip Broz Tito. Especially the younger Yugo-nostalgics, born after Yugoslavia's dissolution, idolize Tito as a leader who gave his people a collective feeling of personal security in the present and a shared certainty for the future.

Yugo-nostalgia generally turns a blind eye to Tito's actions as a dictator who ruled with a heavy hand and violated human rights. Selectively remembering, Yugo-nostalgia celebrates Marshal Tito to mythic proportions. He was the Resistance commander who bravely led the courageous Partisans to victory during World War II. Of all the invaded countries in Europe at the war's end, Yugoslavia under Tito was the only one that had liberated itself with its own military force. And it was Tito who firmly steered the postwar nation fearlessly along a pioneering Third Way disassociated from Stalinism. To some admirers, Tito was an international statesman on the level of a Franklin D. Roosevelt or a Winston Churchill; to some, he was Yugoslavia's Che Guevara. Tito has, in fact, "become canonized as a secular saint…. Tito remains a mythological hero of the people: a Balkan blend of George Washington, Abraham Lincoln, and Russell Crowe."[47]

Yet the Yugo-nostalgic scientist admitted to me: "As time progresses, I see more of the downsides of the system where we weren't allowed to speak of certain things, especially not against the president and, when you criticized, you went to an island prison. At the time, we were convinced that the people who went to Goli otok[48] were guilty. We regular people didn't feel the police state. We could see stuff going on, and knew we had to be careful, but from a young age we were indoctrinated. We only knew one source of information, the government. We did not know differently. That was a minus. Tito lied to us but we all loved him. I miss the feeling of brotherhood and unity, and working for a better tomorrow for your country and your people."

Probably Yugo-nostalgia says as much about romanticizing the past as decrying the present while simultaneously longing for a new Third Way. More people today, also outside Yugoslavia's successor

---

[47] "Bosnia Remembered – Part II: The Lost Generation," by David Danelo, second in a three-part series, *The Legacy of Jasenovac*, available at website of Foreign Policy Research Institute, Philadelphia: www.fpri.org/articles/2012/12/bosnia-remembered-part-i-legacy-jasenovac

[48] Goli otok, "barren island," a desolate island of bare surface without any vegetation in the northern Adriatic Sea off the Croatian coast, was a high-security, top secret prison and forced-labor camp (1949–1989) for male political prisoners; the nearby Sveti Grgur island was a similar camp for female prisoners.

countries, wish for a political and economic system offering social equality and social justice along with personal freedom and privacy.

My own Yugo-nostalgia connects with an appreciation I have for the extinct Yugoslavia. The unique country presented me with surprising life lessons that helped prepare me to live with more awareness. Our path through life moves us forward with ups and downs, standstills and backslidings, sidesteps left and sidesteps right. Having now a larger storehouse of experiences, today I could more ably handle the challenges a Yu-go-*slave*-ia would present.

In Zagreb, I was still journeying through my life quite unconsciously. I had no idea I was progressing on a path to the inner knowing of that "knowing" which dispels one's existential ignorance like Sun over snow. I did not realize that, in Professor Yu-go-*slave*-ia's classroom, my daily experiences were functioning as a master teacher conducting me through the first stage of a de-education, refocusing, and re-education. Not yet did I know the deeper profundity of the truth that every single experience, no matter how large or how small, helps us learn and grow. No experience is a waste or a loss, despite the stubbed toes, twisted ankles, and skinned knees incurred on our travels. However seemingly insignificant, our experiences contain lessons and teachings to help us know life more totally.

When we accept our personal experiences to be our best preceptors, one major difficulty may arise. As Will Rogers, the insightful American political wit and folksy philosopher of the early twentieth century observed: "Sometimes the final exam comes first, then the lesson." Indeed, in the unconventional, twenty-four hour classroom of Yu-go-*slave*-ia, no human teacher proclaimed, "I am giving you a final exam." The "Final" landed on my desk unperceived by me. It called for my answers, conveyed through my attitudes and behavior, before I knew the lessons the Final came to teach. Holding up a mirror reflecting my state of development, the unannounced exam revealed what in myself needed improving.

Unaware I was being tested, I did not study. The very lack of studying let me know myself better through the confrontations that followed one after another. Thanks to the paranoia acquired in a police state, I moved through my days as if there traveled within my mind a conscious watcher consciously watching. As lessons arrived, I was always an outsider looking in, at myself. I became a silent witness of my own being.

Lessons packaged within difficulties, crises, and apparent failures help ripen us toward human maturity, the perfection of our highest human qualities. But simply spotting and possibly understanding a life lesson is not enough. Life lessons we do not learn in the same way we memorized our ABC's and multiplication tables. Life lessons we absorb by changing our attitudes and behavior.

Unlearned lessons may reoccur. The process of "practice makes perfect" has taken me more than once through the same lesson transmitted through different people, places, and circumstances. A lesson may present itself in varied outer guises and with increased potency until I "get it."

Once I integrate a life lesson, that same teaching does not usually revisit me, except perhaps as a check up exam. And, may I never get a check-up exam testing my compassion for animals! My compassion has heightened since Zagreb, but I am not obliged to host any animals unwillingly, especially not microscopic-size "domestic pets" that could do me harm, even if minor.

May I also not get any serious follow-up exams measuring my adherence to "Thou shalt not kill," though mice and biting insects always prove a challenge. In all seriousness, I shudder with horror remembering my diligence in following the instructions of the "louse doctor" at Zagreb Hospital: "Dust your clothes, your body, and your hair with DDT." Dutifully I poured the killing pesticide between my sheets.

Sleeping as a kind of double agent with the enemy DDT for one full week in 1968 in order to kill the enemy lice, also indicates my then-ignorant disregard of *Silent Spring*. Rachel Carson's 1962 bestseller foretold of a dead spring resulting from the toxic products of the chemical industry. She argued that the indiscriminate use of synthetic chemical pesticides, especially DDT, endangers the environment, wildlife, and human health. Once an agricultural and food supply hero, DDT not only kills off unwanted insect visitors to crops. It remains toxic in the environment, entering and harming the food chain. The accumulation of DDT in the fatty tissues of animals, including human beings, causes cancer and genetic damage. Exposing the dangers of DDT, Carson's book raised awareness of nature's vulnerability to human intervention. *Silent Spring* helped initiate the environmental movement.

In my irrational fear of the tiny bloodsuckers holding on to my hair with their sticky little feet, I dusted myself liberally with the pre-scribed DDT. After all, these parasitical creatures had no right to settle into my scalp to gestate a colony of domestic pets. To rid myself of the itching and burdensome invaders, willingly I surrendered myself to DDT's destructive force in a classic case of the cure being worse than the disease.

But I cannot blame the Zagreb Hospital doctor for his lack of knowledge. DDT was then a controversial subject in the West, and East Europeans knew even less about its downsides. Remembering my own uninformed use of the pesticide, I am thankful I took Zagreb's do-mestic pets home with me only once. That type of caring and sharing I prefer to learn solely from books. Infestation with head lice, I now rea-son, was a health risk much less harmful to Zagrebians—the potentially deadly DDT cure notwithstanding—than their picking up the ailments inherent to a fast-paced, stress-based, and highly competitive modern industrialized society.

Referring to the DDT-prescribing doctor reminds me that I erred miserably in not exposing him to the hospital authorities. I acknowledge as cowardly irresponsible my inaction to report a man who misused his position of authority and power to try taking sexual advantage.

Equally irresponsible was my ingesting blindly the chemical pills the doctor offered. Such unwise behavior I rejected four years' post-Yugoslavia, when I switched to an organic diet of plant-based whole foods and natural health aids. Once I discovered the healing benefits of herbs and other natural preparations, I rejected toxic chemical concoc-tions for my health and beauty care. I stopped applying or ingesting chemical products that, while temporarily alleviating symptoms, do not go to the cause of a problem and may additionally trigger negative side effects. But oh, how tough a teacher was DDT! Today I would choose a non-toxic herbal solution or shave off my hair.

Decades later, Amsterdam natural health practitioner Richard J. Smit found traces of the deadly pesticide in my system. During a health consultation in 2008, I did not mention the delousing in Zagreb. Nonetheless, Smit detected DDT when he made a scan of my body using a computerized machine to which he connected me by headphones. The machine analyzed the information of my energy field compared with an ideal energy state based on vibrational rates unique to all physical forms. The machine discovered in my system the vibrational rate identified with the toxin DDT.

"Since quantum physics, we know that everything consists of vibrations and even the human body is a multi-dimensional vibrating body," explained Smit. "Everything is energy. Subtle energy systems run through and around the human body. Disturbances of the energies lead to disease."

When I asked for a simple, lay explanation of how the machine diagnoses and treats health conditions, Smit stated: "The therapy works on the level of cell information. The computer program I use sends the cells impulses of electromagnetic field, sound, and light. Comparing the output of these three signals, the computer makes an analysis. In your case, the presence of the vibrational frequency of DDT indicates a disturbance of the body's subtle energies. Regarding treatment, the computer, using a filter, inverts the DDT frequency, altering its disharmonious vibration, and sends a mirror signal of the original frequency back to the body. The body, reacting to the signal, tries to expel it."

After his explanation, Smit admitted that this system of diagnosis and therapy, while covered for payment by the Dutch health insurance system when someone has a supplementary "alternative healing" package, is not accepted by mainstream medicine.

All in all, personal reinvention and renewal began for me in Zagreb. The instruction underlying all the lessons in Yugoslavia basically was, "Know thyself! Reflect on your life!" How could I reflect in Zagreb if still running the New York City race that had become an integral part of my biorhythm? The habits developed in my hometown reputed for "never sleeping" heavily influenced me.

"Slow down!" Yugoslavia had commanded as soon as my train lumbered over the border. Had I any choice? Life in Zagreb obliterated the conditions and pressures that formerly hurried my steps. The traffic rules of Marshal Tito's Third Way society commandeered my supersized battle tank of a powder blue Buick off the eight-lane superspeed highway. I found myself repositioned on a gentler path I did not know I was already traveling. Slow-moving Yugoslavia both forced and stimulated me to ascertain my own most effective gait. Adjusting to the Yugoslavian turtle tempo allowed me time to reflect, discover greater self-awareness, and recalibrate my life.

The slowing-down process received assistance from my state of aloneness after work hours, brief cultural diversions or occasional visits to Trg Republike notwithstanding. In effect, Aloneness relieved my mind from absorbing an excess of stimuli. Now I perceive that the phenomenon of always being busy and taking in stimuli is another expression of greed and the grabbing wish for "more ever more." In America, my hunger for experience left me precious little time for thoughtful self-examination of the experiences reaped, except when I made jottings in my logbook. My sense is that modern children and youth could benefit from the inclusion of guided periods of aloneness and inactivity into their educational schedules.

My probing mind, true to its training in a consumer society based on "more," had always wanted to know more and more about everything. When Zagreb compelled me to repace and become friends with Solitude, my mind automatically focused its curiosity inward, as if recognizing its own deeper need for "the moreness within." My why-questioning moved decisively inward.

As another permanent effect, the Yugoslav deceleration instilled in me lasting protection from the rushing around that the high-speed, high-tech, high-achievement twenty-first century modern society tries to impose. I was empowered to resist people, places, circumstances, and also "time-saving" machines enticing me to zoom through life. For the record: I do not mind my computer running faster and faster! Or society leaping with no time to lose into a fossil-free, solarized future!

Had Yugoslavia not intervened, perhaps I would be zipping along in the daily societal marathon, whizzing through my days and nights without a second to reflect, so frazzled that I missed the wonder and joy of being alive. Despite outer pulls to go here or there, I try to stick to a discipline balancing my outer with my inner activities. Obviously I do not give fashionable answers to the queries: "How are you?"; "How are things going?" The trendy response is "Busy!" or "Crazy!" or "Insane!" This is modern shorthand language for: "I am excellent; I am constantly active with work and play; I am successful, popular, wanted, not empty, not alone."

Had I continued my intense New York lifestyle, content with fleeting happiness in the illusionary feel-good effects of unbroken activity, pleasurable diversions, and careless consumption, I might be at the mercy of a nonstop, stressed, and distracted mind. I might be a chronically overtired person having limited ability to relax. When finally collapsing into my bed, I might find sleep eluding me as I twisted and turned through the night even while I might fall asleep at work during the day.

Sleep, a necessity of life basic to human functioning, has become a precious commodity some of us acquire only with tranquillizers, sleeping pills, and sleep-inducing techniques, or purchase as quick "power naps" in "sleep shops."

And then, when we step out of our bed or the sleep shop to resume the modern-day survival race, how many of us (perhaps only unconsciously) are asking: "How much faster can I go?" Dashing through life in our brand-name runner shoes or chic high heels, at times doing too much too fast too unthinkingly, do we remember that even light has speed limits? Then we may ask: "To where is everyone hurrying in their fashionable footwear?"

Speaking of footwear, just as the Yugoslavs did not try to walk in my shoes, I failed to try and put myself in theirs, as Svetlana bluntly asserted. Reviewing my progress in feeling genuine empathy for others and acting on that empathy, I see I was as guilty of separatist behavior as my co-workers. I related to my Studio colleagues by our outer differences, not our inner similarities. Empathy, walking with our mind and heart in someone else's shoes, especially when the other person's shoes are in desperate need of repair or replacement, or strolling "on the path of sandals" as Stern cryptically stated, helps us discern that problems, discomforts, and suffering are universal. If we could slip into the sandals of the people of Tuvalo, the small island nation in the Pacific Ocean facing disappearance under climate change flooding, or step into the boots of the Inuit of the Arctic (commonly still called Eskimos) as melting sea ice undermines the fragile ecosystem upon which their cultural survival depends, more of us might work heroically for the needed energy transition.

Lack of empathy on a mass scale has manifested as an unbalanced, unjust, antilife global society undergoing one survival crisis after the next. When we can empathize with others, we expand beyond our I-centeredness. When we are able to share feelings and understanding, it becomes easier to share on the material level. We can ponder whether Muhammad Ali had transcended his own ebullient "I-ness" and was attuning with a greater whole when he recited, during a Harvard University lecture in 1975, his shortest poem ever: "Me, We."

Me-to-We-aspiring Yugoslavia helped loosen me from the need to compete. My realization in Zagreb that *there is no one to compete with in life except myself, the better person I can grow into,* helped extract me from the old paradigm of competition. Unexpectedly, I landed in a new mental space. I lost interest in continually having to sharpen my competitive and self-promotional skills to enhance my position in society and my material wealth.

Pre-Zagreb, my mind had been stuffed to its rafters with the persuasions of competing. I could not have guessed that the loss of the drive to compete would in fact help empty my mind and my heart of the fears, desires, and restlessness inherent to competition. Such purging obstructs the build-up of the envy, jealousy, and greed that a lifestyle based on competitive struggle invariably stimulates. Distancing myself from competition nurtured my heart's kindliness and compassion, readying me to know the benefits of cooperation and selfless service. Although in Zagreb I took steps in the transformational process unconsciously, those steps moved me closer to knowing my deeper identity and purpose as a human being.

My sojourn in Yugoslavia called my attention to the original significance of the term "American Dream." Terminology in society often takes on different meanings than intended. Growing up in America, I dutifully accepted that "American Dream" simply points to material accomplishment. While writing this book, I investigated the source of the expression. American writer and historian James Truslow Adams coined the term in his book *The Epic of America*, published in 1931 during the severe economic depression.

The American Dream, he wrote, is: "that dream of a land in which life should be better and richer and fuller for everyone, with opportunity for each according to ability or achievement. . . . It is not a dream of motor cars and high wages merely, but a dream of social order in which each man and each woman shall be able to attain to the fullest stature of which they are innately capable, and be recognized by others for what they are, regardless of the fortuitous circumstances of birth or position."[49]

Hear hear! Who could not subscribe to such a dream? Until Yugoslavia twirled my life upside down, the film images viewed with Stern proving to be quite prophetic, I associated "American Dream" with only its subsequent, grossly material significance. Yugoslavia woke me up to question the materially seeped conception of the contemporary American Dream. I saw that the American Dream does, indeed, belong to a state of the mind during sleep. Yugoslavia made me aware

---

[49] www.en.wikipedia.org/wiki/James_Truslow_Adams

I had been asleep, unconscious, to the limiting egoistic concept of insistently pursuing material reward. For all its enticing material glamour, the contemporary American Dream is one from which we have to awaken.

The years post-Yugoslavia strengthened my resolve not to go after the dreamlike things of life but, rather, to pursue the *source* of the things of life. The epitome of being free, rich, and successful is to be yoked with our existential origin, to know our true identity as a life form.

Those defining success as material affluence may not appreciate the value of spiritual wealth. In my case, surely no one will ever place me on the world's richest people list, at least not as "rich" is popularly defined. In my mother's last years, I may add, she compared me, despite my skimpy bank account, to the well-off people she knew. I received her pat on my head and my life when she favorably concluded: "You have what they lack: peace of mind." After knowing me for so many decades, she finally recognized the "net worth" of my nonmaterial wealth. Similarly, the process of rethinking the significance of life and what is really important is enriching more people with higher dividends than the stock market ever can offer.

The contemporary, incomplete, version of the American Dream, heavily stressing materiality, dishonors what "success" implied only two generations earlier to my émigré ancestors. I believe that when they arrived in the Promised Land, material good fortune was less important to them than the intangible dream of religious freedom, equal opportunity, political liberty, and justice. The original American Dream transcends national borders.

Growing numbers of Americans and people elsewhere are connecting with a new dream. Dreams evolve, as do concepts, awareness, and understanding. The new "Global Dream" is the postconsumerist dream of a durable world established on environmental and ecological values and moral, ethical, and spiritual principles applicable to all.

Likewise, my understanding of freedom keeps evolving. In the society Titoism created, I realized that although in America I had considered myself to be a free person, I was not free. Funnily enough, "coincidentally," the photo in my Andrew Jackson High School yearbook,

The Pioneer, illustrating the boy and girl graduate "Most Likely to Succeed," portrays Joel Blatt and me behind bars, as if we are in a prison cell! The photo shows fashionable me—at age eighteen still following my mother's dress code—wearing a silk dress, pearl necklace, wristwatch, and a golden ring set with two small diamonds gifted by my Hungarian grandmother for my sixteenth birthday.

Not that photo, but Yugoslav society, helped me perceive that I was not free. Yugoslavia, giving me the time to explore who and what I existentially am, helped me grow in my understanding of what it truly means to be free. As an American, I always felt myself a free person. Yet my unawareness had deluded me into living in America as a slave. How free was I when caught by a competitive system teaching me to pit myself against others, to note the differences in others rather than the similarities, to kowtow to those "above" and to look down on those "below"?

The conceptual thrust of mainstream American thought had shackled me to the "I-I-me-me" syndrome. To help me find equilibrium between love of self, self-interest, and selfless love for others was never a priority of my schoolteachers, except the unique Professor Yu-go-*slave*-ia.

My top-rated American schools had supplied excellent breadwinning education tailored for material success in the dog-eat-dog world. Based on competitive testing, grades scored in exam upon exam, and personal accomplishments, we compared ourselves incessantly with others. But there was no assessment of our inner achievements. "Know thyself" remained words connected with ancient history and philosophy. The prominence given to external activities did nothing to help me know my mind's intuitive capacity or the subtler dimensions of life. Improvement of the ability to identify and understand people's situations and feelings, hopes and struggles—to love selflessly and empathically—did not figure into the scholastic packet. Specially designed tests calculated our IQ, our Intelligence Quotient, but no exams measured our LCQ, our Love and Compassion Quotient. There was no competition encouraging us to vote for the senior graduate "Most Likely to Love the Most Unconditionally, the Most Selflessly." As I learned later on, to live a truly successful life we need wisdom more than book knowledge.

The competition in our high-achievement world has become so extreme it is robbing adults of their health, and children of their childhood. Preoccupation on external achievements and success has caused a dramatic rise of teen mental health problems.[50] As a result of exhaustion caused by long-term stress, even children have become victims of burnout.[51] Moreover, childhood burnout is as rampant in Asia as in the Western world.[52] The root cause of youthful burnout during school years is not the excessive homework itself; it is the long-term goal of material success and the short-term competition underlying the phenomenon.

Outer achievements do not constitute total human development. Never in any of my schools did I hear: "Education is the manifestation of the perfection already in man [woman]."[53] None of my schools gave attention even to the humanistic meaning of human perfection: a state of completeness reflecting a fulfillment of the highest "good" potentialities inherent in the human nature. There was no focus on helping us mine our highest inner potential for good so we might attain a genuine fulfillment and contentment. I was not made to feel the necessity to

---

[50] Founder and Director of the SOS: Stressed-Out Students Project (SOS) at Stanford University, Dr. Denise Pope wrote a book whose very title sums up the phenomenon: *Doing School: How We Are Creating a Generation of Stressed-Out, Materialistic and Miseducated Students*. See: "Teenage fixation on 'success' bad for mind and spirit, according to panelists" by Annie Jia, May 21, 2007, www. News-service.stanford.edu/news/2007/may 23/sos-052307.

[51] "No More Teachers, Lots of Books," op-ed by Sara Bennett and Nancy Kalish, *New York Times*, June 19, 2006, online edition.

[52] Quote by Chinese woman interviewed in the TV documentary about China, *Niet van hier* ("Not from here") made by the Dutch broadcasting group VPRO and broadcast in the Netherlands (Nederland 2) on July 23, 2006.

[53] Statement by Swami Vivekananda, the Indian monk who was the chief disciple of Sri Ramakrishna, nineteenth-century Indian sage, published in the chapter "What We Believe In" in *The Complete Works of Swami Vivekananda*, Volume IV, Mayavati Memorial Edition, Advaita Ashrama Publication Department, Kolkata, India, 2006, p. 358.

cultivate and expand my inner life. "Inner development" and similar phrases never came up in my classes.

The inner facets of my education received their first ABC's in the classroom of Professor Yu-go-*slave*-ia. Yu-go-*slave*-ia compelled me to recognize myself from both without and within. I began to experience that my outer life is not my whole life, and that changes in my inner life were necessary. In so doing, I saw my slaveries and had to acknowledge: the chains binding me to *slave*-ia are inside myself. I was in servitude to the conditioned thinking that often dictated my actions.

Living in the monitored capital of Croatia engendered in me the tangible feeling and meaning of both personal and societal freedom. Walking through my days in Zagreb as a witness of myself, while looking over my shoulder for any possible watchers also witnessing me, I could not avoid seeing that I was not the free person I had fancied myself to be.

In Yu-go-*slave*-ia, I also became consciously aware, still minimally, of the ultimate nature of freedom. I asked questions that pierced through the borders of freedom I had previously explored while living in my birth country: What is "freedom"? What is "true freedom"? Mahatma Gandhi spent years in prison; does this indicate he was not "free"? Does not true freedom have less to do with outer circumstances and more with awareness?

Once upon a time—not in Yugoslavia but four years later, in 1972, in India—I would experience, if briefly at first, an "ultimate freedom." This is the freedom beyond all human-legislated freedoms as free speech, free press, and free assembly, and also beyond the individual's freedom of consumer choice, and even beyond the existential freedom from suffering. The final freedom, to live awakened to the nondream of the true nature of Reality, in oneness with the highest truth of existence, remained an aspiration still hidden from me in 1968. Back then, I took the physical world of appearances for the whole of Reality instead of only a limited and fleeting aspect. I could not imagine that my Yugoslavian experiences were preparing me for a next stage in the self-growth process. I had no clue I was being guided to real human maturity. Little did I suspect I was already walking a road leading to the transcendental knowing of life's true success.

The inner awakening in India provided affirmative answers for the existential questions about inner guidance, Higher Purpose, and Greater Power that had plagued me during the Yugoslavian period. I came to look at "coincidence" and "good luck" as the fruit of karma, the cosmic law of sow and reap governing the effects of our actions. Therefore, no longer do I ask why any experience has come. I inquire: "What is this experience trying to teach me? What karmic debt am I paying off?"

When we perceive (and can continually remember) that all our experiences yoke with helping us discover and connect with what we truly are, from within, then we can more easily accept our everyday challenges and difficulties. We can become free from slavish identification with the outer forms and conditions of our life.

Looking at my stay in Yugoslavia from the viewpoint of Now, with an eye toward the future, has enabled me to enter more deeply into matters that, although appearing negative at the time, actually turned out positive. Experiences that initially seem poisonous may ultimately resemble nectar when we understand they help nudge us along life's educational road.

For instance, I think about the influence on me of Zagreb's physical environment. A place, like a person, has a singular personality and invisible energy field able to affect us to greater or lesser magnitude, depending on the stage of our personal development.

My New York eyes, accustomed to the razzle-dazzle of the superabundant "Big Apple," saw the Croatian capital in 1968 as plain, gray, and drab. Just as living creatures make themselves alluring for sexual partners, cities in a capitalist society decorate themselves to attract consumers. Many American cities adorn outdoor spaces and shop windows with catchy images, clever designs, and hypnotic slogans devised by advertisers and marketers. The epitome of commercial display is Times Square, Manhattan's super-illuminated advertising hub not so many streets from where I was born.

Habituated as I was to the flashy and splashy gigantic advertising billboards and excited buzz of "The Crossroads of the World," Zagreb provided no color, no life. And that was at a time when the Times Square billboards came nowhere close in size to the mammoth digital advertising screen, eight stories tall and nearly the size of a football field, erected there in November 2014.

The physical environment of Zagreb, mostly ad-free except for some officially sanctioned state products, was clearly unsoiled by the seductive expressions of commerce. I, however, was unable to recognize the city's refreshing authenticity and purity. Now I am conscious that the deepening of gray approaching black that I experienced in the Croatian capital had less to do with the historic city and its Old World charm, and more to do with my own shortage of awareness.

In Zagreb, even with my limited perception, I also attained receptivity to a subtle environment my outer eyes could not detect. Apparently I was able to "see," rather "sense," an "invisible Zagreb." This was a mental and emotional landscape created by Zagrebians, both those contented with the Yugoslav experiment and those not. Numerous factors apparently made me more responsive to the negative elements of the subtle, invisible Zagreb. Perhaps, in addition, I reacted to subtle historical remnants of the fear that terrorized the city during World War II, when the citizens suffered many forms of wartime agony.

I can only imagine the fright that was generated in May 1943, when Heinrich Himmler, overseer of all the Nazi concentration camps, visited Zagreb. A few days later, the Croatian collaborationist wartime government rounded up for deportation to Auschwitz the area's remaining Jewish population. Whatever sources created the gloom I felt in Zagreb, a dark atmosphere suffocated my American optimism, at least temporarily.

Simultaneously, my new habit of regular introspection attuned me, unknowingly, with the personal cloud of darkness hanging over my own me. For all the successes and rewards of life in my homeland, I had undergone disappointments, pain, and sorrow. One cannot live a competitive, rushed, and stressful "good life" without acquiring some toxic character qualities and bearing their negative side effects. In Zagreb, I was not cognizant of a personal dark cloud, of my own making, overshadowing my thoughts and actions. But the society's difficult lessons unmasked certain of my accumulated negative attitudes and behavioral patterns. Gaining insight into some of the negativities embedded in my mindset, such as the tendency to judge others and to avoid the Germanic, figured heavily in my Yu-go-*slave*-ian de-education.

As I trust may be clear, I am a very changed person from the young American woman in the tight jersey minidress who arrived at the Zagreb train station on a very hot July day in historic 1968. Changed not merely because the succeeding years took alcohol and flesh foods off my menu, removed my watch from my wrist, wrinkled my skin, salted my hair—and lengthened my skirts! I am fundamentally changed because authentic, enduring, and ongoing transformation of inner level firmly integrated with my outer life.

My experiences in Yugoslavia, a country that experimented with cooperation and unity as a national policy, helped broaden the understanding of my heart. My thinking formerly centered on *my* blood family, *my* city (New York), and *my* country (America). My mindset expanded to encompass *our* human family, *our* society, *our* world. Until we as a species recognize our unity in the diversity of *our* one world, and accept that we are all relatives in *our* one human family, we run the risk of competing with each other in a manner that could well yield the destruction of ourselves, nature's bounty, and planetary civilization itself.

Durable social reform arises first as motivational energy in our loving, compassionate, and empathetic human heart before materializing in practical systems, structures, and programs. In our individual heart resides that understanding of goodness by which we know what ought to be done and what not. We need to let the power of our convictions stand us up in courage to connect with others in goodness and cooperation. The power of goodness will always overcome the power of a Hitler.

Yugoslavia, for all its contradictions, suggested a hopeful message: Human beings can create a society functioning between the extremes of the competitive Western mindset of I-me-mine and the old Eastern Bloc's totalitarian we-us-ours. Workers' Self-Management was a twentieth-century experiment in the "We" direction. The concept of worker-owned enterprises and worker profit-sharing promoted horizontal cooperative democracy. More people had more rights in the workplace. Having a voice and participatory power in the work process assured workers that their wages and benefits would not inevitably erode or stagnate, as may occur in "top-down" management and organization faced with shareholder pressure for continually higher profits and dividends.

Workers' Self-Management was to Yugoslavia what democracy is to Western countries following free market economics. Yugoslav communists saw true democracy not as political but economic, with the working people themselves controlling the conditions and products of their work through self-management. The role of the state was envisioned to weaken as associations of free producers became stronger and took over state functions. Despite the system's imperfections, problems, and obstacles, WSM as practiced in Yugoslavia, and in several countries of Latin America, deserves reexamination and reconsideration.[54] Aspects of WSM may resonate with people today who, seeking solutions for humanity's manifold problems, appreciate the spirit of cooperation and sharing inherent to economic democracy and social participation. Study would be needed, however, based on existing documents and statistics from the former Yugoslavia, if available, to try and ascertain to what extent WSM yielded a smoothly functioning economy that could fend for itself in the world without having to rely on loans and additional forms of assistance from other countries and international organizations.

The same principle of democratization emerged during the student activism that gripped France in May 1968, which John Grierson called "the most astounding revolution" in his lifetime. The May events

---

[54] See "The Third Way: The Experiment of Workers' Self-Management in Socialist Yugoslavia," by Zoran Erić: www.academia.edu/4223251/The_Third_Way_The_Experiment_of_Workers_Self-Management_in_Socialist_Yugoslavia

in Paris started when French students addressed themselves in part to the undemocratic management of the universities. French students sought to participate directly in the running of their educational institutions.

Today more people than ever believe that the right of direct participation in society, in any enterprise, institution, or activity, belongs to everyone. Ours is evolving away from the hierarchical set up in some societies and communities, at least on a grassroots level. It can be easier and less time-consuming to let one person or a small elite make decisions, but the principles of participatory politics, economics, and self-management are finding bottom-up support among growing numbers of people who want to be involved in issues and decision-making.

A new model is arising to displace the old "higher and lower" relationship between the governing and the governed. More people in the work world are questioning the traditional boss-employee/master-slave-servant approach. Courageous folks are swimming against the reigning stream to bring on a new work culture.

New-style leaders see themselves as part of a team. They do not tell and order what needs doing. New-style leaders make sense of what is happening and help workers be part of the company's decision-making, if not profit-sharing. As with WSM, new-style leaders emphasize communicating, listening, cooperating, and facilitating based on a horizontal relationship between all members of the workforce. New-style leaders can recognize themselves in words written thousands of years ago by the Chinese sage, Lao Tzu. In his classic, *Tao Te Ching*, Lao Tzu notes that when a good leader's work is done, the people say, "We did this ourselves."

Recently I met an eleven-year-old girl who told me her goal in life is to be a manager. I asked her, "What is a manager?" A manager, she said, is someone who works with a team of people to bring about the best of everything for everyone. She wants to be a manager of a soccer club or something in music. "What about husband and children?" I inquired. "I can combine," she answered.

The young girl's emphasis on teamwork particularly struck me. I got the idea that she automatically assumes that society should be playing itself out, for the advantage of all, in team formation, on a level playing field, using the peaceful means of cooperation, horizontal relationships, social concern, and sharing.

To get to the future cooperative society, we need inspiration not only from innocent, eleven-year-old idealists. We also require engagement from practical visionaries who, besides advocating positive changes for humanity and society, themselves live or try to live those changes in their own lives. We envision new-style leaders to work in the spirit of caring, giving, and sharing rather than with the calculating attitude of "What's in it for me (and my bank account)?" We visualize leaders who live according to the simple truth that, "If it is not right, do not do it; if it is not true, do not say it."

The needed societal and planetary repair and renewal begins nowhere else than with our own changed attitudes and actions. Former United Nations Secretary-General Kofi Annan zoomed in on one aspect of our multifaceted global challenge when he stated: "Lifestyle, especially that of Western society, is the biggest stumbling block to sustainable development in the world."

Just as Yugoslavia activated my initial awakening to the sustainable lifestyle decades ago, the fading of the huge consumer economy in the twenty-first century is freeing people from preoccupation with materialism, possession, and ownership. Although reduced income and tighter budgeting may seem hellish to us in the beginning, our altered economic circumstances may be recognized, eventually, as leading us to a happier condition than when we had ample funds to spend without having to count every penny. Forced reduced spending and tempered consuming may seem temporary, but the recalibration is, I suggest, part of the twenty-first century's evolving redefinitions of the good life, success, family, happiness, progress, and security, both personal and national, among other aspects of living in this world.

Contemporary living leaves most of us little, if any, time and energy to take quiet pauses for the self-reflection that Yugoslavia granted me back then, enabling me to come closer to the deeper self hidden within my societal personality. Of course, in Zagreb, I was in a unique position as an economically privileged person from the West. I am sure that Yu-go-*slave*-ia did not similarly grant much time and energy for self-reflection to its hard-working citizens. As well, the citizens knew that self-reflection in their totalitarian society could possibly give a voice to their potentially dangerous, critical self-expression. Even in private, who knew which listening ears might belong to "faithful correspondents" of the secret police —and could lead one to Goli otok, the prison island that in no way resembled the paradisiacal refuge of Robinson Crusoe?

The speed and pressures of modern life prod us to rush ever faster to keep up with endless activities, demands, and distractions that tend to keep our attention focused outwards. Nonetheless, the force of global crises is pressing more of us to live the examined life. Lasting social reform derives from our individual self-awareness and self-improvement put into service for the whole.

My own continuing self-examination also brought me to define "work" quite differently from the I-centered materialistic definition I held upon my arrival in Yugoslavia. By the time I waved "*Doviđenja* [goodbye]," to Mario and Zagreb, and boarded the train for the Netherlands, my definition of "work" had expanded to the wider, humanistic, We-definition inspired by John Grierson: to labor in the service of humanity.

By the way, the reader may have noticed that never in the story have I referred to "Miss Green" by a first name. This is because my name in Zagreb was not Surya, but Norma. "Norma" is the name my parents gave me, to honor my grandfather Noah. "Surya" is the name mystical experiences with our Sun gave me in India in 1972, as described in my first book (which, although written earlier, is actually a sequel to this present book).[55]

India, fulfilling its traditional role as spiritual guru of the world, opened my inner eyes to the eternal spirit and the need to reach the

---

[55] *The Call of the Sun: A Woman's Journey to the Heart of Wisdom,* by Surya Green, Element Books, UK/USA/Australia, 1997. Earlier versions appeared in German and Dutch translations. *Once Upon a Yugoslavia* is a prequel to *The Call of the Sun.*

ultimate human perfection and inner realization. In India, four additional years of post-Yugoslavia life-lessons having further prepared my mind, I received the "Sun-revelation." During a series of miraculous mystical occurrences, I experienced our Sun as incredibly more than simply the shining golden disk I loved to worship in my bathing suit.

One wondrous disclosure of my spiritual awakening and rebirth was the Sanskrit name *Surya,* "Sun, the Source." I narrate my renaming from "Norma" in my first book. Written in the 1990s, the book gives the background of my complete trust in humanity's ability to rise from the depths of materialism, the philosophy that this sensory world alone is true.

Now it is luminously clear to me that in 1968 I was not just the adventurous Norma (Linda) Eisner Green heading to a summer temp job abroad. Waving goodbye to my parents at the airport in New York City, I was, unintentionally, an American emigrant embarking on foreign explorations that would move me toward borderless living. Like my European forebears, I, too, was part of a mass exodus. But I was leaving not so much a geographical region as a state of mind. Unconsciously, involuntarily, I was traveling away from an I-lifestyle based solely on my own self-interest and material success. I was shifting to the more inclusive We-mentality and heart space.

It is true that I had criticized my homeland for its I-istic lifestyle revolving mainly around competition, money, power, things, and appearances. I had complained about America's imbalances, injustices, abuses of minority groups, and more. But I had not gone to Yugoslavia as a comparison shopper, looking for a new political or economic system. In 1968, I had not one thought about exchanging my American life for any other life elsewhere. One day, I knew, America would rise up from all that was pulling it down, and I trusted to be on the spot to help in the renewal process. For a temporary period, however, I was open to investigate another lifestyle abroad. Well, sometimes "temporary" can last as endlessly as a Yugoslav minute.

Leaving New York in 1968, I was also saying—without any awareness, quite unconsciously—"*Dovidenja,* goodbye" to residing full-time in

America. As much as I loved my birth country, little did I know I would immerse myself in numerous non-American societies during my life's journey of self-discovery. I was en route to experiencing that wherever I am, I am home as long as I feel at home in my own house, my own unity of body-mind-spirit.

When I was Yu-go-*slave*-i-an, I was Am-er-*I-can*. Additionally, I was starting to expand past national borders, passports, and visas to encounter my larger identity as a citizen of the world, not to mention the Cosmos. I was beginning to grasp the elementary aspects of a cosmic truth: we are all workers for a better world within a universal, transformational, evolutionary process. This ongoing process is steering humanity toward spiritualization. Simultaneously, the spiritualization process is moving Earth society in the direction of social justice, economic fairness, resource sharing, and ecological sustainability.

At the same time, there are forces working against spiritual regeneration. In this worldwide battleground, I get an unpleasant Yu-go-*slave* déjà vu every time I read, or learn about, new ways that we, citizens of our countries and of the world, are being monitored. John Grierson's advice to retain both in art and in life itself "a secrecy, a privacy," calls up a human right we are fast losing, if we have not already completely lost. Privacy used to be a citizen's unwritten individual right, equated with freedom and liberty. But technology in the digital age, besides providing immense benefits, can be, and is, used in ways that deprive people of basic human rights and civil liberties.

Just as in twentieth-century Yugoslavia, in our twenty-first century modern global society we have the expectation that we are being watched. The prying eyes of the high-tech Orwellian world are examining our cyber storage files, banking activities, and online photos. Privacy does not mean very much as our phone calls, land post, emails, and Internet traffic are subjected to tracking and archiving. Our thinking, interests, and habits may be deduced from our Internet searches. What we speak, type, send, or attach may be tapped, data based, and tracked within a global mass surveillance state. Facial recognition, iris scan, radio frequency ID chips, and palm scan technologies collected for one purpose can be used for another purpose, virtually carte blanche, without our permission or knowledge.

The surveillance camera has become a humdrum but chilling part of daily living. High-tech cameras observe us on the public streets, in public transport, airports, shops, shopping malls, buildings, crowds, and sometimes in our private homes. Handheld radar devices enable law enforcement agencies, bypassing the use of legal search warrants, to see secretly through the walls of houses to detect if anyone is inside, where they are, and whether they are moving.[56] Supermarkets track our smart phones to know the products we look at and for how long. Electronic camera sensors in food shelves can scan our facial structure, age, and weight, and record when we take something from the shelf. Internet businesses may ask us to log in with our voice and/or fingerprint. Camera technology can detect something so personal as our heartbeats. Retina-scan technology, monitoring our eye movements, can predict what ingredients we want on our fast food pizza.[57] Marketers amass money from our data by identifying our consumer preferences, predicting our buying patterns, and targeting us with personalized ads.

Present-day technologies can give direct access to our inner being, making us vulnerable to a subtle form of abuse and exploitation. Advanced technology is giving governments more power over our individual mindset than ever existed in totalitarian nations. At which point is the technological intrusion intolerable?

And then, to travel "freely" from country to country, we may be compelled to show the contents of our luggage, if not sometimes our body cavities. Please never dare to ask airport authorities, "*Zašto*? Why?" Even our water bottle, filled if only with blessed liquid obtained at miraculous Lourdes or at holy river Ganges, is subject to scrutiny and

[56] "New Police Radars can 'See' Inside Homes," by Brad Heath, *USA Today*, January 20, 2015. www.usatoday.com/story/news/2015/01/19/police-radar-see-through-walls/22007615/

[57] "Pizza Hut to retina scan customers' eyes to create 'perfect' Orwellian fast food," by Jonathan Benson, *Natural News*, December 11, 2014. www.naturalnews.com/047953_Pizza_Hut_retina_scan_biometrics.html

confiscation. We may be asked to give our fingerprint and/or the scan of our face, our iris, and our entire body, or submit to a full physical pat down. Notations are made of our data. Our border crossings in and out of an increasing number of countries are documented and may be kept for years.

Modern society appears to be traveling the quickest route possible to prove George Orwell negatively prophetic with his book *Nineteen Eighty-Four*, published in 1949. As the esteemed nineteenth-century American author Mark Twain observed, "Truth is stranger than fiction, but it is because Fiction is obliged to stick to possibilities; Truth isn't."

Today some democratic governments, abusing transparency, oversight, and accountability, exhibit "Big Brother is watching" characteristics similar to the authoritarian societies they formerly condemned. Fear and secret policies prevail. Surveillance around the world violates the private lives of the citizens, at home and in public, on line and off. Governments reference prevention of terrorist attacks and national security to justify the gathering of our personal information. But what and how much is being done to address and fix the problems at the source of terrorism?

Besides the obvious physical limitations on our freedoms, on the emotional level we absorb into our lives the fears of the projected terrors against which the legislative laws ostensibly protect. Our fear-filled minds sustain a fear-filled world. This process occurs even when we intellectually understand our government's explanation of the necessity to impose limits on our human rights. The absorption of societal negativity into our consciousness, or at least into our unconscious, contributes to a negative mindset tending to fear, demean, and hate while also nourishing distrust, despair, and depression, if not suicide.

Some people, fearing international terrorism and possible future harm, regard the loss of civic liberties, including free expression and privacy, as a minor inconvenience. The monitoring of our activities by digital surveillance is rationalized with the argument: "The innocent have nothing to fear or hide." This may be so, yet do we not have the right to keep our private matters and our private communication private

if we so choose? Is not our privacy our own intangible personal possession to increase or decrease at our own wish? Without privacy, can there
be free intellectual exploration of the World Wide Web of information?
Without privacy, do we not self-censor to some degree our Internet
searches and online expression? Self-censorship is a reverse freedom.
Privacy is a freedom.

Or does freedom for a citizen in modern society mean swimming
"freely" around in a global goldfish bowl not caring who watches?
Having nothing to hide, we swim naked, except for the blindfolds or
rose-colored glasses we wear. "Who watches the watchers?" What
guarantees our protection from abusive monitoring and misinterpre-
tation of our data? We can ponder the deeper meaning of Benjamin
Franklin's caution to Colonial Americans: "They who can give up essential liberty to obtain a little temporary safety, deserve neither liberty
nor safety."

As Dr. Henry Breitrose noted in his foreword to this book, the
experiences "in a society that ran on 'Yugo-*slave*' time also made Surya
re-examine the conflicting values of personal security, which was what
Yu-go-*slave*-ia offered its people, and the lack of personal freedom,
which was the price." Having paid that price to some limited extent while
living for a short time under Tito's Third Way, I have to say that staying
in a monitored society back then was for me a form of psychological
torture. Decades later, I am feeling tortured again.

Perhaps today's democratic and freedom-touting nations, feeling under threat and wishing to protect the citizens, would like all the
people to feel grateful for stepped-up security measures. But once such
measures become ho-hum accepted everyday procedures, embedded
in society, what is to prevent them from being used beyond perceived
current threats to take on a wider and self-perpetuating function?
Yugoslav dissident Milovan Djilas sounded the deep ring of truth,
timelessly applicable as a warning to all individuals, nations, and situations, when he stated: "By justifying the means because of the end,
the end itself becomes increasingly more distant and unrealistic, while

the frightful reality of the means becomes increasingly obvious and intolerable."[58]

Future peoples may very well wonder how we *slave*-ians in the twenty-first century surrendered our privacy—freedom and liberty, that is—so easily and with so little resistance. Perhaps, in our existential loneliness, we actually get comfort from knowing we are more often than not a focus of attention, possibly being watched, assessed, judged, and archived. If we cannot know with absolute certainty that there is an all-seeing Divinity always witnessing and influencing us, at least we are sure there is an omnipresent technological god whose observational presence in our lives is scientifically provable. We are not alone in this mysterious existence.

It is hard to determine the long-term consequences of the lack of privacy and the psychological components associated with the fears upon which monitoring is based. This is another issue that is everyone's in the twenty-first century. Massive general surveillance and the elimination of privacy undermine personal mental health, societal democracy and freedom, and liberty and justice.

In so many areas, we the people have to decide what kind of a society we want. We know real change is needed. But mere transformation of political, economic, and social machinery cannot effectuate the better life comprising basic human rights and securities that the greater part of humanity desires and deserves. Yugoslavia taught me that politics, the political system, and political revolution are not the source of durable social transformation. Political and governmental processes are only partial tools for realizing social change that lasts. It is questionable whether we can create a humane human society solely by legislation. The break-up of the Socialist Federal Republic of Yugoslavia along ethnic lines is another proof that brotherhood and sisterhood and unity cannot be imposed.

---

[58] *The New Class*, ibid, p.163.

On the contrary, governmental rules to enforce cooperation, sharing, and communality may heighten people's sense of separation, selfishness, and possession ("mine is mine"). Dictates compelling the individual to deny personal aspirations and wishes cannot bring about the elimination or diminution of selfishness and greed. Governments suppressing or suspending rights and freedoms—except the supposed "rights" and "freedoms" claimed by some to discriminate against minorities and abuse others in criminal and/or violent ways—will not inspire the emergence of a citizenry in which noble values and the power of goodness prevail. Curbing free expression of discontent or punishing public exposure of governmental abuse creates suppressed, fearful, and also angry people. Forcefully stopping criticism, dissent, and protest will control citizen unrest only temporarily.

Ignoble acts cannot produce noble results; pure goals can never justify impure methods. Mahatma Gandhi pointed to the cosmic truth of "As you sow, you reap" when he said: "As the means, so the end."

The hope of societal transformation may flame brightly when we elect promising change-promising leaders, yet enduring social change requires our own individual, aware, committed, and purposeful adjustments of attitudes and behavior. Yugoslavia's disintegrated social experiment is but another confirmation that human beings cannot establish a positively transformed society until human beings themselves change, from inside out. The outer changes of a society have to synchronize with the inner transformation of its citizens.

To effect durable social reform, it is necessary to overcome dependency on governments, institutions, and corporations as the fountainhead for policy innovations. We ourselves can contribute to societal betterment by working for the larger whole in the areas of our everyday expertise and influence. Instead of complaining (privately, as the Yugo-*slaves* had to do out of fear), we have to speak out (as most Yugo-*slaves* dared not unless they wished free room and board at Goli otok). In our democratic societies we have to exercise our freedom of speech and expression and share publicly our advice and suggestions. And we have to help implement changes before rising rivers sweep us away, or massive droughts dry up our drink water, or the global economic system destabilizes life on Earth completely. If individual courage and mass peaceful action could help collapse Soviet communism, so can we the people organize and act together to help effect the positive transformation of this world for the good of all.

Yes, I know—my trust in human beings ultimately creating a (spiritualized and solarized) global society of loving unity, peaceful cooperation, harmonious comaintenance of the planet, and fair sharing may seem unrealistic, ridiculous, and absurd, at the very least. But if I am a dreamer, if I am an idealistic optimist, I am not the only one.[59]

We all know that human beings possess a brain able to penetrate the mysteries of the universe and discover the physical secrets of the stars, comets, planets, Moon, and Sun. Human beings have hearts large enough to feel compassion, empathy, and unconditional love. Human beings have the potential to manifest their inherent, latent, human perfection in the same way that humanity has made astounding material progress in its external life.

Humans fly through the skies? Moon walk? Are our modern human minds open to the possibility that what yesterday struck us as improbable and inconceivable, could one day become reality? The sudden fall of the Berlin Wall in 1989, followed by the astonishing end of Soviet communism and the USSR, and the uniting of the divided Germany, serve as only three matter-of-fact examples that startling alterations can come to a reigning system with a minimum of bloody revolution.

My trust in a future humane humanity and harmonious global society is also rooted in my personal history. My unsought, authentic, ongoing reversal of focus from outer to inner, with the gradual balancing of the two perspectives in my daily life, lets me recognize the force of genuine awareness-awakening and the positive transition from "I" to "We" energizing today's changing world.

That is why I picked up my pen to describe how, once upon a time in Yugoslavia, I became motivated to pinpoint and carry out more

---

[59] With thanks to John Lennon for his iconic inspirational song, *Imagine.*

persistently my own individual work for humanity's better tomorrow. My transformed life is, I suggest, only one expression of the larger trend. We are all traveling the same human evolutionary road in our own unique way.

Realists, dreamers, and visionaries know that every morning, Sun always "rises." Although skies may turn stormy black, Sun ever blazes. If we can be sure of anything in life besides change, it is the unchanging truth of Sun's continually shining presence, even when clouds fill the sky and we see only grayness. So too, a solarized society of caring and sharing is dawning on Earth

How far into the future am I looking ahead?

Short Yugo-Historical Afterword

Yugoslavia's form of socialism did not result in the true or lasting Third Way to which Josip Broz Tito aspired. Yet, to some degree, during its relatively flowering years well before the war that then tore it apart, when it stood out internationally in an almost positive light among the nations of the East Bloc, Marshal Tito's Yugoslavia had a beneficial impact, in a hard to measure but not negligible manner, on the growth of humanity's recognition of its brother-sisterhood. For all its deficits, Yugoslavia's social experiment has helped drive forward what I do believe (recognizing that some would argue otherwise) is the world's steady movement toward unity and peace (though at the slower pace that characterized the Yugoslavia I knew). The mantra "Brotherhood and Unity" all Yugoslavs spouted has surely influenced the collective consciousness on a subtle level.

Socialism and communism, just like democracy, have at their roots the ideals of compassionate caring and sharing, as well as the ideal of equality. It seems that the spiritual basis of Tito's political ideology was not a real truth to him, as it was not to any of the communist leaders, Mikhail Sergeyevich Gorbachev excepted. Otherwise, they could not have used dictatorial and violent means en route to the idealized society.

Tito had great charisma and influence. But, like many political leaders, he lacked the spiritual aspiration, discernment, and detachment that can prevent a national leader from placing his or her own ego, desires, and personal ambition above the needs and welfare of those who are led. Had Tito developed the humility to allow himself to be the true servant of his people rather than the master, perhaps a genuine and lasting social transformation might have occurred in Yugoslavia. Had his strong personal power been even stronger, perhaps he could have used his force to bring to Yugoslavia democratic governance with much greater, sustainable personal and political freedoms.

Within the Socialist Federal Republic of Yugoslavia, Tito had to work hard for the unity of the various ethnic groups—a formidable challenge given the lingering animosities that presumably existed, for example, among many Serbs toward Croatians on account of atrocities committed during World War II, and to some extent vice-versa. Yet, to a certain degree, Tito attained his goal, however short lasting, of brotherhood and unity. To achieve that unity, however, he repressed the nationalistic tendencies of the Balkan peoples.

But even in an "ideal" Yugoslavia, a society embracing democratic socialism, which does not throw people in jail for vocalizing against the government, Tito would probably have tended to stifle potentially destabilizing expressions of nationalism in the republics. As well, he was not willing to give citizens the freedom to voice either their grievances or their wishes for reforms. Although in 1968 Tito condemned the Soviets for invading Czechoslovakia and crushing the Prague Spring, he himself suppressed reform movements in his own country.

In 1967, a group of Croatian poets and linguists published the "Declaration Concerning the Name and Position of the Croatian Literary Language." The goals of the document were more political than linguistic. The Declaration helped shape the Croatian civil and nationalist rights movement *masovni pokret*, or MASPOK, for "mass movement." A highly politicized period between 1969 and 1971 became known as the "Croatian Spring," *Hrvatsko proljeće*. The Croatian Spring gave outer expression to greater rights for Croatia within the Federation of Yugoslavia. It called for democratic and economic reforms and transparency of economic relations between the republics. The movement steadily picked up support, especially among students.[60]

Croatia's yearnings did not mesh with Tito's policy of national unity. Setting one's own republic above any other was considered a threat to federal Yugoslavia. Tito decisively suppressed the nationalistic tendencies lest they lead to tensions and instability among the federation's various ethnic groups. When student activists staged protests in Zagreb in 1971, the police arrested many demonstrators. Thousands were criminally prosecuted, some receiving prison sentences of up to several years. A parallel reform movement emerged in Serbia. The Serbs, like the Czechs before them, wanted "socialism with a human face." Tito quashed both the Croatian and the Serbian reform movements. He removed leaders with nationalistic leanings, putting hard-line centralists into place.

The Croatian Spring, which gathered force from the early 1970s on, nonetheless influenced the new Yugoslav federal constitution of 1974. The constitution gave more autonomy to the individual republics and protected the Workers' Self-Management system from state interference. One of the longest constitutions in the world, the document proclaimed Josip Broz Tito Yugoslavia's president-for-life (after he had been elected to the office a further five times after first becoming president in 1953).

In 1980, on the fourth of May, just after three p.m., sirens throughout the country announced that Yugoslavia had lost its charismatic leader. Josip Broz Tito died after thirty-five years in power. Millions of people wept. One hundred and twenty-eight nations sent two hundred and nine political delegates to the funeral, making it the largest funeral of any political figure in the twentieth century.

Following Tito's death, three days short of his eighty-eighth birthday, no one emerged commanding the combination of ability and charisma and respect he had to keep the Balkan peoples together.

---

[60] *Zagreb: A Cultural History*, by Celia Hawkesworth, Oxford University Press, 2008, New York, pp. 156–161.

Also, a committee-type government, as in the Soviet Union, did not emerge. The rival policies of the constituent republics gradually replaced Titoism.

With the 1989 collapse of communism in the Soviet Union and most of Eastern Europe, suppressed nationalism and ethnic tensions resurfaced in the six, nominally equal, Yugoslav republics. Yugoslav turned against Yugoslav. Eleven years after Tito's passing, the Yugoslavian experiment concluded with the traumatic series of civil wars between regions and ethnic groups. Some two decades after I left Zagreb, the Yugoslav Wars of the 1990s ruptured the country. It has been estimated that between 130,000 and 140,000 people died as a result. In 1991, the Federal Republic broke up into its constituent ethnic parts.

Croatia, Slovenia, Bosnia and Herzegovina, and Macedonia became independent nations. Croatia held its first democratic elections. In 1992, Croatia gained recognition from the European Union and the United Nations as an independent state. By 2005, the *Lonely Planet* travel guide book termed Croatia the "world's hottest travel destination."

Serbia and Montenegro made up the Socialist Federal Republic of Yugoslavia until 2006, when Montenegro voted for independence. In 2008, the parliament of Kosovo declared the Republic of Kosovo independent from Serbia.

In 2013, Croatia, with its high-income market economy joined the European Union. In the Croatia of the former Yugoslavia, Tito's birth in Kumrovec on the seventh of May had been celebrated eighteen days later as "Youth Day." Independent Croatia revived the tradition of celebrating Tito's birthday.

In Serbia, every year on the occasion of Tito's death anniversary, admirers travel to his mausoleum in the "House of Flowers" in a residential area of Belgrade. Carrying Tito's photo and Yugoslav flags, they gather and sing songs from the Titoist era. After the death of Tito's wife Jovanka in 2013, she was buried next to him.

In 2001, Alexander Karadjordjevic, the only son and heir of Yugoslavia's last king, Peter II, returned to live in Serbia. He is known as "Crown Prince Alexander," the title he legally held in Yugoslavia from his birth in mid-1945 until his father's deposition by the Communist Party of Yugoslavia that same year. Crown Prince Alexander promotes a constitutional monarchy for Serbia, envisioning a king as a stabilizing, nonpolitical figure representing national continuity and unity.

The one unifying figure for the former Yugoslavia was, of course, Josip Broz Tito. Paradoxically, Yugoslavia's breakup testifies to Tito's able, if authoritarian, rule. His iron will, strong personal leadership, and synthesizing political skills kept Yugoslavia's six republics, five nationalities, four languages, three religions, two alphabets, one political party, and about fifteen million fiercely individualistic citizens living together for decades in mutual tolerance and peace (while jailing some of those whose aspirations might have changed this status quo). Even while various republics resented the disproportionate amount of power exerted by Belgrade, Tito's seat of power, the six disparate Yugoslav republics stayed intact in one federal unit. But the imposed values of communality and cooperation had not taken hold in the hearts of the diverse peoples. The disappearance of Yugoslavia is additional proof that human law can bring human beings only a limited, and fleeting, interdependence and unity.

The federation's disintegration dealt Zagreb Film a nasty blow. As war raged in 1991, state funding ended. Production at Zagreb Film came to a full halt. Four years later the city of Zagreb, in line with Croatia's new capitalist economy, took over the company. Restructuring was undertaken with the aim of helping Zagreb Film adjust to a market economy and assume a new place in the film business internationally.

Zagreb Film started following the Western model of contracting artists per project on a freelance basis. The artists lost the employment securities of the former socialist times along with the luxury of being able to create artistic films without concessions to commercial success.

On a more positive note, another big change was that female artists found their place in Zagreb Film.

The Zagreb School of Animated Film has its own permanent exhibition at the Zagreb City Museum. In 1972, Zagreb Film inspired the establishment of the biennial World Festival of Animated Films Zagreb, aka Animafest Zagreb, with Želimir Matko the first festival director. After 1990, other companies took over the festival organization, but Zagreb Film remained involved as partner. In 2005, the festival became an annual event. The festival's "Mr. M Audience Award" was named after Matko. Animafest Zagreb is considered one of the world's four most significant animated film festivals.

The unraveling of Yugoslavia naturally ended the Yugoslavian experiment of Workers' Self-Management. Milovan Djilas, who always claimed credit for the adoption of WSM, served nearly ten years in jail for his critical writings. Yugoslavia banned his books for decades. Although released from prison in 1966, he could not publish his views at home or travel and speak abroad until toward the end of his life. Milovan Djilas died in Belgrade in 1995 at the age of eighty-three.

Josip Broz Tito died in 1980.

The Socialist Federal Republic of Yugoslavia died in the Yugoslav Wars of the early 1990s.

And Yugo-nostalgia lives on.

GLOSSARY

Blažeković, Milan (1940–) Croatian animator; part of the creative animation team for the cartoon series **Professor Balthazar**; still works with **Zagreb Film**.

Bratstvo i jedinstvo "Brotherhood and Unity"; Serbo-Croatian translation of the popular national slogan of the Communist Party of Yugoslavia, coined during World War II; became guiding slogan of the postwar nation, championing Yugoslavia's official policy of peaceful coexistence between its ethnic groups.

Chetniks One of the two resistance movements active in Axis-occupied Yugoslavia during World War II; consisted mainly of troops from **Serbia**; unlike the resistance movement of the **Partisans**, remained loyal to the Yugoslav monarch, King Peter II, who set up a government-in-exile in England.

Croatia Republic of Croatia; parliamentary constitutional republic at the crossroads of Central Europe, Southeast Europe, and the Mediterranean; capital Zagreb; first established as a duchy in the eighth century; after World War I, joined the newly formed Kingdom of Yugoslavia; during World War II, occupied by Nazi Germany and fascist Italy; after the war, became a socialist unit within the federation of Yugoslavia; during the Croatian War of Independence (1991–1995), gained independence from Yugoslavia; joined the European Union in 2013.

Dedijer, Vladimir (1914–1990) Yugoslav **Partisan** fighter, politician, human rights activist, historian; sole member of the Communist Party of **Yugoslavia** to defend freedom of expression and side with **Milovan Djilas** (1954) for his criticism of the Yugoslav system; his book *Tito: A Biography* was translated into twenty languages.

Djilas, Milovan (1911–1995) born in Montenegro; helped **Tito** establish the Yugoslav **Partisan** resistance during World War II; held key posts in the postwar government until expelled for criticism of the Yugoslav system; prominent dissident of Yugoslavia and the entire Eastern Bloc; became internationally known for his US-published *The New Class* (1957); used his ten years in prison to write (on toilet paper) additional books.

Goli otok barren island off the coast of **Croatia**; site (1949–1989) of a high-security, top secret prison and forced labor camp for male political prisoners in the former Yugoslavia.

Grgić, Zlatko (1931–1988) Croatian animator; worked with **Boris Kolar** and **Ante Zaninović** on the animated series **Professor Balthazar** for **Zagreb Film**; emigrated to Canada in the late 1960s; the **Zagreb World Festival of Animated Films** awards the Zlatko Grgić Prize for best first production apart from educational institutions.

Kolar, Boris (1933–) Croatian animator and film director; worked with **Ante Zaninović** and **Zlatko Grgic** on the TV series **Professor Balthazar**.

Kumrovec village in northern **Croatia**; birthplace (1892) of **Josip Broz Tito** when Croatia was part of the Austro-Hungarian Empire; since 1953, the house in which Tito was born has been the Memorial Museum of Marshal Tito.

Non-Aligned Movement (NAM) founded in **Belgrade** (1961) by thirty-five Third World countries wanting to steer a middle course between the Western and Eastern Blocs and maintain neutrality in the Cold War; largely conceived by President **Tito,** who served as NAM's first Secretary General, and India's first prime minister, Jawaharlal Nehru; Egypt's second president, Gamal Abdel Nasser; Indonesia's first president, Sukarno; Ghana's first president, Kwame Nkrumah; and

Burma's first Prime Minister U Nu; today the organization has one hundred and twenty members and seventeen observers, many of them also United Nations members. The end of the Cold War caused NAM to redefine its main purpose and place in the world.

Partisans national liberation army in Yugoslavia during World War II, comprising mainly workers and peasants; led by the Communist Party of Yugoslavia under the military command of **Josip Broz Tito**; carried out resistance actions against the Axis Powers; considered Europe's most effective anti-Nazi resistance movement.

Professor Balthazar amusing-eccentric-altruistic-inventor cartoon character who solves problems with imagination and positive energy; featured in the animated, children's television series of the same name created by **Zlatko Grgić**, **Boris Kolar**, and **Ante Zaninović**; produced (1967–1978) by **Zagreb Film**; became internationally popular.

Pula seafront city on the tip of Croatia's Istrian Peninsula; founded tenth century BC; known for its many well-preserved ancient Roman structures; its first century amphitheater, the Arena, is site of the **Pula Film Festival**.

Pula Film Festival established (1954) as Festival of Yugoslav Film; annual summertime festival; film lover President **Tito** served as patron; 1991 festival canceled because of the Yugoslav Wars; restarted (1992) as Pula Film Festival; in 2001, the festival introduced a competition for European films; in 2010, introduced a competition solely for Croatian films; awards the Golden Arena, (Yugoslav) Croatian equivalent of the American Oscar.

Serbia Republic of Serbia; parliamentary constitutional republic (since 2006); at the crossroads between Central and Southeast Europe; capital Belgrade; as the Kingdom of Serbia, cofounded Yugoslavia after World War I; occupied by Nazi Germany and fascist Italy during World War II; during the Yugoslav wars of the 1990s, formed a union with Montenegro that dissolved (in 2006); candidate for membership in the European Union.

SFRY Socialist Federal Republic of Yugoslavia, socialist federation founded during **World War II** under the leadership of **Josip Broz Tito**; experimented with a **Third Way** governing system positioned somewhere between Soviet-style communism and Western capitalism, with some distinctive features, such as **Workers' Self-Management**; consisted of six Balkan republics (Bosnia and Herzegovina, **Croatia**, Macedonia, Montenegro, **Serbia**, and Slovenia), plus the autonomous provinces of Kosovo and Vojvodina; existed from 1943 to dissolution in 1992 amid the Yugoslav Wars.

Third Way Tito's Third Way; political and social ideological experiment and national path forged by **Josip Broz Tito** in Yugoslavia; refers to a distinctly Yugoslavian twentieth-century form of socialism that incorporated some communistic ideas of Karl Marx with some economic principles of capitalism; featured **Workers' Self-Management**; straddled Yugoslavia between the Eastern Bloc led by the USSR and the Western Bloc led by the US; further development of Tito's Third Way lessened with the leader's death (1980) and certainly with the disintegration of Yugoslavia (1990s).

Tito, Josip Broz (1892–1980) military-political leader, communist warrior, and international statesman born as Josip Broz into a peasant family in **Kumrovec** in **Croatia**; used the code name "Tito" working underground for the then-illegal Communist Party of Yugoslavia (1930s); given the title "Marshal of Yugoslavia" (1943) as chief commander of the **Partisan** resistance during World War II; leader of Yugoslavia until his death. His independent ruling style brought Yugoslavia to a relational break with Joseph Stalin and prevented Yugoslavia from becoming a Soviet satellite state; forged a Yugoslav **Third Way**, Tito's Third Way; proclaimed president-for-life in 1974 after election as president five times since first obtaining the presidency in 1953; during the Cold War cofounded the **Non-Alligned Movement**.

Vukotić, Dušan (1927–1998) animator-director born in Bosnia and Herzegovina; most internationally known member of **Zagreb Film**;

animation pioneer recognized with a Golden Arena award at the **Pula Film Festival**; winner (1961) of the first Academy Award for best animated short film outside the US.

Workers' Self-Management WSM, workplace decision-making by the employees; a characteristic of various forms of socialism; one of the experimental features of **Tito's Third Way**; basis of the economic and social order of Yugoslavia; a form of direct participatory democracy.

Zagreb Film film production company known primarily for its animated films; established in Zagreb, **Croatia** (1953); in the late 1950s, attracted international attention when noted French film theorist Georges Sadoul coined the phrase, "Zagreb School of Animated Film"; with the cartoon *Surogat* (Substitute) by **Dušan Vukotić**, won the first Hollywood Oscar awarded a non-American animated film (1961); most famous for the **Professor Balthazar** cartoon series for children. The disintegration of Yugoslavia brought its state funding largely to an end; after the independence of **Croatia** (1991), Zagreb Film was restructured in accord with the country's new, free market economy.

Zagreb World Festival of Animated Films aka Animafest Zagreb; established (1972) under the inspiration of **Zagreb Film** with Želimir Matko the first festival director; in 2005, the festival became an annual event; the "Mr. M Audience Award" was named after Matko; considered one of the world's four most significant animated film festivals.

Zaninović, Ante (1934–2000) Croatian animator; created, with **Zlatko Grgić** and **Boris Kolar,** the **Professor Balthazar** cartoon series for children.

INDEX

ALSO AVAILABLE
FROM NEW EUROPE BOOKS

New Europe Books

Williamstown, Massachusetts

Find our titles wherever books are sold,
or visit www.NewEuropeBooks.com for order information.

ABOUT THE AUTHOR

Surya Green, who grew up in New York City and received degrees from Stanford University (MA in communication) and Barnard College (BA in American studies), is the author of *The Call of the Sun: A Woman's Journey to the Heart of Wisdom* (Element Books Ltd., UK, 1997). She has published magazine articles internationally and has led gatherings, given workshops, and spoken on transformational themes in the USA, UK, the Netherlands, and India. A member of the Dutch Association of Journalists and the Society of Authors (UK), she has also worked as a professional actress and singer. She lives in Amsterdam, the Netherlands, where in 2000 she established the nonprofit foundation Sun Conscious.